# Advance Praise for How
## *Trump Is Making Black America Great Again*

"Horace Cooper's incisive strategic insights applied to the plight of Black America under President Trump are forceful and timely. The traditional civil rights establishment has found itself increasingly marginalized amidst the Democratic Party's shift away from African Americans as the 'most favored minority' towards illegal immigrants from south of the border. Cooper's call for a realignment of political priorities among Black Americans is a clarion call for a new self-Emancipation off the Left's 'political plantation.'"

—Sebastian Gorka, Ph.D, Former Strategist to
President Trump, Host of AMERICA First

"We've all heard that President Trump's policies are benefitting Black America, but how? Horace Cooper, one of the great constitutional legal minds of our time, has written this brilliant, nuanced, and fact-filled analysis explaining just that—how President Trump's policies benefit Black America and all Americans. Cooper understands the historical and social dynamics that have given rise to some of the crises the black community has experienced and is currently experiencing. His unique insight gives this book's thesis a powerful perspective, purpose, and validity."

—Janine Turner, Actress, Founder and Co-President of
Constituting America, Creator and
Voice of God On The Go Minute

"I have known my brother Horace Cooper for over thirty years and can attest to his intelligence, integrity, and strong adherence to conservative Christian values. When he advocates conservative social values as a prescription for what ails Black America, he's speaking from personal experience. How Trump is Making Black America Great Again is sure to become a seminal text. It will stand the test of time."

—Armstrong Williams CEO, HSH Holdings, Broadcast Television Owner, Host of The Armstrong Williams Show

"Horace Cooper makes an elegant and convincing case for how Trump's policies can and have worked for black America. He writes with clarity and unique insight. This is a must read, not only for black Americans concerned with their future, but also for any American who seeks to appreciate the impact of Trump's core economic and social agenda. I have been working with Horace as a guest and a friend for as long as I can remember. And much like the relationship between student and sensei, just when I think I have everything I need to know about the Constitution, he presents me with a new intellectual challenge. When the topic of complicated Constitutional issues come up, he is at the top of my list for on-air booking."

—Andrew Wilkow, Political Commentator, Radio Host

# HOW TRUMP IS MAKING BLACK AMERICA GREAT AGAIN

*The Untold Story of Black Advancement in the Era of Trump*

## Horace Cooper

BOMBARDIER
BOOKS

A BOMBARDIER BOOKS BOOK
An Imprint of Post Hill Press
ISBN: 978-1-64293-221-8
ISBN (eBook): 978-1-64293-222-5

How Trump is Making Black America Great Again:
The Untold Story of Black Advancement in the Era of Trump
© 2020 by Horace Cooper
All Rights Reserved

Cover Design by Cody Corcoran

Post Hill Press
New York • Nashville
posthillpress.com

Published in the United States of America

*Dedicated to Jay Parker*

# *Contents*

❧

# *Dedication*

❧

As a new Congressional staffer in Washington, D.C., I came to meet a gentleman whose friendship and mentorship would affect me for a lifetime. James A. "Jay" Parker dedicated his life and career to the pursuit of liberty and lived a life replete with success. He served as an advisor to presidents of the United States. He encouraged and supported conservative jurists. He shaped the minds of intellectual influencers. He exhorted legions of college students to think and act seriously about politics and policy. Parker embodied the importance of personal responsibility and he contributed to his native and adopted hometowns through philanthropy and community service. He sought me and many others out at whatever our stations in life, and continually encouraged us to be exemplars of citizenship, defenders of freedom, and promoters of our great Constitution.

Like many who knew and cherished Jay, I labor to be worthy of his counsel. The consistent theme of his lessons, taught by word and example, was to discern and eschew the "nonsense" of life. He urged us to ignore petty distractions for our own peace of mind and personal betterment.

Although Jay lost his bout with cancer in the fall of 2015, he combated the physical limitations foisted on him with the same enthusiasm he poured into counseling hundreds of young people around the world to soldier forward for personal reliance and independence.

I miss my regular interactions with Jay. I miss his pedagogy. I miss his infectious laugh. But the one thing I will always possess of his is the power to be wise. This book is a testament to my earnest attempts to live up to his investment in me. It serves as the best earthly dedication I can offer in honor of Jay's friendship and guidance, undeserved, yet freely and generously shared throughout my formative adult life and beyond.

Thank you, Jay Parker.

# *Introduction*

~

*H*ow *Trump is Making Black America Great Again* makes the case that President Trump's conservative economic and social policies are improving the lives of black Americans, especially the lower middle class and working poor. I also wish to convey to readers that Trump's core agenda items, which consist of industry deregulation, tax cuts, and strong immigration policy, have already led to significant gains for African Americans—in terms of employment, economic advancement, and improved communities—and that African Americans have made progress under Trump at a faster pace than the electorate as a whole. While many of Trump's policies are not specifically tailored to African Americans, they are nonetheless a great fit for what Black America needs to advance in the 21st century and beyond.

Although it has been at times difficult to come to terms with, blacks who do not tow the Democratic Party line of liberalism and identity politics—who are politically conservative and who care about the fate of blacks and Americans as a whole, and yet dare to think outside the narrow plantation perspective—have been viewed by the progressive left as "unicorns." Being pro-America, pro-black, and conservative all in one seems like a formula for confusion amid the reigning political consensus within both the black community and the Democratic Party. In fact, white liberals with whom I've crossed paths over the years see me as a walking contradiction. How in the world could a black man from the deep south (if Texas can be categorized as such) ever end up working for a Texas Republican Congressman for almost twenty years? Don't Republicans actually hate black people? Aren't they out to roll back the hard-fought gains that blacks made during the battles for civil rights and equal justice? How on God's green earth could someone whose own grandfather was denied the right to vote or even purchase property for his business in the state of Texas a mere eighty-five years ago ever advocate for Republican politics? And why on earth would any black man support a controversial figure like President Donald Trump in his own mission to "make Black America great again?"

Surely, I must have been paid off. I must have sold out. There has to be some sinister, hidden reason why Horace Cooper, an astute law professor, television pundit, counsel to the Republican Leader of the U.S. House of Representatives Dick Armey, and co-founder of conservative black advocacy organization Project 21, chose the dark side and went with Donald Trump. Or so the narrative goes.

But over the years, having spent countless hours writing legislation, fighting congressional battles over policy and appropriations, thinking critically about the issues, and publicly advocating for African American inclusion within the Republican Party, I can firmly and honestly say that the critics have got it all wrong. The au courant wisdom has failed both America as a whole and Black America in particular. The dominant policy view for the last few decades has been that elites in Washington can create government agencies and issue regulations that will provide targeted assistance to some groups and stymie others, all while increasing the overall size of the pie. This hasn't worked, and yet, rather than admit failure, elites have redoubled their misguided efforts. The result: they have merely prevented more opportunity for the groups they claim to promote, and destroyed the hopes and dreams of millions in the process.

And that's why it took an unconventional candidate in Donald Trump to bring to the fore serious problems with the reigning liberal dogma that most present-day politicians, academics, and pundits continue to try and sweep under the rug simply because they cannot stomach the idea of a man like Trump occupying the highest office in the land.

By now, it must be conceded that Mr. Trump, more than any other president in recent history, has broken the mold of what an American President looks and sounds like. Sure, we elected our first black president a decade ago with the historic and—viewed by many voters at the time—mold-breaking election of Barack Obama. But in hindsight, it almost seems as if Barack won by fitting the mold of what the elites expected to a tee, right down to the perfect sound-bites, the well-fitting suits, and the customary bland platitudes about hope and change that had been peddled by previous office holders. In many respects, Obama adhered even more faithfully to Democratic Party dogmas than previous Democratic candidates, although he recited them with an almost lyrical eloquence. At the end of the day, however, could it be said that black Americans or the country as a whole was measurably better off under Obama's leadership? Did significant social and economic gains accrue to blacks under America's first black president?

The answer is no. Obama chose to build on the liberal elite agenda that the Democrats believed would prove to be a winning formula for the 21st century. It embraced values that were not only directly harmful to the interests of black Americans—abortion, identity politics, and accretion of the regulatory state, to name a few—but also it alienated Americans in the middle of the country that found this vision foreign and repugnant to their own small-town realities. Obama was not solely to blame though. The coalition between the Democratic Party and Black America had been fraught with strains for some time before he inherited the mantle. But under Obama, those tensions persisted and worsened. Black unemployment under Obama averaged over ten percent (without even accounting for the dismal labor force participation among black males); black home ownership levels plummeted to their lowest levels in over a generation;[1] and the wealth gap between blacks and almost every other group in America widened. While Obama's eloquent lip service to the ideals of equality and progress sounded sweet, the reality was far

---

[1]    Matt Bruenig and Ryan Cooper, "How Obama Destroyed Black Wealth," *Jacobin*, December 2017, https://jacobinmag.com/2017/12/obama-foreclosure-crisis-wealth-inequality.

more bitter.[2] By almost every measure that counts, Black America lost ground under President Obama. Historians looking back at the Obama years will likely note that, like FDR's failed Depression- era policies, many, if not most of the Washington-driven programs and regulations pursued by Mr. Obama in an effort to fix America, actually exacerbated and extended the duration of the Great Recession.

Moreover, many white Americans, even those inclined to side with blacks on issues of civil rights and equal opportunity, saw the rise of a new evil—identity politics, which they viewed as a shrewd and cruel way of sowing deep and hurtful divisions among Americans for political gain. Predictably, identity politics failed to address the fundamental problems of economic distress and social decline being experienced by the middle and working classes. Instead of bread for the masses, we got massive bank bailouts and racial revenge. And even though folks at both the top and bottom of the economic pyramid saw benefits under Obama, his coalition was crafted at the expense of those in the middle—those who could claim neither the seductive moral power of the poor, nor the sheer economic and political might of the rich and well-connected.

It was to those forgotten people whom Donald Trump appealed most intimately. Hadn't they, in fact, borne the brunt of the "jobless" recovery? Weren't their family and friends and neighbors suffering greatly from the decades-long evisceration of middle class jobs? How, in fact, did working class whites in rust belt cities—those cities that elected both Trump and Obama—benefit from the "white privilege" so often touted in the press as the motivating rationale for greater government intervention against them?

This book is no hillbilly elegy though. That book has already been written. Rather, it is an appeal to blacks, whites, and browns

---

2    Rakesh Kochhar and Richard Fry, "Wealth Inequality Has Widened Along Racial, Ethnic Lines Since End of Great Recession," FactTank, Pew Research Center, December 12, 2014, https://www.pewresearch.org/fact-tank/2014/12/12/racial-wealth-gaps-great-recession/.

to understand the problems that gave rise to Donald Trump, why President Trump is addressing the ills that America is facing, and how Trump's solutions benefit black Americans as well as the rest of America. Nor is this book an attempt to advocate that Trump, the individual, is "pro-black." Rather, it attempts to demonstrate how identity politics can be counterproductive to enacting broad-based economic, social, and foreign policies that benefit all Americans.

In this book, I argue that conventional wisdom has gotten it wrong. The reigning narrative when it comes to African-American politics is that liberalism, particularly the Great Society programs instituted by Democratic President Lyndon Johnson in the late 1960s and early 1970s, ushered in a new era of prosperity and progress for African Americans. But on closer examination, it becomes obvious that no such resurgence occurred. Since the advent of the Great Society and its signature programs—Aid to Families and Dependent Children (aka "welfare"), Food Stamps, Head Start, Affirmative Action, and forced desegregation of public schools (aka "bussing")—blacks have actually fared far worse than the rest of the country and have fallen further behind in many of the core markers of economic prosperity. Since the 1960s, the proportion (and absolute quantity) of black children born to impoverished single mothers has skyrocketed from under a quarter of births out of wedlock in the 1960s to over three-quarters of all black children born to single parents today.[3] This, by any strain of the imagination, is not progress. Illegitimacy brought with it the twins of poverty and crime, each a deep stain which imbues Black America.

Liberals have pointed to abortion rights as the key to women's liberation and advancement. African Americans' experience with abortion has not been so liberating. Abortion is a moral abomination along the lines of de jure slavery, the holocaust, and other human rights catastrophes. As a moral wrong, abortion creates the seeds for

---

3    "African-American Family Structure," *Wikipedia*, last modified January 19, 2020, https://en.wikipedia.org/wiki/African-American_family_structure.

its own destruction, because, like any evil, it is eventually eclipsed by good. But even on a more practical level, abortion rights have not had the effect of liberating poor black women from economic bondage. On the contrary, abortion rights came along with a slate of liberal fallacies—free love, radical individualism, disregard of marriage and religious institutions—that have greatly harmed black women and black families. Rather than build up the black community, abortion devalues lives, family commitments, and community cohesiveness. Liberalism teaches us that whatever the individual chooses to do to express him or herself is paramount. According to liberal dogma, morals, conservative values, and communitarian institutions like church and family, stunt an individual's growth rather than sustain it.

Attitudes like this are especially dangerous for a downtrodden people attempting to move upwards. Blacks are not stronger individually in most cases. Because of the history of discrimination and slavery in this country, blacks have often had very little choice but to rely upon family bonds and faith-based institutions to advance themselves. And even the gains made since the end of slavery would not have been likely if blacks as a community had embraced the radical individualism espoused by the left today.

By adopting liberalism, blacks set themselves up to be picked apart and left for dead by the broader currents of social decline sweeping through modern society. Whereas, for example, a white wealthy individual who gets hooked on drugs may be able to muster the financial and social support to get off of them when they finally hit rock bottom—whether the support appears in the form of an expensive substance abuse rehab center, or in the form of family interventions, or both—most blacks are not so lucky. When white elites cry "uncle!", there is often, in fact, a wealthy uncle around to heed the call. Blacks, by and large, don't have a rich uncle who can save them from their mistakes. Consequently, black drug addicts mostly end up homeless on the streets, or in prison, or simply just dead. In their wake, they leave a depressing legacy of broken families, children born out of wedlock, who too often grow up to be just like their parents, which ends up creating generations of wasted talent, wasted opportunities, and wasted lives.

In short, most blacks do not have the luxury to behave like white liberal elites, and shouldn't hope to fall back on their wealth to recover from the consequences of their poor choices. For most blacks, liberalism as a political philosophy is no freedom suit; it is a straitjacket.

This book goes on to argue that President Donald Trump offers a far better alternative to liberalism for what ails Black America. Let's start with liberalism's most prominent homage to radical self-centeredness: abortion. The president has already appointed two extremely competent conservative judges to the Supreme Court, and almost 150 more to lower courts. These appointments are intertwined in time with changes in state abortion laws, as recently seen in the passage of pro-life laws in Alabama, Georgia, Missouri, and several other states. While the road ahead to end abortion is still a tough one, we see signs of hope that America can come to its senses and respect the sanctity of life, as well as the institutions that safeguard life, namely family and religious organizations. When abortion is pushed into the dustbin of history, then and only then, will "all lives matter"—including black ones.

Another dubious liberal concept is the desire to abolish the Constitution's Second Amendment guarantee for Americans to have an individual right to keep and bear arms. Democrats and many black leaders have allied with leftists for greater gun restrictions, purportedly in a bid to end gun violence plaguing the black community. It is noteworthy, however, that the communities in America with the highest concentrations of gun violence also have some of the strictest gun laws. Chicago, for example, had the tenth highest murder rate in the nation in 2018, with 24.1 murders per hundred thousand residents. And yet it has some of the toughest gun laws in the United States. Baltimore touted a murder rate more than twice that of Chicago, with 55.6 murders per hundred thousand residents, and it, too, has very strict gun laws. Similarly, with regards to Detroit, Michigan; Cleveland, Ohio; and Newark, New Jersey.[4] All these cities are among America's deadliest for black folks, and yet all have strict gun laws. Tragically, they each also have years' long backlogs of hundreds and hundreds of unsolved murders committed against young black males.

How could this possibly be? If liberals contend that people don't kill people, but guns do, how could cities where guns are essentially outlawed be littered with the bullet-riddled bodies of black folks? The grim reality again runs directly counter to the narrative. The cities with the highest per-capita registered gun ownership have some of the lowest homicide rates. According the Pew Research Center, more than 70 percent of legal gun owners lived in rural and suburban areas in 2018, whereas the concentration of gun violence in the U.S. has been in cities where the majority of homicides have been committed with illegally owned firearms.

Rather than joining in the chorus of voices opposing legal gun ownership, African Americans should be clamoring for less-restrictive gun regulations in the places they live, and championing greater efforts by law enforcement to end the chaos in their communities. African Americans have a long history of using firearms to protect themselves against racist violence, especially during early efforts to fight the Ku Klux Klan and lynching. That same approach is needed today where black communities are plagued by rampant crime. The Second Amendment stands for self-protection today just as it has for over 200 years. Donald Trump has been a strong proponent of the Second Amendment, and is the first sitting president to speak at the NRA convention, in thirty-four years.

President Trump's championing of the Second Amendment helps black Americans who are disproportionately affected by violent

---

4     Grace Hauck, "Donald Trump is Visiting Chicago, a City He's Called a War Zone. But What's Really True About Guns There," *USA Today*, October 28, 2019, https://www.usatoday.com/story/news/nation/2019/10/28/ trump-chicago-presidential-visit-highlights-gun-crime-violence/4072445002/.

crime. In fact, in the two years since Trump's election, more African Americans have become legal gun owners than in any other recorded period in American history. The National African American Gun Association's numbers tripled after President Trump's inauguration.[5]

When asked why he thinks membership has swelled in recent years, Philip Smith, NAAGA's president, replied, "I think, one, people are looking at the state of the United States in terms of robberies, burglaries, things that are happening on your daily basis. I believe that the best way to stop someone with a gun other than law enforcement is to have a gun yourself. I think too often as African Americans we've been told to not arm ourselves. And I think too often we are just sitting back and letting someone come and save us. If you look at our communities right now across the country, they are in a wreck because we cannot protect those communities."

Coupled with a reinvigorated effort to welcome and praise the role that law enforcement and other first responders play in keeping our communities safer, Donald Trump's actions directly challenge the elite view that guns and cops are the great problem facing our neighborhoods. *We need more of both, instead of less of each.*

By promoting and advancing public policies that help American workers—like confronting America's trade partners about their unfair trade laws and actually implementing tough punitive measures—Trump is in the process championing African-American jobs.

Thus, Chapters 1–3 focus on Trump's core economic policies—tax reduction, deregulation, international trade, and immigration policy—as a powerful mix of incentives that drive labor market expansion, especially at the semi-skilled rungs of the labor force. Low-wage, low-skilled labor is the sector of the labor force that is most highly impacted by illegal immigration. In the black community

---

5     Brakkton Booker, "With a Growing Membership Since Trump, Black Gun Group Considers Getting Political," NPR, July 10, 2019, https://www.npr.org/2019/07/10/738493491/with-a-growing-membership-since-trump-black-gun-group-considers-getting-politica.

the displacement of low-wage labor caused by illegal immigrants has produced dire economic and social consequences. By some estimates, the increase in low-wage labor performed by illegal immigrants has caused a forty-percent decline in African-American male employment over the past three decades. Jobs traditionally performed by African Americans, from childcare to farm work to hospitality services to construction and building trades, are now largely done by immigrants. Poor black men—like poor whites and browns—are seen as less attractive partners for women, and their economic deprivation operates to depress overall marriage rates in the black community when they desperately need to rise the most.

Perhaps most maddening is that too many of these competitors entered the country illegally and have failed to undertake measures to obtain lawful residency, all the while overburdening education, health, and community service centers set up to serve needy American citizens (and legal immigrants), including blacks.

On the other side of the aisle, Democrats are practically climbing over themselves attempting to ingratiate with America's newest "most-favored" minority, namely Hispanics. Blacks, who were once their most-favored minority, have been left out in the cold, with their votes taken for granted and therefore discounted. The Democrats' legislative agenda of chasing God out of the public square, advocating amnesty for illegal immigrants, saddling America with an ever-growing government bureaucracy, and fettering businesses with job-killing regulations is not working for most of Black America. On the other hand, President Trump's efforts—reminiscent of the successful policies of the early 20th century—to reset unfair trade imbalances, curb illegal immigration, promote faith-based organizations, and eliminate government red tape and growth-stifling regulations all help Black America.

Whereas illegal insourcing of low-skilled labor and the outsourcing of American manufacturing to Asia and Central America eventually caught up to the middle class, who saw their own wages, employment, and educational prospects suffer, blacks saw their entire communities ravaged, seemingly beyond recovery. In rust belt cities that once held thriving populations of middle class workers, the flight of manufacturing jobs left behind a legacy of decay and decline. Detroit, once home to a thriving black middle class, today is a wasteland of corruption, headed by an entrenched black political elite that continues to prey upon its most vulnerable citizens amid an ever-shrinking pond of taxpayer supported jobs and businesses.

When Donald Trump went to speak at a Detroit church during the run-up to the 2016 election, and issued the rhetorical challenge to black Americans, "What do you have to lose?!?" he forced a reckoning among many of the congregants who had already lost almost everything. They had lost their jobs, their homes, and a great many of them had lost friends and relatives to Detroit's culture of predatory criminal violence.

This book does not make the argument that President Donald Trump is the second coming of Christ. He is not Moses coming to lead black people out of bondage. He is not a man with a biblically ordained mission from God to rescue black Americans. But what he does offer is a practical plan to revive the areas of the U.S. that have fallen into decay and decline. With blacks disproportionately impacted by this decay and decline, they have the most to gain.

The president's approach is a practical plan that has worked in America's past, and if adopted today, will work again. American presidents in the past, like Taft, Harding, Coolidge, and Kennedy, embraced low-tax and low-regulation policies during their administrations, and it led to remarkable economic growth for the country overall and it especially benefited black Americans.

Like the successful presidents of the 20th century, President Trump has aggressively pursued low-taxation, low-regulation policies for America. By eliminating sixty-seven regulations in 2017 alone, and following it with another fifty-seven in 2018, the Trump White House unleashed billions of dollars' worth of badly needed economic growth and innovation all over the U.S. economy. In terms of new regulations with costs having more than $100 million in impact issued over that period, Mr. Trump's administration issued only 229 rules, in contrast to the job-strangling 647 new regulations issued during the first two years of the Obama administration.

Combined with the comprehensive Tax Cuts and Jobs Act, which cut taxes by $1.5 trillion, Trump's deregulation agenda, which is valued at almost as much, has produced not only sustained growth, but also produced an acceleration of economic growth. His plans aren't just for the haves; the have-nots benefit, too. Trump's tax reform included Opportunity Zones to spur private investment into hundreds of blighted communities in the United States, and it is already proving effective. Opportunity Zone legislation is driving public-private partnerships and capital investments in underinvested areas like Louisville, Kentucky; Baltimore, Maryland; and Detroit, Michigan. There has been a renewed sense of localism and inspired hope in areas that were once considered America's wasteland.

One of the major sticking points in terms of addressing America's lack of sustained socioeconomic growth has been labor immobility. Many of the individuals with labor skills who could move to areas of better opportunity during the initial years of the Great Recession did so. But significant numbers of people could not afford to move and found themselves stuck in job-poor places. Many of them could not sell their homes, as they were experiencing declining home prices and negative equity on their mortgages. Others were constrained by family considerations. Even those who did manage to escape to large cities with plentiful jobs, did so at great expense. Many of them ran up exorbitant student loan debts in an attempt to re-tool their skills. Some moved to crowded cities run by progressives whose urban policies resulted in the costs of living outpacing their increased earning abilities. Consequently, even if these U.S. migrants were able to move away from declining communities, thereby delaying their downward economic spiral, the move did not lead to upward mobility.

By contrast, since January of 2017, there has been a dramatic change in the economic prospects for all Americans—black, white or brown. Middle class incomes, after adjusting for inflation, have surged by $5,003 since Donald Trump became president in January 2017. By the fall of 2019, median household income reached $65,976—an all-time high, and up more than 8 percent in 2019 dollars.[6] In contrast, during the period that Barack Obama was president, incomes inched up by only $1,043.

Higher household income is directly related to the extremely tight labor market, which has given workers new bargaining power to demand higher pay. As of the winter of 2019, there were more than seven million unfilled jobs in America—the highest number ever recorded—providing even more ability to working Americans to command higher pay.[7]

Even as the positive data continues, critics abound. Notably, at the beginning of 2019, a left-leaning think tank (the Economic Policy Institute) criticized what it called one of President Trump's favorite statistical claims: record-low unemployment among blacks. According to the EPI, the real test for Trump's policies is not the low rates at present, but whether the rate stays low long-term, and more importantly, whether the black unemployment rate continues to be more than twice that of the white unemployment rate. Well, by the end of 2019 unemployment rates for blacks have not simply remained steady for the last three years, they've gone lower, and most importantly, blacks are getting hired at faster rates than whites for the first time in nearly fifty years, ending the pernicious two-to-one hiring rate. At the beginning of the fall of 2019, black unemployment was 5.4 percent, edging ever closer to the white unemployment rate of 3.2 percent (and breaking the two-to-one barrier). One thing is

---

6    Stephen Moore, "Middle-Class Incomes Surging—Thanks to Trump Policies," The Heritage Foundation, October 10, 2019, https://www.heritage.org/markets-and-finance/commentary/middle-class-incomes-surging-thanks-trump-policies.

7    "Economic News Release: Job Openings and Labor Turnover Summary," U.S. Bureau of Labor Statistics, U.S. Department of Labor, January 17, 2020, https://www.bls.gov/news.release/jolts.nr0.htm.

for certain—2019 marks the highest number of blacks in the workforce in America's entire history.

Chapters 4–6 address some of the social policies that Trump has championed: pro-life, pro-Second Amendment, and the relationship between blacks, the military, and law enforcement.

Black folks have traditionally served as the proverbial "canary" in the "coal mine" of the American social experiment. Policies that ultimately hurt most American families and American workers first hurt black Americans and with worse overall consequences. Whereas, for example, liberalizing sexual behavior (through easy access to abortion and school programs promoting condom use and so-called sex education) and expanding the welfare state has caused an overall increase in single-parent births among all Americans, it has hurt the black community even more. Whereas overall single-parent births in America have increased to more than 40 percent of all children born, the figure sits at more than three out of four black children born to single parents.[8] This staggering level of out of wedlock births for all Americans cannot be sustained and must be reversed. Liberalism's championship of licentiousness *über alles* is one of the greatest threats to blacks and America as a whole.

Turning to international matters, President Trump's foreign policies are driven by an America-first focus that recognizes that Americans are weary of playing sheriff for the world in recovery. Although most of the battles were waged on foreign soil—with the exception of the odious terrorist attacks of September 11—Americans paid the wages of war at great cost to our economy and armed forces. President Trump's outlook from an America-first perspective seeks to reduce America's military adventurism abroad. He has not abandoned our European and Asian allies, but he has demanded they make good on their long-term commitments regarding the cost for

---

8      Paul Bedard, "77% Black Births to Single Moms, 49% for Hispanic Immigrants," Opinion: Washington Secrets, *Washington Examiner*, May 5, 2017, https://www.washingtonexaminer. com/77-black-births-to-single-moms-49-for-hispanic-immigrants.

our mutual security. President Trump also believes in a strong U.S. military, and has committed unprecedented resources to training, equipping, and compensating American soldiers—including the largest pay increases for American troops in over a decade.

Trump's foreign policy also contributes to restoring Black America to greatness. First, the military is and has been the most stable employer in America, and the skills and training provided by military service have proven over time to be a remarkable tool for moving black Americans out of poverty and into the middle class. Just this past May, a record number of female African-American officers graduated from the military college at West Point. They are poised to rise through the ranks to positions of leadership in the American Armed Forces. Trump recently appointed highly decorated Col. Lorna Mahlock to serve as the first black female brigadier general in the U.S. Marine Corps. General Mahlock currently serves as the chief information officer of the entire corps. African Americans, particularly African-American women, enlist at far higher rates than Americans as a whole.[9] They are also far more likely to continue their military service beyond a first term, thus enabling them to achieve non-commissioned officer status at a higher rate than other American groups.[10] Moreover, Americans with significant military service are preferred candidates for domestic public sector law enforcement and private security roles.

Why is black participation in law enforcement important? Law enforcement is a key tool to restoring vitality in black communities, just as it does in the rest of the country. To the extent that there is a disconnect between law enforcement and the black community, it has traditionally been for two principal reasons. First, black leaders in

---

9     George M. Reynolds and Amanda Shendruk, "Demographics of the U.S. Military," Council on Foreign Relations, April 24, 2018, https://www.cfr.org/ article/demographics-us-military.

10    Lutz, Amy, "Who Joins the Military?: A Look at Race, Class, and Immigration Status," *Journal of Political and Military Sociology* (Winter 2008):167-188. https:// surface.syr.edu/cgi/viewcontent.cgi?article=1002&context=soc.

our communities have often sided with the criminal element against the police, acting as if the police were out to target all black Americans rather than black criminals. See Al Sharpton generally. Liberal politicians such as Hillary Clinton and former President Barack Obama cynically exploited the fraught relationship between black America and police in a way that further alienated black Americans from law enforcement while doing little to reduce crime rates. When national political leaders join in this activity by highlighting concerns such as racial profiling and isolated instances of police misconduct, and also stoking flames in Ferguson, MO, and Sanford, FL, they encourage African Americans' ambivalence towards law enforcement, thereby emboldening the criminal elements in their communities. These criminal elements and their apologists within Black America have effectively tarred the overall impression of blacks by law enforcement, even when the men and women in blue are black themselves. Notably, black males are overrepresented in law enforcement and yet their sacrifice and service often go unappreciated.

But the reality, unfortunately, is that a small subset of Black America, particularly young black males between the ages of fourteen and thirty-four, are responsible for the lion's share of the crime that is committed in black communities. The number of police-involved shootings of African Americans is in no way comparable to the mayhem against blacks caused by this group of blacks. Police are not the problem. Criminals are. And when innocent blacks get caught up in the war between police and criminals, a lot of the blame has to be placed on leaders within the black community whose self-identification with criminality and the vastly disproportionate amount of crime committed by black males in particular is either downplayed or ignored. Black males constitute less than 6 percent of the American population, and yet account for over a third of America's prisoners. Unless one believes that hundreds of thousands of African Americans have been convicted of crimes in the U.S. due to black victims falsely singling them out, the problem is obvious. A criminal element within communities of color is running rampant and must be expelled. In other words, black interactions with law enforcement occur more frequently today—not due to bigotry or "profiling", but instead because black communities are disproportionately victimized by violent crime. To paraphrase famed bank robber Willie Sutton, police are often seen in black neighborhoods because that's where the crime is.

Unlike the progressive candidates running for president, Donald Trump is the "law and order" candidate, and he fully supports our law enforcement officials. As president, he has directed the attorney general to give grants to support local law enforcement, and since becoming president, has vocally supported the efforts of America's leading law enforcement organizations. What if, instead of being the largest targets of law enforcement, blacks instead became the largest enforcers of the law? To the extent that Trump's policies have the effect of enabling more blacks to enter law enforcement careers, we could soon see a situation in which African Americans are more associated with solving and preventing crimes than committing them. If crime rates in the black community were to substantially drop, real estate values would rise, businesses would thrive, and black neighborhoods would come to be seen as oases of prosperity and security.

Chapter 7 addresses what, at first glance, may seem the most counterintuitive benefit of Trump's presidency. Specifically, it is that Trump's presidency represents an opportunity to finally achieve Martin Luther King's vision for a colorblind America. By eliminating the vestiges of de jure discrimination—including Affirmative Action in higher education—the Trump administration helps to firmly enshrine equal opportunity under the law for all Americans, regardless of race, color, or creed. Tackling the myth that today's progressive segregationists are on the side of the angels, the chapter shows that there is no moral difference between "evil" race separatists and "good" race separatists. The chapter also addresses the pernicious price of racial hoaxes in perpetuating some of the divisions that prevent America from truly achieving its potential as a colorblind society.

This book, then, is written from a conservative world-view—which at one point was the dominant perspective of blacks—that seeks to address several issues affecting Black America which are being made better by Trump's presidency. The basic philosophical framework presented herein is that we can use historical parallels to find success strategies, that when adopted, lead to greater prosperity, stronger family formation, and enhanced community vitality in today's environment. Similar strategies worked for Black America during the latter part of the 19th century and up to the Great Depression. Whenever these success strategies are abandoned or forgotten within Black America, stagnation and deprivation have followed.

In sum, the case for understanding Trump's success in improving the station of Black America is divided into three parts. First, the conventional wisdom that blacks' relationship with the Democratic Party assures them a seat at the table is wrong. Democrats have replaced blacks with a new *most-favored minority*, namely Hispanic immigrants. In order to fully participate in the new political world, blacks must reassess their strategic relationship with the Democrats. Second, the pernicious idea that identity politics is the best approach for benefiting Black America has tragically backfired. In fact, black Americans are far better off eliminating the hyphenation and embracing a mainstream American mindset. Mainstreaming has worked effectively in the past and is now the only real option for success today. Third, I argue that President Trump's America-first policies don't have to be specifically targeted at black Americans in order for blacks to benefit from them. In fact, it is precisely their racial universality that is the key to their success.

I ask the reader to bear with me as we engage in a frank and thoughtful discussion of the principal features of the Trump presidency and how it is making Black America Great Again.

# Chapter 1

༄

# MAGA-NOMICS IS RESTORING AMERICAN PROSPERITY— AND THAT'S GOOD NEWS FOR AFRICAN AMERICANS

MAGA-nomics, n. meaning: the set of government policies aimed at restoring American economic prosperity by reducing taxes, eliminating market-distorting regulations, and negotiating fair terms with America's largest trading partners to improve business formation, employment, and income growth. The Trump administration's MAGA-nomics policies are driving unprecedented economic growth, and blacks are greatly benefiting from it.

Why MAGA-nomics? And why now?

Imagine first that you are a driver in a car race. You've had an accident on the track, and the car ends up in a roadside ditch. You eventually get towed, the car gets fixed, and you get refueled. Of course, having been in a wreck, you've now fallen behind. To catch up, you'll need to move faster. But oddly, you find that your car, although it is being pulled around the track by the world's most powerful engine, is still falling further behind. How could that possibly be? Well, as it turns out, the previous driver installed electronic governors that constrained the car's performance capacity, ostensibly to save on fuel costs. Imagine that fuel costs a fraction of the potential earnings from winning the race, say 20 percent of your gross winnings. The previous driver, as it turns out, made the unfortunate calculation that saving a bit of money on fuel was worth losing the entire race. This is essentially the trade-off the Obama administration made while ostensibly attempting to dig America out of its worst economic crisis since the Great Depression.

Why would a driver make that choice? Well, perhaps it is because he is not primarily interested in winning. His primary goal is to demonstrate a novel concept—that it is better to be pro-green than win the race.

Would you ever invest in a racing division that was more interested in "saving fuel" than winning the race? For eight years of the Obama administration, America made a choice like this in many areas and American households suffered.

President Trump's MAGA-nomics policies are squarely focused on helping Americans come from behind, overtake the competition, and win the race. By removing the limiters placed on the economy by the Obama administration, the Trump administration has improved the U.S. economy, and more importantly, increased household incomes for Americans of all stripes.

This isn't new. Trump is following in the footsteps of 20th century presidents like Harding, Coolidge, Kennedy, and Reagan. The president has deployed the low-taxation and government deregulation model that has always worked in the past to revitalize our nation's economy.

Most Americans aren't familiar with the Great Recession of 1920. Economists note that its economic impact was actually more severe than that of the Great Depression. The difference is that although severe in intensity, in duration it was significantly shorter. Within eighteen months of the start of the downturn, the economy had turned around and would ultimately go on to become so strong that now the entire period is referred to as the Roaring 20s. Spending reduction, tax reduction, and paying down the national debt were all major aspects of Presidents Harding and Coolidge's economic policies.[1]

A decade later, another economic downturn would occur that would remain enshrined in the nation's consciousness. But this time, policymakers changed their strategy, and as a result America experienced the Great Depression. Economists and historians now note that the depth and duration of the Great Depression was actually extended as a direct result of the macro-economic policies of Franklin Delano Roosevelt.[2] As part of the "planner's vision," FDR undertook all of the steps that would worsen things. He dramatically raised taxes, adopted expansive new regulations of the private sector, and undertook a campaign of unprecedented government expenditures.

The resulting economic disruption had never been experienced by so many Americans for so long. The experience changed our culture and permanently shifted expectations Americans have for government. What it didn't do was make things better. White, and especially Black America, suffered severely.

Black men who had just a decade earlier been the highest-employed group in the U.S., became the nation's most unemployed.[3] According to the Library of Congress, the unemployment rate for blacks exceeded 50 percent during this ten-year period.[4] The

---

1    John Hendrickson, "President Coolidge's Economics Lesson," Calvin Coolidge Presidential Foundation, August 8, 2014, https://www.coolidgefoundation.org/blog/president-coolidges-economics-lesson/. Economists Richard Vedder and Lowell Gallaway argue that "the seven years from the autumn of 1922 to the autumn of 1929 were arguably the brightest period in [the] economic history of the United States.

2    Jim Powell, "How FDR's New Deal Harmed Millions of Poor People," Cato Institute, December 29, 2003, cato.org/publications/commentary/how-fdrs-new-deal-harmed-millions-poor-people.

3    *Philip Greenspun's Weblog*: "Black Unemployment: The Effect of 80 Years of Government Intervention," blog entry by Philip Greenspun, July 10, 2008, https://philip.greenspun.com/blog/2008/07/10/black-unemployment-the-effect-of-80-years-of-government-intervention/.

4    "Great Depression and World War II, 1929-1945: Race Relations in the 1930s and 1940s," Library of Congress, http://www.loc.gov/teachers/classroommaterials/presentationsandactivities/presentations/timeline/depwwii/race/.

economic devastation would have a detrimental impact on blacks for decades; the black unemployment rate would exceed, by as much as two times, the rate of whites for the next ninety-seven years.[5]

Utilizing MAGA-nomics, President Trump has returned to the time-tested strategies that brought wealth and prosperity to America and helped it fully and rapidly recover from economic downturns. Trump's accomplishments to date include tax reform, deregulation, implementing fairer trade policies, and leading the U.S. withdrawal from the job-killing Paris Accord. The president has also made strides towards bringing more energy infrastructure online, including opening additional lands for oil leasing, reducing the Outer Continental shelf royalties, expediting implementation of the Dakota Access and Keystone XL pipelines, and enacting rollbacks of Obama-era fracking and methane emissions rules.

Because MAGA-nomics policies are spurring unprecedented economic growth and driving full employment, they are having a beneficial impact on African Americans. African-American employment has reached a fifty-year high. In fact, women and minorities accounted for a majority of new hires for the first time in 2019.[6]

## TRUMP TAX REFORM IS SPURRING UNPRECEDENTED ECONOMIC GROWTH

The first prong of MAGA-nomics, historic tax reform legislation passed in 2017 as the Tax Cut and Jobs Act, marked not only a lowering of taxes on middle class Americans, but also a fundamental

---

5    Christopher Klein, "Last Hired, First Fired: How the Great Depression Affected African Americans," History.com, April 18, 2018, updated August 31, 2018, https://www.history.com/news/last-hired-first-fired-how-the-great-depression-affected-african-americans.

6    Heather Long and Andrew Dam, "For the First Time, Most New Working-Age Hires in the U.S. are People of Color," *The Washington Post*, September 9, 2019, https://www.washingtonpost.com/business/economy/for-the-first-time-ever-most-new-working-age-hires-in-the-us-are-people-of-color/2019/09/09/8edc48a2-bd10-11e9-b873-63ace636af08_story.html.

change of the way the federal government incentivizes business and consumer activity. Since the election and passage of the tax cuts, dozens of businesses have announced bonuses and wage increases. One hundred and twenty utility companies announced rate cuts for their customers. Amazon, the online retailer, recently announced it was increasing the minimum hourly wage paid to U.S. workers to fifteen dollars, about a 28 percent increase over the current minimum of eleven dollars per hour. Walmart and Target have also announced significant minimum wage increases to their workforces.

One of the less frequently discussed impacts of the Trump tax cut legislation is the impact it is having on state tax regimes and regional economic investment. Under the previous tax code, an individual could deduct the full amount of state and local taxes paid from one's federal taxes when filing April 1. The new tax code limits the combined deduction of states' property, income, and sales tax to $10,000. States with high property and sales taxes cried foul, because this change means their own citizens, particularly those at the higher income levels, will bear the brunt of the tax load rather than transferring the cost of the deduction to taxpayers in low tax states. Before this change in the law, people living in high tax states could spread their federal tax burdens to the rest of the country, since once they received their local deductions, they barely paid any federal taxes. This new change now puts pressure on states and localities to become more tax attractive to businesses and individuals.[7]

High-tax, high-service states like New York, New Jersey, and California face an almost certain reckoning, as lower allowed deductions of draconian state and local taxes will put pressure on income earners to leave the state. California is also among the states with

---

7     Ben Casselman, "Federal Tax Cuts Leave States in a Bind," *The New York Times*, May 12, 2018, https://www.nytimes.com/2018/05/12/business/economy/state-tax.html.
Jesse McKinley, " New York and New Jersey File Suit Against Trump Tax Plan," *The New York Times*, July 17, 2018, https://www.nytimes.com/2018/07/17/nyregion/salt-taxes-deduction-lawsuit-trump-cuomo.html.

the most income inequality in the nation. It is home to both Mark Zuckerberg, with an estimated net worth of $70 billion, and record numbers of homeless people crowding its cities. California is what happens when a vision for a liberal utopia runs amok. California's state pension obligations, environmental regulations, and liberal immigration laws—all the result of virtue-signaling liberal elitism—have had the unfortunate, although not unpredictable effect of squeezing the life out of the middle class.

California ranks among the highest taxed states in the country. It's state tax regime is onerous and usurious. Tolls, DMV fines, and other "policy rents" drain residents of their hard-earned money to the tune of billions of dollars. Excessive environmental zoning in the state has constrained home building, driving average rents on sub-par housing to over $1,440 per month, among the highest averages in the nation. Most California residents spend more than a third of their after-tax household incomes on rent or mortgages. While the elite enjoy basking in the rarified air of their liberal fantasy, the middle class and the poor bear the brunt of these well-meaning but ultimately job-killing and soul-crushing policies. With only 12 percent of the national population, nearly a third of all Americans on welfare live in California.[8] As a result, the state now faces massive government spending deficits—primarily in the form of underfunded state and municipal pensions, but also in the form of incapacity to perform basic public services such as fire, police, and disaster management. By some accounts, California's homeless problem, and dire infrastructure and public services crises are converting it into a "pre-modern" society.

California and other high-tax states also face an ongoing demographic exodus. There is already ample evidence that individuals, especially retirees and folks on fixed income, are moving in droves

---

8    Kristin Tate, "Middle Class is Disappearing in California as Wealth
     Gap Grows," The Hill, October 24, 2018, https://thehill.com/opinion/
     finance/412928-middle-class-is-disappearing-in-california-as-wealth-gap-grows.

to states with low or no state income taxes where they they are not penalized by limited deductions for state and local taxes due to the new law.

Furthermore, economists, including Arthur Laffer and Stephen Moore, believe that over the next three years more than a million more people will likely migrate from high-tax states like California, Connecticut, New Jersey, Minnesota, and New York, to states with lower taxes.[9] Most of those people will be high-income and wealthy individuals, which will of course initially leave the poorer residents behind, thus compounding the fiscal burden on those remaining.

It remains to be seen whether something similar to the mass migration of the 1930s, where millions of blacks left the South and headed North in hopes of the end of economic misery would occur in the twenty-first century. But such a move from high-tax/high regulation states to low-tax/low-regulation states wouldn't just speed up prosperity within Black America, it would also have significant socio-political effects, and change the racial and economic demographics of cities like Baltimore, Detroit, and Chicago.

Although the primary reason for reducing taxes is to acknowledge that Americans should be able to keep the lion's share of the hard-earned money they make, one huge additional benefit of tax reduction is that it spurs overall economic growth. Over the years, the U.S. has become far less competitive than other developed nations in encouraging new business expansion and attracting foreign investment, and that is mainly because the U.S. corporate tax rates were high relative to other industrialized nations.

Before the Trump tax cuts took effect, the untaxed income of the foreign subsidiaries of U.S.-based businesses continued to sit offshore as businesses feared the consequences of having most of it taken away in the form of taxes. Thanks to the Trump tax cuts, capital that

---

9    "Doug Schoen: Democrats Face Trouble From Population Losses in High-Tax Blue States," Fox News, June 23, 2018, https://www.foxnews.com/opinion/doug-schoen-democrats-face-trouble-from-population-losses-in-high-tax-blue-states.

now sits offshore in those corporate accounts is moving onshore. In April 2018, Apple announced that in response to the Trump tax cuts it would repatriate to the U.S. its entire overseas cash hoard of over $250 billion. It also announced that it would use some of that cash to create twenty thousand new jobs and open a new corporate campus. Apple will commit $10 billion to capital expenditures in U.S. data centers. Apple added that it will spend $5 billion as part of an innovation fund, up from the $1 billion CEO Tim Cook announced in 2017.[10]

Kevin Hassett, former Chair of The President's Council of Economic Advisors, noted, "[before the tax cuts] we were the highest taxed place on earth. Now we are not… The adjustment to having all the industry come home is not something that happens overnight, it spreads out over three to five years."[11]

By reducing corporate rates, the U.S. government is signaling to corporations that the nation is open for business and will create a welcoming climate for businesses to invest here, and for others already here to expand domestically instead of heading overseas. Because business investment growth generally leads to job growth, reducing corporate tax rates is great for the U.S. worker.

MAGA-nomics is focused squarely on spurring economic growth. The president's economic goals and proposals designed to "Make America Great Again" aim to return America to "sustained 3% economic growth" consistent with the country's historical 3.5 percent average from 1940 to 2007. Already there have been signs of a significant uptick in economic growth. Second quarter GDP growth in 2018 growth reached 4.2 percent, the highest since 2014,

10    Anita Balakrishnan, "Apple Announces Plans to Repatriate Billions in Overseas Cash, Says It Will Contribute $350 Billion to the U.S. Economy Over the Next 5 Years," CNBC, January 17, 2018, https://www.cnbc.com/2018/01/17/apple-announces-350-billion-investment-20k-jobs-over-5-years.html.

11    Lydia DePillis, "4 Ways Trump's Tax Cuts Changed the American Economy," CNN Business, April 15, 2019, https://www.cnn.com/2019/04/15/economy/trump-tax-cuts-impact-economy/index.html.

and third quarter 2018 growth reached almost 3.5 percent.[12] If the current state of the economy is any reflection on the effects of the 2017 tax cuts, it appears that they are working. Overall U.S. economic growth in 2018 increased nearly a full percentage point to 2.9 percent, whereas global growth slowed in the same period.

By some estimates, the Trump tax cuts accounted for about 40 percent of the GDP growth we saw in 2017-2019. It is remarkable that only two years ago, most economists were stumped about how we were going to get to the economic growth target of 2 percent, and now we are actually debating whether economic growth numbers above 3 percent can be sustained. This is a completely different ball game from three years ago, when the economy sputtered around at near zero growth.

Over the course of the Obama administration, average economic growth was 2.1 percent, even though the recession officially ended in June 2009. Under President Trump, average economic growth has accelerated to 2.9 percent and appears to be quickening.

In 2017 through 2018, half the economic growth came from the declining unemployment rate and an uptick in labor market participation. Labor force participation was actually double the forecasted improvement of 0.2 percent, and went up by almost 0.5 percent over the period. One key factor in making economic growth work for all Americans is to increase labor productivity.

During the Obama administration, the country experienced above average income growth in capital-intensive businesses such as real estate and technology, but extremely poor increases in labor productivity. Labor productivity has in fact been slowing in the U.S. since 2005, growing at an average annual rate of 1.1 percent over the period—essentially a standstill. This rate of growth in labor productivity cannot sustain continued economic growth above 3 percent.

---

12    Bob Bryan, "Trump Got a Dynamite GDP Number Last Quarter—and Early Signs Point to the Next One Being Even Better," *Business Insider*, August 2, 2018, https://www.businessinsider.com/trump-gdp-growth-q3-third-quarter-strong-2018-8.

One of the primary lag measures of labor market productivity is "capital deepening," increases in the amount of capital deployed per worker hour. Capital deepening eventually leads to greater labor market productivity. This started to recover during 2018, and continued into the fourth quarter of 2019.

The corporate tax cuts were specifically designed to reduce user cost of capital—that is the after-tax cost of a company's investment in capital assets (property, plant, and equipment). As taxes go down, capital deepening starts to increase.

Liberal orthodoxy, as Ronald Reagan explained, is: "If it moves, tax it. If it keeps moving, regulate it. And if it stops moving, subsidize it." For eight years, the Obama administration's economic policy followed this model. He subsidized green energy, taxed households making over $250,000 in income, and harshly regulated the energy industry. It's no wonder the economy limped along.

In 2017, Americans spent more than 1.5 times more on taxes than they spent on food and clothing. According to the BLS, American households spent on average $9,562 on food and clothing, and $16,749 on state, local, and federal taxes.[13] If there is any plainer demonstration of how taxes and regulation crowd out economic growth, this is it. When Americans are paying the government more than they are paying local businesses or saving for themselves, the government is no longer helping the average citizen—it is literally feeding on them. MAGA-nomics is the first major step in over a generation to reverse that trend.

As the economy moved into full employment in 2018, President Trump repeatedly urged the Federal Reserve to pursue a more accommodative monetary policy, including lowering interest rates on dollar-denominated securities. The reasons for this were several. First,

---

13    Terence P. Jeffrey, "BLS: Americans Spent More on Taxes Than on Food, Clothing Combined in 2017," CNSNews.com, September 24, 2018, https://www.cnsnews.com/news/article/terence-p-jeffrey/bls-americans-spent-more-taxes-food-clothing-combined-2017.

the Trump administration believed that banks were overcapitalized due to provisions in the Dodd-Frank Act financial industry regulations enacted by Congress in the aftermath of the Great Recession. Increased capital requirements were preventing banks from lending, thus impeding capital investment and growth in wages and employment. Secondly, efforts to get our trading partners to come to the table resulted in lower U.S. exports as some of those countries—notably China—pursued retaliatory sanctions. Thirdly, U.S. exporters faced a decline in orders due to a global economic slowdown.

And yet, despite these headwinds, the U.S. economy beat expectations in November 2019 by posting better than expected job growth, adding 129,000 jobs in October. This was significant because it occurred amid a General Motors Strike that forced roughly 42,000 workers onto the sidelines. Absent the GM strike, job growth in October would have reached 187,000, far exceeding expectations. As of November 2019, unemployment sat at a near fifty-year low of 3.6 percent, marking more than two consecutive years of full employment in the U.S. 2019 closed with an additional 145,000 new jobs in December resulting in more than 2.1 million jobs added for the year.[14]

While the jobless rate reached a fifty-year low in 2019, the unemployment rate for African Americans dropped further to 5.4 percent in October 2019, the lowest level ever recorded since the U.S. Bureau of Labor Statistics started keeping track in 1972.[15] Blacks also made incredible relative gains compared to the overall labor force. During the Great Recession, when the overall unemployment rate hovered around 6.6 percent, the black unemployment rate was more than double that, reaching an alarming 14 percent. The current overall

14    Annekin Tappe, "US economy adds 145,000 jobs in December," CNN Business, January 10, 2020, https://www.cnn.com/2020/01/10/economy/december-jobs-report/index.html.

15    Bethany Blankley, "Black Unemployment Drops to Lowest Level in Recorded U.S. History, Job Numbers Soar," The Center Square, November 4, 2019, https://www.thecentersquare.com/national/black-unemployment-drops-to-lowest-level-in-recorded-u-s/article_d3c4c5ca-ff0f-11e9-ae61-a36920bfdad1.html.

rate is about 3.6 percent, and the black unemployment rate is 5.4 percent, representing a narrowing of the employment gap by almost three quarters—quite a remarkable improvement in the race for equality (*and notably resulting in black unemployment breaking through the historic two-to-one ratio for unemployment*).

## THE TRUMP TAX CUTS ARE SPURRING A RESURGENCE OF CAPITAL INVESTMENT IN THE U.S.

One of the most exciting developments of the MAGA-nomics economy is that companies have been encouraged to make major capital investments in plant, equipment, and human resources. Preliminary indicators suggest that the economic growth trend is accelerating. In the weeks immediately following the Tax Cuts and Jobs Act's passage, over 300 companies announced wage and salary increases, as well as bonuses and supplementary 401(k) contributions of $2.4 billion affecting 4.2 million workers. By February of 2018, there was an estimated $190 billion in newly announced corporate investment projects publicly attributed to the Trump tax cuts. Tina Hodges, CEO of Advance Financial, a Nashville, Tennessee-based firm, announced in a January 5, 2018 press release, "Because we believed the new administration was committed to doing what it takes to get America's economy back on track, we are already ahead of the curve this year in terms of capital investments. We dramatically sped up our plans to open new locations—we're opening the 85th one this morning in Jackson—and hire more employees—we are bringing on 100 new people in January. We have also exponentially expanded our reach outside of Tennessee. In 2017, for the first time, we began offering our services outside the state."

Almo, a Philadelphia-based appliance, consumer electronics, housewares, and pro A/V distributor, is investing its savings from the Trump administration's new tax legislation in its employees and infrastructure. President/CEO Warren Chaiken said Almo's newly lowered tax structure will allow it to reward its employees with an incremental bonus of $1,000, stating that "they are the greatest asset we have to offer as a business." It is also making capital investments, including a new three-hundred-thousand-square-foot distribution center in Philadelphia, plus warehouse relocations in Nevada and Ohio to larger facilities. Almo is also going to fund a headquarters renovation that includes a reconfigured first floor and a new seven-thousand-square-foot second floor that can accommodate sixty-five additional employees, a new central office in Fort Lauderdale, and a new, larger headquarters office in Baltimore.

American Airlines granted $1,000 bonuses to every employee (excluding officers). The bonuses, which totaled $130 million, were paid out in the first quarter of 2018. In a press release announcing the bonuses, the company stated, "There is no doubt that our country's new tax structure will have positive long-term benefits for Americans. We will be able to invest even more in aircraft and facilities, and we will be able to do so with even greater confidence about the future."

Amgen, a California-based pharmaceutical company, announced that it was planning $3.5 billion in capital expenditures over the next five years, including construction of a "Next Generation" manufacturing plant in the U.S.—a $300 million investment to implement Amgen's next-generation biomanufacturing capabilities, and manufacture products for the U.S. and export markets. The construction and validation work is expected to add 220 jobs to the local economy. In addition, Amgen expects this new facility to employ up to three hundred highly skilled full-time workers. The company announced, "We will make product in the U.S. and export it to cover 85% of our international sales."

Increasing capital expenditures and paying employees more is what drives economies forward. Imagine how wonderful it would be if we could also transform our government such that it could invest in badly needed infrastructure, too. Imagine how many jobs would be created. Imagine how much more efficiently we could work as a nation with a domestic infrastructure that is at least as developed as the world's best. We should strive for that. The second necessary step in that direction requires reducing the regulatory burden imposed on American infrastructure development.

## REGULATORY POLICY: UNSHACKLING AMERICA'S PRODUCTIVE POTENTIAL

The second prong of MAGA-nomics involves taking a hard look at existing business regulations and our approach to regulatory policy in general. The governing framework, going back at least forty years, is that regulation should guide business activity rather than merely referee it. A case in point, consider President Obama's expansive clean energy policy. Not only did the policy seek to drive business activity by, for example, implementing drastically accelerated fuel economy mandates for automobiles, but it also made billions of dollars in direct grants and loans to "clean energy" firms. Many of these firms would not have been able to attract capital in the private market because their projects were too speculative for prudent risk-taking investors to take on. But government-supplied capital disrupted the markets for fossil fuels, making them more expensive to produce, and artificially inflated the value of "clean energy" companies. In the end, most of them failed because their business models simply were not economically viable. The regulatory crowding-out of fossil fuels and government-mandated fuel economy standards—part of a multi-decade effort—also made cars more expensive to purchase and own. This consequently delayed consumers' purchases of new automobiles, leaving older, less safe cars on the road and stunting job growth in the U.S. auto industry—an area where black Americans traditionally could be employed and expect to receive middle class wages and benefits.

MAGA-nomics is attempting to change that framework, making economic activity, not government regulation, the primary driver of economic growth. Governmental regulation pervades the lives of ordinary Americans, impacting decisions by both firms and individuals.

Regulations can have intended benefits, along with expected and unexpected costs. Those unexpected costs can sometimes be greater than the realized benefits. Some of these costs are not recognized on company balance sheets, but can accrue in the form of dampened growth, diminished capital formation, stunted business dynamics, hampered productivity, decreased employment, and lower labor mobility. As regulation in the United States has marched upward in recent years, many of these maladies beset the U.S. economy.

The Trump administration has prioritized the elimination of unnecessary regulations in the U.S. economy in order to clear the pathway to more robust economic growth. The administration's specific and far-reaching actions will ensure that only those rules that *provide benefit in excess of their costs* will be imposed on Americans. The record of the administration's first year reflects these efforts, because the number of deregulatory actions that eliminate unnecessary and harmful regulations exceeds the number of new regulations.

President Trump revolutionized regulatory practice when he came into office, essentially constraining regulatory costs at the federal agency level. The president's policies forced bureaucracies to make cost-benefit decisions about new regulations by forcing them to get rid of existing regulations if the cost of the combined regulations exceeded the capped level. Again quoting the President's Chief Economist, Kevin Hassett, "The successes have been impressive. For example, the 2017 Drug Competition Action Plan and subsequent reforms have led the Food and Drug Administration to approve dramatically more generic drugs, which has increased competition and helped push prices for prescription drugs 1.2% lower during the 12 months through February 2019."[16]

But by far the biggest battle over industrial policy and regulation during the Trump administration has been the fight to remove the

---

16    Kevin Hassett, " Former White House Chief Economist: The Case for the Trump Economy," CNN Business Perspectives, updated August 27, 2019, https://www. cnn.com/2019/08/26/perspectives/kevin-hassett-trump-economy/index.html.

regulatory carve-out given to the state of California to set its own fuel economy standards for cars. California imposes quite stringent fuel economy standards relative to the rest of the nation, which in turn forces automobile manufacturers to produce all of their cars in the U.S. market in conformity to California's standards. After all, it would be fatally inefficient for auto manufacturers to produce cars only for the California market. Hence the tyranny of the minority reigns. Virtually all cars produced and sold in the U.S. conform to California's stricter standards.

Recently, however, domestic automobile makers joined with the Trump administration to attempt to reassert federal authority over fuel economy standards in California, and to embrace Trump's efforts to lower the average annual fuel economy standard increases mandated at the federal level. Especially, as America has become a net producer of energy along with the related reductions in energy costs thanks to domestic production, letting American consumers have the option of lower priced cars would be good for families and the economy.

## TRUMP LABOR MARKET POLICIES ARE UNSHACKLING AMERICA'S WORKERS

Americans want not only to have jobs, but also to have jobs that sustain family and community growth. A driving factor of stagnant job and income growth in the U.S. since 2009 has been a failure of policymakers to understand an important concept: easy to fire, easy to hire, and its corollary, hard to fire, hard to hire.

When government acts to provide "employment" protections for certain categories of workers, it can also inadvertently disadvantage those very same workers. When firing an employee can lead to penalties or lawsuits, those other employees not covered by a new labor protection are suddenly more attractive. Whether layoffs are necessary, an employee just isn't working out, or any other reason that leads to a discharge, the person most likely to get a new job is the person perceived to be less costly to terminate. Ironically, it is illegal immigrants, who receive little to no federal employment protection, who have become the most attractive employee in America, as they are easy to hire—often under the table—and easy to fire for any or no reason.

Myriad job-killing regulations were adopted or promoted during the Obama years, and they collectively acted like a wet blanket on job creation. In 2012, for example, the Obama administration updated the Equal Employment Commission (EEOC) guidelines regarding the use of arrest or conviction records in employment decisions. The agency stated that employers' reliance on arrest and conviction records may have a disparate impact on people based on race or national origin (because black and Latino applicants are more likely than whites to have criminal records for felonies). Employers were cautioned to be more judicious about basing hiring decisions on applicants' criminal records. Rather than categorically exclude applicants with criminal records, employers were instructed to conduct an "individualized assessment" and speak with an applicant before disqualifying him or her based on criminal history. Instead of opening doors for those with a criminal history, it raised the cost of hiring such individuals. Imagine an employer having to engage in such a nuanced determination of whether this or that individual's felony record is less disqualifying, and which felons deserve to be hired despite their criminal conduct. This is a virtually impossible rule to apply, and yet easy to avoid by the shrewd employer who does not explicitly and categorically deny applications from ex-felons.

The state of Texas sued the EEOC, alleging that the regulations infringed on the state's authority to impose categorical bans on hiring felons for certain jobs. "The Obama administration overreached its legal authority by imposing EEOC hiring directives that preempt state law and ignore the very real risks to public safety," said Texas

Attorney General Ken Paxton. On August 6, 2019, the 5th Circuit Court of Appeals sided with Texas and struck down this guidance.[17]

But rules like these stymie economic growth and innovation, and most importantly, tend to harm the so-called beneficiaries the most. Employees whose firing or failure to hire could result in fines or civil judgments are far less attractive to employers and will, in fact, encourage employers to spend scarce hiring and business resources trying to avoid them.

Because Trump signaled that he would unshackle industry from growth-killing regulations, the four quarters of 2017 marked a positive turning point in terms of economic growth. From 2010 through 2016, real output in the United States grew at an average annual rate of 2.1 percent, while labor productivity grew, on average, by less than 1 percent. The pace of economic recovery was slow by historical standards. Deeper recessions are typically succeeded by steeper expansions. The recent recovery since 2009 is a rare exception. The anemic growth since the recession officially ended in 2009 is a direct reflection of policy choices centered around market intervention and regulation rather than promoting economic growth.

The evidence of anemic growth suggests that the Obama administration's emphasis on regulation and taxation helped to weaken capital formation, thereby restraining capital deepening, productivity growth, and ultimately, output and real wage growth. As a result, labor productivity turned net negative in 2012 and 2013 for the first time since World War II.

Increases in transfer payments (welfare, food assistance, and unemployment benefits) accounted for one-third of the overall decline in labor market participation during the recovery. Under the

---

17    Lisa Nagele-Piazza, J.D. SHRM-SCP, "Texas Wins Challenge to EEOC Guidance on Criminal Background Checks," SHRM (Society for Human Resource Management), August 8, 2019, https://www.shrm.org/resourcesandtools/legal-and-compliance/employment-law/pages/texas-wins-challenge-to-eeoc-guidance-on-criminal-background-checks.aspx. The 5th Circuit, found specifically that EEOC and the U.S. attorney general may not treat the guidance as binding in any respect.

Trump administration, there are two million fewer people currently receiving food assistance than under President Obama. MAGA-nomics sees employment and skills development through on the job training or more formal education as key to reducing government transfer payments that encourage rather than discourage work.

Curbing the opioid crisis, another policy priority of the president, is of critical importance for ensuring a stable or growing employment rate among prime-age workers. The president has focused on curtailing the supply of illegal drugs, therefore reducing addiction rates. Individuals who are currently out of the labor force because of drug addiction may struggle to re-enter without additional investments in skill upgrading. Progress on the opioid addiction front might stem the tide of workers into nonparticipation, and over time, even improve the labor participation rate.

## INTERNATIONAL TRADE: A RESTORATION OF "FAIR TRADE"

The third prong of MAGA-nomics is fairer trade. Many have mistaken some of the president's actions in penalizing imports from China and other countries as "protectionist" measures. They are not. These are merely corrective measures. There is a massive amount of asymmetry in trade practice around the world. While the U.S. has some of the lowest tariffs among economically developed countries, many of our trading partners impose significant tariff and non-tariff barriers on imports from the U.S. This isn't fair trade or free trade. The EU imposes a 10 percent tariff on U.S. autos sold into Europe, while we have only a 2.5 percent tariff on auto imports from Europe.

The steel industry is another prime example of how MAGA-nomics is improving the lives of Americans. Previous administrations have struggled to address the protectionist industrial policies of our trading partners around steel exports and imports. A whole cottage industry of lawyers and law firms has grown up around the various unfair trade practices of our trading partners. The bilateral trade deal the Obama administration negotiated with South Korea, for example, did not address the non-tariff barriers preventing U.S. autos from being sold in South Korea.

The U.S. trade policy framework that has been in place over the past fifty years was characterized by our cold war diplomacy. The U.S. was trying to sell democracy and capitalism around the world in order to curb the spread of communism. One way it did that was by permitting asymmetric terms (i.e., we were willing to allow the economic benefits of trade to disproportionately benefit other countries rather than the United States). We gave countries we wanted to influence, preferential access to our markets without requiring that they similarly open their markets to us.

And it worked. We were able to stem the tide of communism and move the world to a more democratic vision. But the trade incentives we employed also came at some significant cost to the American worker. At the same time we were fighting communism, domestically we dramatically raised the cost of manufacturing, and related blue collar industries in the U.S. with various regulatory interventions.

It is now time that we evolve to a more mature posture of requiring our trading partners to carry more of their own weight and simultaneously relax some of our industry regulation. The Trump administration is addressing this by successfully renegotiating key aspects of existing agreements, such as NAFTA, and by requiring the EU to shoulder more of the financial responsibility for joint military defense commitments under NATO. Trump's successful push to get NATO countries to actually live up to their obligations of committing 2 percent or more of their GDP to defense commitments was a major win for the American people, who have had to shoulder far more than their share of the NATO commitment in the past.

Combined with new measures rolling back regulation of the domestic automobile industry as well as the energy sector, Trump's focus on trade equity internationally is likely to revitalize the U.S. economy.

China's entering the World Trade Organization has greatly harmed American communities. Not only has China manipulated its own markets and currency in contravention of WTO rules, it has also targeted American industries through import subsidies and other transgressive trade practices, including intellectual property theft and piracy. The problem is that the remedies pursuant to the WTO have not been an effective deterrent against China's rule-skirting trade practices. It gains far more from breaking the rules (while the U.S. follows them) and paying the eventual penalty, which is often five or more years in the future, than by following the rules and playing fairly. This is a classic problem in economics, reminiscent of the Prisoner's Dilemma in which the cheating party unfairly seizes the shared benefits of free trade, thereby leaving the entire relationship worse-off than if each side had abided by the rules.

One thing is certain. If every country on earth adopted U.S. liberal international trade practices, global GDP would explode. As things stand today, many of our trading partners skirt the line with respect to bilateral and multilateral trade agreements with the U.S., and thus reap benefits while disadvantaging the U.S. By insisting on renegotiating trade agreements with our largest trading partners, the Trump administration is actually honoring America's commitment to free trade in the truest meaning of the term.

In October 2018, the Trump administration announced its most important trade achievement to date, an updated NAFTA, which will be called the United States-Mexico-Canada Agreement, or USMCA, after a year of intense negotiations that were often fraught with dramatic protests by our Mexican and Canadian trading partners. The USMCA is a major improvement over NAFTA in that it protects American jobs, particularly in the transportation and logistics sectors, brings more manufacturing onshore, and grants fairer access for U.S. firms to consumer markets in Mexico and Canada.

In yet another sign of how progressives in Congress thwart the economic ambitions of Americans—especially blacks—after the mid-term elections, Congress forced the USMCA to wait more than a year for ratification to prevent a political victory for Donald Trump.

It is one thing to signal a tougher tone on trade, but quite another to implement tougher trade policies and use them as a negotiating tool. One of the most impactful measures that Trump has enacted are the tariffs against China. In 2019, President Trump announced significant tariffs affecting more than $250 billion in Chinese imports to the U.S. In retaliation, China began to impose its own set of tariffs, primarily on its imports of American agricultural products. An interesting thing about the Chinese—they love their pork. In fact, pork is a dietary staple in China, comparable to chicken in the U.S. China's leverage to increase tariffs—and pass on pork price increases to their domestic market—was severely curtailed this year amid a catastrophic swine flu epidemic that is said to have affected nearly a third of the world's pork production. The rise in pork prices due to the combination of domestic tariffs and sharply curtailed global supply proved to be a significant factor in the political unrest that arose in Hong Kong—China's offshore mercantile colony.

The rising political unrest in Hong Kong has brought China back to the negotiating table and forced it to begin, in earnest, negotiating a "fair trade" framework that would protect American intellectual property and open its markets on fairer terms, to U.S. imports. China backed off from further planned sanctions, and a new deal seems likely to be struck soon.[18]

# HOW MAGA-NOMICS ARE IMPROVING THE LIVES OF BLACK AMERICANS

Americans are only recently coming to terms with record low black unemployment in the U.S. But we still haven't yet understood the

---

18    Conrad Black, "Trump's Economic Triumph," *National Review*, September 26, 2019, https://www.nationalreview.com/2019/09/donald-trump-economic-success-prosperity-increasing/.

strong correlations between employment, poverty, and crime. A look at the historical record of blacks and employment, as well as the role of the Democratic Party as the former political auxiliary of the Ku Klux Klan, are helpful in understanding how things have changed.

As then-director of the Office of Management and Budget (and formerly the president's chief of staff) Mick Mulvaney explained in The Wall Street Journal, "MAGA-nomics is for everyone, but especially for those who left for work this morning in the dark but came home after their kids were asleep. It is for those who are working part-time but praying for a full-time job. It's for folks whose savings are as exhausted as they are.

"This president hears you. He knows America's greatness does not spring from higher taxes, unnecessary regulations, or broken welfare programs. It does not come from government at all. It comes from you." The OMB Director succinctly described Black America beleaguered by eight years of President Obama's failed economic policies.

## MAGA-nomics Helps Distressed Communities by Spurring Much-Needed Private Investment

The first and foremost sign that MAGA-nomics is working for Black America is the record unemployment rate for black Americans. However, more broadly, the labor market policies adopted by the Trump administration have the potential to expand opportunities for the communities in which black Americans live. One of the most challenging and intractable aspects of the recent recovery is the lack of mobility among Americans experiencing economic distress. Unlike in the past, many Americans will stay in distressed communities rather than simply pick up and leave.

Over the first three years of Donald Trump's presidency, there have been six separate records broken for low unemployment for blacks. As of the fall of 2019, the unemployment rate for blacks broke through the historic barrier that black unemployment is traditionally twice as high as that of whites.[19] Breaking that barrier isn't just psychological. It means that black employment is improving faster than that of whites.

BET founder and former CEO Robert Johnson, who is America's first black billionaire, stated in an interview for CNBC in September 2019, "For African Americans, the trend continues to be favorable. There used to be an old saying, 'When White America catches a cold, African Americans get pneumonia.' It's going the opposite way now. White unemployment is going down, African American unemployment is going down. That's a plus-plus that you can't argue with.... I give the president credit for doing positive things; when I see a president doing positive things, particularly for African Americans."

Black Americans were particularly hard-hit by the housing crisis. Black wealth has been traditionally concentrated in their home equity, and black communities were the most deeply harmed by the decline in housing values during the recession. Reminiscent of the Great Depression, blacks also suffered disproportionately from job losses during the last recession. As mortgages went under water, even blacks who held onto their homes were frequently unable to sell or lease their homes and move to areas where employment opportunities became more plentiful. While homes in exurbs and rural areas declined precipitously in value, the exodus of many workers to urban areas caused a steep and rapid rise in prices and created relative unaffordability of housing in these areas. These dynamics only compounded the geographic immobility experienced by Americans in general, but especially African Americans. There are places that are still suffering—Baltimore, Maryland; Flint, Michigan; Stockton, California; and other rust belt cities—but people are still unable to move away, in part because of the higher cost of living in big cities where the jobs are more concentrated. As a result, some of the most

---

19    "Record-Low Black Unemployment Applauded by Black Activists," Project 21, The National Center, November 1, 2019, https://nationalcenter.org/project21/wp-content/uploads/sites/4/2018/12/black-construction-worker.jpg.

vulnerable people are left stuck amid concentrations of poverty in distressed communities.

The Trump tax bill includes market-based incentives for firms to invest in distressed communities. The new tax law created new organizational forms to help distressed communities, called "Opportunity Zones." Opportunity Zones use tax incentives to draw long-term investment to parts of America that continue to struggle with high poverty and sluggish job and business growth. The provision is the first new substantial federal attempt to aid those communities in more than a decade.

One in six Americans lives in what the Economic Innovation Group calls a "distressed community," where median household incomes remain far below the national level, which is $59,000 a year, and the poverty rate is well above the national average. Those communities are urban, rural, and suburban.[20] They also contain a significantly larger proportion of African Americans than the nation at large.

While most economic development funds have been flowing to the large cities, major investment companies are sitting on an estimated $2 trillion of unrealized capital gains. These will be either taxed at the capital gains rate once the projects are completed, or they can be rolled over to investments in distressed cities without incurring any tax penalty.

Over the past year since the tax law came into effect, investment in these Opportunity Zone funds has attracted intense interest and development. It could also have potentially significant social and cultural effects as the wealthy see investing in poorer communities as a wealth preservation strategy rather than a handout. The potential realignment of interests is huge. We will revisit Opportunity Zones in action in the next chapter.

---

20    Jim Tankersley, "Tucked Into the Tax Bill, a Plan to Help Distressed America," *The New York Times*, July 29, 2018, https://www.nytimes.com/2018/01/29/business/tax-bill-economic-recovery-opportunity-zones.html.

## Black Employment and Labor Market Participation Are Exploding Under Trump

Black unemployment stands at the lowest levels ever recorded. The gap between black unemployment and white unemployment has also narrowed significantly, representing strong relative gains for African Americans. Since the black unemployment rate is catching up with the overall rate, it stands to reason that economic conditions among blacks are improving relatively more rapidly than for Americans overall.

President Trump's recent federal action in drastically reducing the number of green cards granted for low-skilled labor, as well as labor protections built into the newly renegotiated USMCA (formerly NAFTA), promise even more opportunities for African-American workers. This is excellent news, but it is not the end of the struggle for African Americans seeking to achieve the American dream.

The massively disproportionate incarceration rates experienced by African Americans stand in stark contrast to some of the progress we see on the employment front. It is important to mention this here, since incarceration greatly inhibits opportunities for full employment among African Americans.

African Americans today, despite making up only 12 percent of the population, make up more than a third of the nation's prisoners.[21] Black men are six times more likely to be incarcerated than white men are. Black incarceration has devastating sociological effects on the black community, including reducing family formation, reducing fatherhood, and reducing opportunities for skill development and wealth attainment. It is the single-most pernicious social pathology in our society.

Policies that increase black labor market participation, which continues to lag behind that of the overall country at around 62.4

---

21    John Gramlich, "The Gap Between the Number of Blacks and Whites in Prison is Shrinking," FactTank, Pew Research Center, April 30, 2019, https://www.pewresearch.org/fact-tank/2019/04/30/shrinking-gap-between-number-of-blacks-and-whites-in-prison/.

percent (vs. an overall rate of 66 percent) is the best way to improve overall employment among African Americans. And that involves significantly reducing incarceration rates among black males in particular. As the growth in the economy has shown already, by having millions more positions than applicants, some employers are voluntarily recruiting workers with criminal histories—yet another reason why a hot economic market is good for blacks. But here again, agency is important. Blacks—young males in particular—also must take responsibility to not undertake the criminal activities that cause them to be harder to employ or force them out of the workforce altogether.

On the one hand, criminal justice reform is long overdue, and Trump's policies, as we shall explore later in this book, have taken an important first step in this direction. But on the other hand, African Americans' attitudes and philosophical orientation around criminal justice and law enforcement also bear closer examination. One of the most common refrains one hears from black leaders and intellectuals—including former President Barack Obama—is that blacks have been "set up" to fail, and end up in the prison system by design. Others, such as Berkeley Law Professor Michelle Alexander, have gone as far as to say that incarceration among African Americans constitutes a new "Jim Crow," stating, "My experience and research has led me to the regrettable conclusion that our system of mass incarceration functions more like a caste system than a system of crime prevention or control."

These alarmist prevarications are not only untrue, but counterproductive. The *overwhelming* majority of the individuals who are incarcerated are in fact guilty of the crimes of which they have been convicted. They are in prison for a reason—they broke the law. That is not to say that the prison system or criminal justice system is always fair; in some instances it is not. But the principle issue that gets disregarded in this debate is the personal agency one can have in avoiding incarceration by not committing crimes. If blacks cannot seem to get control over that central act of free choice, of volition, if they are merely pawns in a system that controls their every thought and behavior—including acts of violence against other blacks—then it is difficult for blacks as a group to argue that they are worthy candidates for the freedom they are seeking.

## Before Rosa Parks There Was Claudette Colvin

Claudette Colvin's case is illustrative of this principle. An interesting fact about the civil rights movement that many people may be unaware of is that Rosa Parks was not the first black woman in 1955 to be arrested in Montgomery, Alabama, for refusing to give up her bus seat to a white passenger. In fact, nine months before Rosa Parks' refusal to give up her seat and the subsequent boycotts that became famous in the annals of civil rights, Claudette Colvin, a young African-American teenager, also refused to give up her seat to a white passenger and was beaten by police, dragged off the bus, and arrested.

Colvin, who at the time was a fifteen-year-old student at Booker T. Washington High School, relied on the city's gold-and-green buses to get to school. On March 2, 1955, she boarded a public bus, and shortly thereafter, refused to give up her seat to a white man.

"I'd moved for white people before," Colvin later said. But this time, "[t]he spirit of Harriet Tubman and Sojourner Truth was in me. I didn't get up." Colvin was handcuffed and taken to the city jail, where she was charged with disorderly conduct, violating the segregation ordinance, and assault and battery, presumably because she clawed the officers with her fingernails. At the time, Colvin was active in the NAACP's Youth Council, and she was actually being advised by Rosa Parks, who was the secretary of the local Montgomery Chapter of the organization.

The local chapter of the NAACP had been waiting for a test case to challenge bus segregation and vowed to help Colvin. But then came the second-guessing: Colvin's father mowed lawns; her mother was a maid. They were churchgoing people, but they lived in King Hill, the poorest section of Montgomery. The police, who took her to the city hall and then jail, also accused the teenager of spewing curse words. Some black leaders believed she was too young and too dark-skinned to be an effective symbol of injustice for the rest of the nation. Then, as local civil rights leaders continued to debate whether her case was worth contesting, that summer came the news that Colvin was pregnant—by a married man.

Local black leaders felt that this moral transgression would not only scandalize the deeply religious black community, but also make Colvin suspect in the eyes of sympathetic whites. In particular, they felt that the white press would manipulate Colvin's illegitimate pregnancy as a means of undermining Colvin's victim status and any subsequent boycott of the bus company.

Civil rights leaders decided that she was not an ideal test case for the proposition that de jure segregation was a per se violation of the constitutional rights of all African Americans. Even before the Colvin incident, the NAACP had considered and rejected several earlier objectors deemed unsuitable or unable to withstand the pressures of a direct legal challenge to racial segregation laws. The leaders paid her fine and waited for someone else that they could all stand behind.

The Claudette Colvin case illustrates the initially successful 20th-century strategy employed by civil rights organizations to stake their claims for equality using a "model citizen." They pointed out that a professional family man, who was a deacon at his church, was denied the right to buy a home because of racially restricted zoning, or how an upstanding Christian lady (like Rosa Parks) was forced to give up her seat for a white man on a segregated bus.

Unlike the successful techniques of the civil rights era in the '50s and '60s, today it has become fashionable to use the worst-case examples as a basis for more justice and inclusion. This is an ineffective approach to gaining sympathy from the broader society, and more critically, it sends the wrong message to vulnerable youth. Instead of being encouraged to model the best behavior, they are taught to reflexively distrust law enforcement and side psychologically with a criminal element. Prisoners have rights, sure, but is that really where blacks as a group want to plant their flag for equal rights and social advancement? Only if they are unconsciously self-identifying as criminals.

When Rodney King rather than Ben Carson is the subject of your best case for a representative of your race, you signal to the broader society a near complete rejection of the consensus idea of Americanism.

A few of any group can ruin the reputation of all. Not all used car salesmen are liars. Neither are all lawyers schemers. A small group of mostly teenage blacks have created a negative impression for the rest of the country regarding blacks and criminal violence. As criminologist Heather MacDonald points out, a subset of blacks, teenage males, engage in disproportionate lawbreaking, and by doing so, create in the minds of fair-minded Americans—white, black, and brown—a degree of apprehension of black men that hinders job opportunities and broader societal acceptance.

A far better strategy for Black America would be taking the opposite tack. African Americans should return to the practice of celebrating black achievement and education. We should make becoming a "model minority," a social and cultural norm. Blacks must take more agency in how they are perceived by the broader society. All things being equal, it would be far better to be perceived as industrious, studious, educated, and law-abiding than potentially criminal and anti-academic, which is unfortunately the perception too many people hold about blacks today.

In fact, from the end of the slavery to beginning of the modern civil rights era, this was in fact, the perception of blacks.

## A Brief History of Racism and Organized Labor
At the beginning of the 20th Century, *black male unemployment was lower than white male unemployment.* But the dual effects of the Great Depression and new labor laws that tilted heavily against blacks led

the black male unemployment rate to soar from 3.3 percent in 1929 to over 50 percent by 1932.[22]

With support from labor unions, politicians and bureaucrats often intervene in labor markets, creating laws and regulations that (they say) are needed to improve working conditions. The truth is that many of these efforts do great harm to the economic interests of blacks, particularly black males. Most people would be surprised to learn that this harm to blacks has historically been an intentional strategy on the part of organized labor.

The National Recovery Administration, one of the first post-Depression pieces of legislation aimed at protecting labor, did not fare well in the African-American press. "Negro Removal Act," "Negroes Ruined Again," and "Negroes Robbed Again," were only a few of the epithets launched at the program. The NRA, a component of the National Industrial Recovery Act (NIRA), created national minimum wage and maximum hours laws, guaranteed collective bargaining rights and industrial production codes, and it poured vast amounts of tax dollars into public works projects. But it did so at the expense of black workers. Because the projects mandated a "prevailing" union wage—unions from which blacks were explicitly excluded at the time—it tended to undercut opportunities for black workers to offer competitive labor.

Racist preferences and exploitation were masked, hidden beneath the banner of economic "fairness" by "progressive" politicians like Hugo Black of Alabama, the chief sponsor of the Federal Labor Standards Act (FLSA), and a long-time champion of wage and hour limits. Black took the oath to become one of ten thousand members of the Robert E. Lee Klan No. 1, on September 11, 1923, in Birmingham, Alabama. He became an officer of the organization and read the Klan oath as members were initiated. Black was elected to the U.S. Senate in 1926, with the Klan's support just three years later. The Exalted

---

22    Dr. Tomas Sowell, "Ruinous 'Compassion,' " Creators, March 17, 2015, https://www.creators.com/read/thomas-sowell/03/15/ruinous-compassion.

Cyclops of the Lee Klan was his finance chairman, while the Grand Dragon served as his unofficial campaign manager, arranging for Black to visit nearly all 148 Klaverns in Alabama.

Once a member of the Senate, Black championed Roosevelt's social reform legislation and fought against anti-lynching legislation—filibustering that legislation at a time when filibusters meant stand-on-your-feet, talk-until-you're-hoarse, all-night monologues. When a filibuster killed anti-lynching legislation in 1935, the Pittsburgh Post-Gazette reported, "The southerners—headed by Tom Connally of Texas and Hugo Black of Alabama—grinned at each other and shook hands." Given that Hugo Black was the legislative father of the Fair Labor Standards Act, it should come as no surprise that the act was seen as part of an effort to keep black men down. But it was the actual language of the measure that did the most damage.

The early "progressive" labor laws all but eviscerated opportunities for blacks, particularly unskilled black men, and the racial consequence—to use a liberal term, the disparate impact of these laws—continues today.[23] Regulations that limit the ability of an individual to offer to undercut his competition by offering his services at a lower price (even if only temporarily) actually validate bias. Early during the Jim Crow era, blacks overcame racial hostilities in the workplace by underbidding white workers. Even the most bigoted employer understood the benefit of the bargain. But here's the thing, to keep a good worker, employers end up having to increase their pay. And their white counterparts were often either unwilling or unable to match their performance and their labor price bid.

How did they respond? By developing regulations and rules that made "low bids" all but impossible. Consider this example: ground beef costs less than Kobe beef. Many people perceive Kobe beef to be

---

23    Horace Cooper, "The Untold, Racist Origins of 'Progressive' Labor Laws: Protecting 'White Jobs' Was the Purpose of Union-Backed Legislation," Capital Research Center, June 17, 2014, https://capitalresearch.org/article/the-untold-racist-origins-of-progressive-labor-laws-protecting-white-jobs-was-the-purpose-of-union-backed-legislation/.

substantially better in taste and texture. Some could care less. Most, however, are unwilling to pay the premium to get Kobe beef, and are perfectly satisfied with ground beef burgers.

What if the minimum price of ground beef were raised to that of the minimum price for Kobe beef? With the perception that Kobe is better in taste and texture (an acknowledged preference) wouldn't almost everyone only buy Kobe beef, giving short shrift to ground beef? Even people who can't really tell the difference would be inclined to get the beef which is perceived to be superior. And those who can't afford the premium would substitute a new alternative—fish or chicken. Consequently, overall burger consumption would drop, but we'd see a dramatic shift from ground beef to Kobe beef.

So it is with the minimum wage and race. Even if some people perceive white workers to be superior, most won't value that "superiority" enough to pay a premium for white labor. Those that don't perceive white workers to be superior at all will also hire blacks or any other worker at the market rate; and only those that really insist on having a white workforce will pay the premium labor rate. Note that those who place a premium on white workers (and are paying higher labor costs) still must compete with all the other companies that have lower labor costs. Over time, the rightness or wrongness of that perception will be borne out by the profitability of the firm. In the end, what happened in the early 20th century shouldn't come as a surprise. An overwhelming number of employers will select the value proposition—black workers.

But look at what happens when you raise the labor rate or minimum wage above the market rate to the "premium" level. In that case, almost all employers will shift their hiring practices. Instead of hiring the laborer with the lowest cost, employers will validate their biases and hire more whites, who are perceived to be superior. Companies that can't afford to pay the premium will reduce their number of workers and/or make mechanical or computer substitutions. In the end, there will be fewer workers overall, and of those that remain, they'd end up being white. This phenomenon isn't related solely to race. Unnaturally raising pay rate minimums above the market hurts any and all groups—women, youths, immigrants, and so on—that are not *favored* by rewarding the selection of favored groups over the disfavored.

Artificial cost elevation always shifts hiring decisions away from the best value to other ancillary concerns. In the past, when hiring decisions were made based on best value, blacks thrived.

A primary example today is the movement to enact a "living wage." Many blacks have forgotten their abysmal history with the labor movement, and align themselves with labor activists in seeking raises to the federally mandated minimum wage requirement, or even higher state and local "living wage" laws. The argument today is that when low-skilled workers receive a "living wage," they can move off of the government assistance rolls and become more self-sufficient. The evidence thus far has served to reinforce the very traditional predictions one might find in any micro-economics textbook.[24] It is axiomatic—raising the cost of labor will incentivize employers to seek out alternatives—alternatives that validate their perceptions of premium value. Consequently, marginalized groups will suffer.

Employers desperate to stay afloat almost always find a way around market-distorting regulatory interventions. When employers are required to pay more for labor, they choose workers with more skills and seek to implement new technology, such as digital ordering.

---

24    Neumark, David, Wascher, William, "Employment Effects of Minimum and Subminimum Wages: Panel Data on State Minimum Wage Laws," ILR Review: Sage Journals 46 (Cornell University), 1 (October 1, 1992), https://journals.sagepub.com/doi/abs/10.1177/001979399204600105.
Using panel data on state minimum wage laws and economic conditions for the years 1973–89, the authors reevaluate existing evidence on the effects of a minimum wage on employment. Their estimates indicate that a 10 percent increase in the minimum wage causes a decline of 1–2 percent in employment among teenagers and a decline of 1.5–2 percent in employment for young adults, similar to the ranges suggested by earlier time-series studies. The authors also find evidence that youth subminimum wage provisions enacted by state legislatures moderate the disemployment effects of minimum wages on teenagers.

As a result, low-skill workers lose their jobs. Minorities—black men in particular—tend to be overrepresented among the unskilled and suffer disproportionately.

A National Bureau of Economic Research report by economists Jeffrey Clemens and Michael Wither of the University of California, San Diego found that minimum wage increases substantially reduced employment. Increases in the minimum wage were responsible for 14 percent of the decline in the share of the working-age population employed between 2006 and 2012.[25]

Employers generally will pay what the market bears. Fewer than 1.8 percent of American workers actually earn the minimum wage. And in today's full employment environment, employers are actually competing for workers, even in low-skilled sectors such as retail, causing them to offer wages much higher than the minimum wage.

When President Trump announced that he was cutting the corporate tax rate, arguing that firms would use the extra money to hire more workers and pay higher wages, many critics countered that companies would simply pay out the windfall profits to shareholders and keep wages constant. That certainly does not seem to be happening. Note, these companies are not raising wages out of the kindness of their hearts, but out of economic necessity. The market is signaling that workers can demand a higher wage because the demand for labor has exceeded the supply. Once again, we see that a hot economic market is far better for households than government intervention.

Black male unemployment has been substantially elevated above white males since the Great Depression. Progressives blame a broader racist American society, yet history shows that the very market-distorting polices the left advocates for are the biggest cause of the phenomenon. Is this unwillingness to reconsider the harm of the

---

25    Diana Furchtgott-Roth, "Column: Raising the Minimum Wage
      Lowers Employment for Teens and Low-Skill Workers," PBS News
      Hour, December 16, 2016, https://www.pbs.org/newshour/economy/
      column-minimum-wage-lowers-employment-teens-low-skill-workers.

policies just a form of foolish stubbornness or is it a modern form of bigotry?

## Blacks Should Take Greater Advantage of Private Industry and Rely Less on Government Employment for Middle Class Growth

MAGA-nomics is all about private sector growth. The shift from the government being a primary source of economic activity, shrinking state and local budgets, and the shrinking of the social safety net means that black folks who have traditionally relied upon "good government jobs" to secure a sort of middle class status face a reckoning.

Over the last three plus years, the economic environment has been strikingly good for all Americans. The policies of President Trump have created this once-in-a-lifetime climate. While the fire is hot, now is the time for all Americans—in particular blacks—to take part.

Government jobs are not the bastion of safety and security they once were. At the federal level, whole agencies are being restructured and downsized by the Trump administration. Under rules put in place by the administration, it is becoming easier to fire federal workers. Public sector benefits at the state and local level, particularly public pension funds, are under increasing strain. During the last Great Recession, pension authorities in several large American cities with significant African-American populations of government employees simply went insolvent and failed to honor their obligations. Even major appropriations for national priorities such as defense are coming under increasing scrutiny as the federal government is coming to grips with massive debt burdens. And with the passage of the Jobs and Tax Cuts Act, which limits the deductibility of local and state taxes, state governments are under significant pressure to reassess their public sector commitments.

Today, black Americans constitute nearly 20 percent of the federal workforce, the only sector of the economy in which they are over-represented. In fact, blacks are 30 percent "more likely" to join the local, state, and federal public sector workforce, compared with 16.3 percent of non-black workers.[26] The simple truth is that relying on government employment as a secure means of attaining middle class status is not a viable long-term wealth strategy for any group—particularly black Americans. Take a look at the top 1,000 wealthiest Americans in the country; how many are career government employees?

With rapid technological change, global competition, and increased economic stratification, average no longer cuts it. The better economic strategy for African Americans is to obtain an education or competitive skills and enter into private industry. It is noteworthy that most immigrants to this country encourage their children to enter only three fields: science and medicine, engineering, and business. They are not doing this because they hate law, liberal arts, or music. They are doing it because they do not have the luxury of failing to advance economically in a society that is increasingly winner-take-all. African Americans should absolutely adopt this strategy going forward.

Blacks must take the stance of former president and signer of the Declaration of Independence, John Adams, who, in a letter to his wife, Abigail, remarked, "I must study Politicks and War that my sons may have liberty to study… Mathematicks and Philosophy. My sons ought to study Mathematicks and Philosophy, Geography, natural History, Naval Architecture, navigation, Commerce and Agriculture, in order to give their Children a right to study Painting, Poetry, Musick, Architecture, Statuary, Tapestry and Porcelaine." African Americans have not even evolved economically as a group to the point Adams envisioned for his children. But they often behave as if they are in the position of leisure he envisioned for his grandchildren.

---

26    Steven C. Pitts, "Black Workers and the Public Sector," UC Berkeley Labor Center, April 4, 2011, http://laborcenter.berkeley.edu/black-workers-and-the-public-sector/.

# CONCLUSION

Everyone wants to earn more money, and certainly African Americans are no exception. But by aligning politically with free market *interventionistas*, such as organized labor, they have often found themselves excluded from the vastly higher financial rewards afforded by success in the private sector. By aligning with free market economics, African Americans have a better chance of both obtaining full-time employment, earning higher wages, and building generational wealth. The same strategies that led to job attainment and prosperity for blacks in the early 20th century—hard work and industriousness, attaining in-demand skills, and aligning themselves politically and culturally with private industry—will work again in the 21st.

President Trump's policies have already greatly helped black Americans economically. Record low unemployment and expanded home ownership, as well as blacks participating in new business creation, have all improved under the Trump administration. Another term could be transformative for blacks and the nation as a whole.

# Chapter 2

❧

# CHA-CHING!

Let's face it, money talks. When people begin to feel as if they have some control over their job prospects and their economic destinies, they tend to feel more confident and optimistic about the future. Since Trump's election, confidence in our economy has skyrocketed, as measured by Gallup's Economic Confidence index, which reached a twenty-year high in January of 2020.[27] This increasing optimism is reflected in the record increases in small business starts among African Americans.[28]

Over the past three years since taking office, the Trump administration steadily pushed for Congress to pass tax reform that lowers corporate and individual tax rates, signaling President Trump's confidence that Americans are smarter than their government when it comes to putting their hard-earned money to work to their greatest benefit. The tax reforms already proposed and adopted have helped

---

27    Justin McCarthy, "U.S. Economic Confidence at Highest Point Since 2000," *Gallup.com*, https://news.gallup.com/poll/283940/economic-confidence-highest-point-2000.aspx.
      Americans' confidence in the U.S. economy is higher than at any point in about two decades. The latest figure from Gallup's Economic Confidence Index is +40, the highest reading recorded since +44 in October 2000.

28    Gene Marks, "African American businesses grew 400% – but they still need investment," *The Guardian*, February 17, 2019. https://www.theguardian.com/business/2019/feb/17/african-american-small-business-growth-investment.

black Americans financially, putting more money in their pockets and bank accounts.

These measures are also spurring new capital investment, increasing economic productivity, and contributing to rising worker pay, especially among African Americans. An atmosphere of general prosperity is prompting special employee bonuses across industries, and of course, creating jobs for the under-employed. The Trump administrations' pro-business policies have also spurred new confidence among African-American entrepreneurs, and are inspiring what appears to be a renaissance in black business endeavors.

The economic and social policies—especially tax reform—pursued and implemented by the Trump administration have also increased household income and helped small business owners succeed. Since 2016, black Americans are earning more, saving more, and investing more. The average year-over-year wage increase for January through March 2018 was the highest for any three-month period since mid-2009. Corporate announcements provide further evidence of tax reform's positive impact on wages, with nearly five hundred employers already having announced bonuses or pay increases, affecting more than 5.5 million American workers.[29]

---

29    John Kartch, "List of Tax Reform Good News," Americans for Tax Reform, October 31, 2018, https://www.atr.org/sites/default/files/assets/NationalListofTaxReformGoodNews%20%287%29.pdf.

## Partial List of Companies Announcing Raises and Bonuses in Response to Trump Tax Cuts

| Company | State | Action | Scope of Impact |
|---|---|---|---|
| Almo Corporation | Philadelphia, PA | $1,000 Incremental Bonus | The capital improvements include a new 300,000-square-foot distribution center in Philadelphia. |
| Allsup's Convenience Stores, Inc. | New Mexico | One-time cash bonuses of $1,000 for all full-time, non-executive full-time and part-time employees | Operates 317 stores in New Mexico, West Texas, and Oklahoma and employs 3,200 |
| Altria Group Inc. | Richmond, VA | $3,000 bonus to approximately 7,900 non-executive level employees | A total of $24 million in bonuses, increased charitable contributions |
| American Airlines | Ft. Worth, Texas | $1,000 bonuses for every employee (excluding officers) | The bonuses will total $130 million. AA had 127,600 employees as of Sept. 2017. |
| American Family Insurance | Madison, WI | 11,000 workers will receive a $1,000 bonus | Reduction in the corporate income tax rate also would help fuel permanent changes to its employee benefits program, such as expanded tuition reimbursement, paying student loans, and scholarships for workers who pursue a post-high school degree. |
| BancorpSouth Bank | Tupelo, Miss. | Pay raises for over 70 percent of employees, $1,000 bonuses for nearly 20 percent of employees | BancorpSouth employs some 4,000 employees in more than 230 locations in Alabama, Arkansas, Florida, Louisiana, Mississippi, Missouri, Tennessee, and Texas. |
| Bank of America | Charlotte, NC | $1,000 bonuses | 145,000 U.S. employees will receive bonuses |
| Best Buy | Richfield, Minn. | $1,000 bonuses for full-time employees, $500 bonuses for part-time employees | Over 100,000 employees will receive bonuses. |
| Big River Steel | Osceola, Ark. | Investing $1.2 billion in expansion and creating an additional 500 jobs | The jobs will pay on average about $75,000 annually. |

In 2018, Walmart, the nation's largest private employer, announced a two-dollar-an-hour increase in starting wages, and a one-dollar-an-hour rise in its base wage for current employees. That means up to $3,040 per year in additional pay for full-time workers.

And it's not just big business on the rise. Crain's Business Daily reported, "Ohio's small and midsized business owners are more optimistic about their businesses and the overall U.S. economy today than any point since the Great Recession began to recede, according to a new report by PNC Financial Services. PNC's spring economic outlook and survey of small-to-midsize businesses finds that, in Ohio, more than half of business owners are expecting sales increases in the next six months, which is the highest level of optimism seen since 2012."

Ohio is not an outlier. Small and midsized businesses in Pennsylvania and Florida have also demonstrated unusual optimism about the growth prospects of the new economy, and many plan to raise employee pay and hire more staff. Such rising optimism helps explain why black Americans are better off today than they were before President Trump took office, and why black unemployment continues to break new record lows.

## TRUMP'S ECONOMIC POLICIES ARE DELIVERING RECORD-BREAKING RESULTS FOR AFRICAN AMERICANS

African-American unemployment fell to a record low of 5.9 percent in August 2018, and to another record low of 5.6 percent in October 2019. Over the three years through 2019, African-American employment has increased by more than 1.2 million new hires. African-American labor force participation has similarly increased, and the gap has narrowed compared to overall labor force participation. Blacks' share of the labor force has increased from 9.9 percent in 1976 to 12.3 percent in 2016. This increase is expected to continue, reaching a projected 12.7 percent by 2026.[30] Even more promisingly, unemployment among African-American teenagers fell to 19.3 percent in 2018, which is the lowest figure on record. That number stands in marked contrast to the 2010 rate of 48.9 percent under the Obama administration.[31]

For a president decried by progressives as hostile to the interests of black America, these results provide positive proof that Donald Trump is not the bogey man blacks should fear, but he is absolutely someone for blacks to revere and appreciate.

The primary driver of these record improvements in employment for blacks is the nearly 3 percent average annual GDP growth resulting from Donald Trump's economic policies.[32] Median household income rose 2.3 percent since Trump took office. Average income rose 2.8 percent, and the poverty rate and food stamp rolls fell.[33] Astoundingly, there are 350,000 fewer African Americans in poverty during the Trump presidency. To paraphrase HUD Secretary Dr. Ben Carson, if Trump is racist, he's certainly a bad one. What kind of self-respecting racist would help employ over a million more African Americans and oversee the elevation of hundreds of thousands more out of poverty?

A rising sea tends to float all boats. But the most encouraging aspect of Trump's economic record for African Americans is that job

---

30 Emily, Rolen and Mitra Toossi, "Blacks in the Labor Force," U.S. Bureau of Labor Statistics, U.S. Department of Labor, February 2018, https://www.bls.gov/careeroutlook/2018/article/blacks-in-the-labor-force.htm.

31 Paul Davidson, "Jobs report: Black teen unemployment fell to 19.3 percent in September, lowest on record," *USA Today,* https://www.usatoday.com/story/money/2018/10/05/jobs-report-black-teen-unemployment-lowest-record/1536572002/.

32 "Economy Reaches Longest Expansion in U.S. History in Third Quarter of 2019, Beats Market Expectations," Council of Economic Advisors, The White House, October 30, 2019, https://www.whitehouse.gov/articles/economy-reaches-longest-expansion-in-u-s-history-in-third-quarter-of-2019-beats-market-expectations/.

33 Brooks Jackson, "Trump's Numbers: October 2019 Update," FactCheck. Org, October 11, 2019, https://www.factcheck.org/2019/10/trumps-numbers-october-2019-update/.

and wage growth have been concentrated among lower-skilled and entry-level workers, which coincides with President Trump's effort to curb illegal immigration and imported labor. Blacks, especially black males, are over-represented among lower-skilled and entry-level workers. Thus, the net result of the expansion of opportunities at the lower end of the employment pyramid has been to empower minority job applicants in ways not seen in over half a century. Far from marginalizing blacks, Trump's message is that every American worker is now a critical part of maintaining and growing the red-hot economy. In a job-short economy, laborers suddenly have a lot of leverage over their employers, and wages are rising to the tune of nearly 2.9 percent over the course of Trump's presidency thus far.

As mentioned above, the strongest wage growth over the past two years came among workers in the bottom tenth of the income distribution. Furthermore, according to data collected and analyzed by the Federal Reserve Bank of Dallas, blacks achieved the fastest annual wage growth of any ethnic group, at roughly 3.3 percent between 2018 and 2019.[34]

The poverty rate among African Americans reached its lowest level on record in 2017. In 2017, African-American poverty was 21.2 percent, a record low, and less than half the peak rate of 41.8 percent in 1966.[35] President Trump has repeatedly touted the fact that helping blacks to achieve economic success is one of his proudest achievements. In a political rally in Wheeling, West Virginia on September 29, 2018, he exclaimed, "The poverty rates for African Americans and Hispanic Americans—it's been incredible, they've all reached their lowest levels in the history of our country." And he's

---

34    Michael Morris, Robert Rich, and Joseph Tracy, "As Wages Rise, Are Black Workers Seeing the Smallest Gains?" Federal Reserve Bank of Dallas, July 16, 2019, https://www.dallasfed.org/research/economics/2019/0716.

35    Patrick Orsagos, "Is African-American, Hispanic Poverty at All-Time Low?" PolitiFact, October 23, 2018, https://www.politifact.com/west-virginia/statements/2018/oct/23/donald-trump/african-american-hispanic-poverty-all-time-low/.

not merely posturing when he says this. He truly believes that fully restoring America's promise is good for all Americans—including African Americans.

## Promising Employment Sectors for African Americans

One of the key factors necessary to build on the positive trend of African-American employment growth is for blacks to make a concerted effort to seek employment opportunities in the private sector as opposed to the public sector. This is critical for two reasons. The first is that over the past half-century, black middle-class growth has been primarily driven by participation in the government employment sector. As that sector shrinks due to a cultural shift in America away from government services (e.g., to quote President Clinton's famous line from his 1996 State of the Union Address, "The Era of Big Government is Over"[36] ) which in the past competed for private business spending, there will be fewer employment opportunities in the public sector. The second critical factor is that as the private sector becomes more deregulated, it will once again become a remarkably powerful economic growth engine in the country and the place where significantly expanded employment opportunities will exist. For blacks to continue to achieve the gains in employment and wealth creation that they have experienced thus far, they will need to take full advantage of this generational shift towards private sector development.

Every economically successful ethnic group in America has ultimately achieved success, not through government employment, but by a significant presence in the private sector. A casual look at the racial makeup of the top 5 percent of wealthy individuals in America is quite revealing. Asians, whites, and East Indians in America are the wealthiest ethnic groups, and they are overwhelmingly dominant

---

36    William J. Clinton, "*State of the Union Address,*" January 23, 1996, https://clintonwhitehouse4.archives.gov/WH/New/other/sotu.html.

in the private sector, especially in fields like telecommunications, science, management, and finance. To measure the impact of wealth attainment in income terms, consider that the highest paid 10 percent of workers earns nearly six times as much as the lowest paid 10 percent. Black income earners are disproportionately situated in the lower income distribution, and are all but non-existent in percentage terms in the highest income distribution. Compare this to Asian Americans, who as a group constitute a full 40 percent of the highest income distribution (above $200,000).[37]

Today, black workers are heavily concentrated in job fields related to office administrative support, transportation logistics, food preparation and service, production and manufacturing, health care administration, and personal care and services. Of those sectors, the fastest growing in terms of the overall economy are transportation and logistics, and health care. The Trump administration's renegotiated trade agreements with Canada and Mexico stand to greatly increase American workers' opportunities in the transportation and logistics businesses. The freight rolling between Canada and the U.S. was valued at $582.4 billion between 2016 and 2017, according to the U.S. Department of Transportation. In 2017, trucks carried half the $300 billion of goods traveling to the U.S. from Canada, and 65.7 percent of the $282.5 billion of goods from Canada to the United States. Black workers in the transportation and logistics business stand to greatly benefit from the increased market share of transportation business going to U.S. firms, as prescribed under the new agreement.

Over the next decade, overall employment in America is expected to grow by over 11.5 million jobs, to reach a total of about 167.6 million jobs in 2026. Nine out of ten new jobs are projected to be added in the service-providing sector, resulting in more than 10.5 million new jobs in this area. Health care support occupations (23.6

---

37    "Household Income in the United States," Statistical Atlas, https://statisticalatlas. com/United-States/Household-Income.

percent) and health care practitioners and technical occupations (15.3 percent) are projected to be among the fastest growing occupational groups over this period.[38] These two occupational groups—which together account for thirteen of the thirty fastest growing occupations from 2016 to 2026—are projected to contribute about one-fifth of all new jobs by 2026. Additional demographic factors such as the aging baby boom population, longer life expectancies, and growing rates of chronic conditions will drive continued demand for health care services. To the extent that African Americans are already concentrated in health and community and social services occupations (including social work, home health care, and childcare services[39]), they should continue to develop skills and career orientation that put them in position to take advantage of growth in these occupational sectors.

However, black Americans lack proportional representation among the second-fastest growing group of occupations, computer and mathematical occupations, and construction and mining jobs. While the science and engineering occupations account for about 12 percent of overall jobs, blacks perform only 5 percent of those jobs, representing less than half their percentage of the total work-force.[40] As lucrative opportunities in science and engineering expand, these occupational endeavors will offer significant opportunities for wage and income growth, and yet the absence of black representation might pose the most onerous challenge the black community faces in terms of overall growth and prosperity going forward. We have seen miracles in science and technology virtually transform the

38    "Employment Projections—2018–2028," U.S. Bureau of Labor Statistics, U.S. Department of Labor, September 4, 2019, https://www.bls.gov/news.release/pdf/ecopro.pdf.

39    Emily, Rolen and Mitra Toossi, "Blacks in the Labor Force," U.S. Bureau of Labor Statistics, U.S. Department of Labor, February 2018, https://www.bls.gov/careeroutlook/2018/article/blacks-in-the-labor-force.htm.

40    "Scientists and Engineers Working in Science and Engineering Occupations: 2015," National Center for Science and Engineering Statistics (NCSES), National Science Foundation (NSF) https://www.nsf.gov/statistics/2017/nsf17310/digest/occupation/overall.cfm.

marketplace over the past half-century, most notably in computer science and engineering. And most of the new wealth creation in the post-industrial age is concentrated in the tech sector.

Early in his term, the president signed a memorandum dedicating at least $200 million a year to promote STEM education efforts targeted at women and minorities.[41] There are currently 5.6 million jobs available to the workforce, many of which go unfilled due to lack of skilled applicants. Numeracy, the ability to reason and communicate mathematically, is the new superpower of the 21st century—not, as some have advocated, a secret mineral called "vibranium" mined in a fantasy land called "Wakanda."[42] Making numeracy a priority will yield huge wealth gains for blacks and for America.

The sectors with the lowest projected wage and salary growth, and even shrinkage, include jobs in state and local government, which are projected to grow at merely 0.4 percent over the decade ending in 2026. Federal government employment alone is actually expected to shrink by roughly 0.2 percent over the ensuing decade.[43] African Americans should pay particularly close attention to this trend. The government sector is either shrinking or stagnating, and the historical approach of African Americans pursuing government occupations as a path to middle-class income and wealth attainment does not offer a viable wealth creation strategy—especially if blacks aspire to close the wealth gap. Actions of the Trump White House leading to an expanding private sector are presenting the very opportunity many blacks want to narrow that wealth gap.

---

41    Ian Kullgren and Caitlin Emma, "Trump Directs $200 Million to Tech Education for Women and Minorities," *Politico*, September 25, 2017, https://www.politico.com/story/2017/09/25/trump-stem-technology-grants-women-minorities-243115.

42    A reference to the wildly popular *Black Panther* movie, adopted by some African Americans as a symbol of Black achievement. Some it seems would rather adopt a fantasy than pursue real opportunities.

43    "Employment Projections—2018–2028," U.S. Bureau of Labor Statistics, U.S. Department of Labor, September 4, 2019, https://www.bls.gov/news.release/pdf/ecopro.pdf.

## Asteroid Mining: The Real Wakanda

The basic premise of economics—and why it is sometimes referred to as the "dismal science"—is that it primarily concerns the allocation of allegedly "limited" resources. This assumption, in fact, has produced wars and famines, motivated autocratic regimes, and animated failed socialist experiments as well as internecine political conflicts that have divided nations and races. In fact, communism as practiced in the former Soviet Union, and currently in China, was predicated upon the notion that more for some automatically meant less for others. But the history of America belies the notion of limits and scarcity. We are by instinct and creed a people who believe in the growth possibilities afforded to us by a history of expansion, exploration, and innovation. We are not at the end of the arc in that respect. In fact, we have much room to grow.

One such frontier opportunity is to harvest rare earth minerals from asteroids that pass through our solar system. Some estimates place the mineral wealth on near-earth asteroids in the multi-trillions of dollars. American companies such as Deep Space Industries, Kepler Energy & Space Engineering, and Planetary Resources are already at the forefront of this promising new endeavor.[44]

Noted African-American physicist Dr. Neil DeGrasse Tyson thinks the prospect of industrial mining of asteroids is not only possible, but likely. "For me," Tyson says, "those ideas are plausible, but they're also a bit dull. So since we're talking about an industry that could potentially change humanity's relationship with space while also dramatically stretching our ideas of personal wealth, why not come up with a wild strategy for collecting this staggering bounty?"

There are, of course, many technological and financial hurdles to overcome before such a venture becomes immediately feasible. But

---

44     Kyle Maxey, "Asteroid Mining—Who Wants to be a Trillionaire?" Engineering. com, July 21, 2017, https://www.engineering.com/DesignerEdge/ DesignerEdgeArticles/ArticleID/15308/Asteroid-Mining-Who-Wants-to-be-a-Trillionaire.aspx.

that is what was true of all ventures that created the world's current bounty—including space travel, and the discovery and colonization of America. These were each endeavors that many believed were impossible, or at least unprofitable, but whose subsequent achievement created some of the greatest wealth the world has ever seen.

As Dr. Tyson puts it, "Who wants to be the world's first trillionaire?" African Americans were late to the game in terms of dominating the technology sector and other exploratory cutting-edge industries, and many are now clamoring for a seat at the table in sectors (such as social media, digital advertising, and search engine development) that have already experienced exponential growth and are now maturing. Why not plan for the future by developing skills in math, science, and engineering around the profitable extraction of space resources now, and be a part shareholder during the creation of the wealth, rather than seek a share after the fact?

## TRUMP ADMINISTRATION IS INVESTING IN DISTRESSED COMMUNITIES

As previously discussed in the first Chapter on MAGA-nomics, one of President Trump's most promising new opportunities for struggling African-American communities is what are called "Opportunity Zones" (or "OZ"), a critical component of the tax reform act of 2017. Opportunity Zones are a major new investment in economically distressed communities, particularly in cities that have seen their populations and industries decimated by a decline in manufacturing spurred by exporting those jobs overseas, as well as being stymied by failed urban policy solutions that rely on excessive regulation and generous welfare subsidies.

Opportunity Zones are special geographic areas in which the U.S. tax code creates dramatic incentives for the private sector to attract investment and job creation. Typically located in high-unemployment and low-income areas, Opportunity Zones are a remarkable tool for using the private sector to address poverty and blight.

The zones were included in the tax reform law at the initiative of Senator Tim Scott, a South Carolina Republican and the only black Republican member of the United States Senate. Opportunity Zones are based on a bill he co-sponsored in 2017 with several Democrats.[45] In an interview with Bloomberg news in 2018, Senator Scott said:

> "The goal is to bring private sector dollars to come in and challenge some of the poverty that has been too persistent in some of the areas. I'm excited about it because I grew up in some of those communities, in a single parent household. So I understand the potential that we have in some of those communities. We can excavate that potential through economic development. We had a bipartisan coalition who supported the legislation. This is an American piece of legislation focused on those who need it the most. The mayors in these cities, many of them Democrat, are very excited about it. This is not shifting government dollars around. There are two trillion dollars of unrealized capital gains sitting on the sidelines. There have been too many hurdles to reinvest in some of the most powerful communities and high potential communities. This lowers that burden and we will see a surge of opportunities in distressed communities."

The OZ framework provides incentives for private equity and venture capital firms to invest their profits tax-free, in areas that desperately need economic development. As such, it has the potential to become a powerful engine for new job creation. Nearly

---

45    Jim Tankersley, "Tucked Into the Tax Bill, a Plan to Help Distressed America," *The New York Times*, July 29, 2018, https://www.nytimes.com/2018/01/29/business/tax-bill-economic-recovery-opportunity-zones.html.

thirty-five million Americans comprising 8,761 communities in all fifty states, the District of Columbia, and five United States territories, live in communities designated as Opportunity Zones. Fifty-six percent of the residents of community zones are minorities.[46] These tax incentives have the potential to jumpstart American communities and create momentum for economic recovery, especially in racially diverse areas.

One of the primary ways that local government and entrepreneurs in areas with concentrated African-American populations can get involved in attracting needed investment through Opportunity Zones is to provide workforce development programs to draw employers to opportunity zones. Both the private and public sectors—including historically black colleges and universities (Land Grant Institutions)—should be eager to invest in skills training so that there are qualified individuals to fill new jobs businesses will be bringing to the community.

An increased employment skills base will enhance the community's attractiveness for OZ investment and ensure that the new capital coming into your community has a real and positive impact on people's lives. Facilitating OZ investments that hold real potential to create new jobs and increase wages is a great way to get the community to rally behind a development.

Partnering with major employers and anchor institutions (such as historically black colleges and universities) in the communities adjoining an Opportunity Zone can also help generate momentum and help get ahead of the curve on this ground-floor opportunity. In February 2017, President Trump signed an executive order renewing the White House Initiative on Historically Black Colleges and Universities (HBCUs), placing it within the Department of Education, and in 2018, President Trump signed legislation that increased federal funding to HBCU programs by more than 14 percent. The president also signed legislation that forgave more than $300 million

---

in Hurricane-Katrina-related debt that threatened New Orleans, Louisiana-area HBCUs. And perhaps most importantly of all, President Trump signed into law the FUTURE Act, which permanently installs over $255 million in annual funding to HBCUs. Previously, funding for HBCUs was subject to congressional reapproval each year. This funding will benefit students at over one hundred HBCUs, including roughly forty faith-based colleges that had previously been denied access to federal funding for capital projects (buildings unrelated to religious functions).[47,48]

African-American entrepreneurs and small business owners, who disproportionally face difficulties in obtaining traditional financing but want to grow and hire from within their communities, can benefit from the OZ provision by expanding their business in an Opportunity Zone.

The City of Louisville, Kentucky, is developing long-term plans for urban redevelopment that include OZ projects. Louisville is experiencing a renaissance in job and employment growth, particularly in the medical technology manufacturing industry. As part of its long-term growth plan, Louisville has envisioned OZ investments in the western section of the city. West Louisville is a primarily African-American and poor area where approximately 65,000 residents have a median income of about $21,000—less than half the city's median income of $50,000.

The Government of Louisville and the Urban League have already begun several anchor projects in the area, including investments in affordable housing ($30 million) and a professional sports complex ($30 million). Private investors are in the process of building new facilities in the community, most notably Passport Health, which is

47    Sara Weissman, "UNCF Celebrates as FUTURE Act Awaits Trump's Signature," *Diverse*, December 10, 2019, https://diverseeducation.com/article/161945/.

48    Andrew Kreighbaum, "Trump Asserts New Win for Religious HBCUs," *Inside Higher ED,* September 11, 2019, https://www.insidehighered.com/news/2019/09/11/trump-administration-acts-funding-restrictions-religious-hbcus.

building a new headquarters ($150 million) that will bring about five hundred jobs to the community.

One West, a new development corporation with significant financial and civic backing from Louisville-wide stakeholders, wants to "re-knit" West Louisville into the broader civic framework. One West is currently focusing on the acquisition and rehabilitation of retail sites along Broadway, the main thoroughfare in West Louisville. One West plans to use OZ incentives to address technical and financial capacity gaps in targeting capital formation for West Louisville development consortia.

## AFRICAN-AMERICAN SMALL BUSINESSES ARE GROWING AT AN UNPRECEDENTED PACE

The primary obstacles to business and employment growth under the Obama administration were the increased regulatory burdens imposed on business formation, employment, and small business financing. A National Small Business Association survey found that small business owners spend more than eighty hours a year just dealing with regulations. In the first year alone, a small business will spend on average roughly $83,000 to comply with government rules. That can be the margin between staying open or going bankrupt.

The Trump administration is empowering minority business owners by eliminating excessive, unnecessary, and burdensome regulations that too often hinder their growth. One of the most significant regulatory headwinds to small business formation and growth were the new regulatory burdens under the Affordable Care Act. The Obamacare mandate forced small businesses with fifty or more full-time employees to provide health insurance as well as a Medicare Part A increase, or be slapped with a hefty tax penalty.[49]

---

49    "ObamaCare Employer Mandate," ObamaCareFacts.com, August 7, 2014, last updated November 16, 2018, https://obamacarefacts.com/obamacare-employer-mandate/.

Small and medium-sized businesses facing this regulatory burden refrained from hiring and often cut back employee hours to below thirty hours per week, so as to avoid the full-time work threshold that would trigger mandatory employee health insurance coverage under Obamacare.[50] Minorities and low-skilled workers were hurt dramatically by this requirement.[51]Like so many schemes put forward by pro-government/pro-regulation policymakers, yet again an initiative to "help" the least in our society had painful and destructive side effects. All too often, blacks have embraced many of these regulatory "solutions" with the most enthusiasm, and then blamed racial animus when the hoped-for results didn't pan out.

In June 2018, President Trump—still saddled with the Obamacare employer mandate—initiated a new rule that allows small businesses and self-employed workers to buy coalition health insurance plans, a move that will lower the price of policies, expand coverage, and free small businesses from some of the worst regulations imposed by the Affordable Care Act.

The Small Business Optimism Index increased in May 2018, to the second highest level in forty-five years. "Main Street optimism is on a stratospheric trajectory thanks to recent tax cuts and regulatory changes. For years, owners have continuously signaled that when taxes and regulations ease, earning and employee compensation increase," said Juanita Duggan, President of the National Federation of Independent Businesses.[52]

The MetLife and U.S. Chamber of Commerce Small Business Index also recorded record optimism. Of those surveyed, 48 percent

---

50    Jacob Passy, "Business Eliminated Hundreds of Thousands of Full-Time Jobs to Avoid Obamacare Mandate," MarketWatch, November 24, 2017, https://www.marketwatch.com/story/businesses-eliminated-hundreds-of-thousands-of-full-time-jobs-to-avoid-obamacare-mandate-2017-11-24.

51    Paul Sperry, "ObamaCare Threatens Minority Jobs," *Investor's Business Daily*, October 11, 2012, https://www.investors.com/politics/commentary/obamacare-threatens-minority-hiring-restaurants/.

52    Adam Brandon, "Trump Boom Ignites Business," The Hill, June 25, 2018, https://thehill.com/opinion/finance/393803-trump-boom-ignites-small-business.

felt good about their local economies, the highest level in the history of the index. Confidence in the Midwest is at 50 percent, and in the West, confidence is at 55 percent.

So who benefits from all this? A 2017 survey by the Kauffman Foundation found that 24 percent of new businesses were formed by minorities. According to a survey conducted by Guidant Financial Services, the number of African-American small business owners in the United States has increased by a staggering 400 percent in just over a year since 2017. The survey found that in 2018, 45 percent of small business owners were minority ethnic groups. This was already a dramatic increase from 2015, when the number of minority business owners was just 15 percent of the total. The biggest increase among minority small business owners has taken place among African-American small business owners—a year-over-year increase of 400 percent between 2017 and 2018.

David Nilssen, CEO of Guidant Financial, said, "It is exciting to see the growth in minority-owned small businesses, a trend that has steadily been rising since we began our survey in 2015. Growth amongst all minorities, including women, is promising in America as small business ownership becomes more favorable and easier to attain. We anticipate and hope to see a continued increase as the impact of tax reform and economic growth shape small business ownership moving forward." Nearly a third of new African-American business owners (30 percent) said they decided to become a small business owner because an "opportunity presented itself."

All signs point to a renaissance in black business ownership in the age of Trump. Even analysts skeptical about the prospects for African-American progress under Trump have conceded that market forces are driving business formation among African Americans. "Black workers have been harder hit by public-sector cutbacks," said Darrick Hamilton, a professor of economics and urban policy at the New School. "Add to that the biases against hiring blacks in the private sector, and the question becomes: Is it a choice to start a black-owned business or is it blacks being pushed into limited labor choices?"[53]

The answer: it is both. Blacks are choosing to start businesses because of the favorable business climate offered by the Trump administration, and they are being spurred by contraction in public sector employment to develop alternative pathways to middle-class status and wealth attainment. Many blacks assert that there remain "biases" in the private sector, hindering their employment potential. The increased pace of hiring relative to whites belies this view. Furthermore, more skill development and educational attainment will likely lead to an even faster pace of wage growth. But ultimately, even if blacks believe that private sector employers are ambivalent or actually hostile, it's all the more reason that entrepreneurship is a great wealth creation strategy. In a growing and dynamic economy, blacks are empowered to take control over their economic destiny. This approach worked at the beginning of the 20th century for black men, and it will work again for all black Americans in the 21st century.

President Trump has made opportunity, entrepreneurship, and wealth creation both possible and appealing for black Americans. The growing economy means consumers are buying again, tax cuts for the middle class have put more spending power in the hands of the middle class, and businesses can make real investments in growth which include hiring more workers. Wages are increasing across the board, especially among the low-wage, low-skill occupations in which African-American workers tend (for now) to be concentrated. All of this creates a virtuous circle of growth that stands to benefit black Americans. There is broad-based support among small business owners for the Trump administration's deregulatory agenda, which promotes innovation and economic growth.

---

53    Richard Morgan, "A Revival of Black Business and Pride, in Brooklyn," *The New York Times*, June 17, 2018, https://www.nytimes.com/2018/06/17/nyregion/black-owned-brooklyn-businesses.html.

## Armstrong Williams: Über Entrepreneur

Media Entrepreneur Armstrong Williams is the owner and CEO of Howard Stirk Holdings, the largest black-owned broadcast television network in the U.S., which currently operates eight local network television affiliates in several states. His business employs over a thousand people and produces original broadcasting content featured on over two hundred television stations nationwide.

Williams, a third-generation Republican (an original member of the "Party of Lincoln" as he puts it), grew up in South Carolina at a time in which it was very difficult for African Americans, especially in the South, to become entrepreneurs. He recounts times when his father, a local tobacco farmer in the rural Pee Dee region, tried to buy farmland. "At that time, it was difficult for blacks to get farms, even if they had the money," he said. "So my dad would go to a white farmer who was friendly to him and ask him to purchase the farm for him and turn over the deed." Over time, the Williams family became a major supplier to the vast tobacco markets in Charleston, and was well-regarded among the business community there.

"Today you have so many new opportunities, and it behooves young people to take advantage of them. No one has to front for you. You can walk through the front door, not around the back like my parents had to do. And I think more people should take advantage of these opportunities." Williams has long been involved in Republican politics, and runs his media empire from an office in Washington, D.C., a stones-throw away from the U.S. Supreme Court. His public affairs programming often focuses on conservative values, and he maintains a distinctly pro-business broadcasting platform.

"I've been in Washington for over thirty years," he says. "I've seen them all come and go—from Reagan to Clinton to Obama, and now Trump is in office. And I can tell you one thing that's different about black entrepreneurs today that I have not seen in the past is a change in attitude. I see less of blacks being portrayed as victims. In fact, I have never seen them so free to explore. All of a sudden, you're not buying into this story that everyone is against you. There's been a mindset change. It's as if you've been on this drug of defeat for so long and now you're on the drug of triumph. And a lot of that has to do with Trump's optimism. It's infectious."

"Blacks feel more confident because they have more money in their pockets. They feel that they have actually received some tangible benefit from Trump's presidency. More money in their pockets means more options for their children. When people have money in their pockets, they feel good about themselves. They connect money with success, happiness, and stability. Trump likes to talk about money. He says, 'the only way that you'll vote for a Democrat is if you're tired of winning.' Their pie might not be as big as mine, but at least they've got a pie. They may not have a mansion, but at least they have a house. People like money—they like to have options about what they can do with their wives, their children, and themselves. It's one thing to have 'hope and no change,' but when you have a little extra change, you have more hope, optimism, and confidence because it's based in reality."

Williams also says his business has been able to leverage some of the confidence that the Trump administration has helped to foster. "Our media platform has been a direct proponent of Trump's pro-opportunity ethos. We have been able to hire more people, especially African-American professionals, train them and ultimately send them out to other opportunities at major companies—CNN, Facebook, and other technology and media companies. We are able to instill confidence in their skills that translates into amazing opportunities for our employees, whether they advance within our company or go elsewhere."

## Jason Riley: False Black Power Did Not Lead to Economic Prosperity

The counterintuitive situation we are seeing—that blacks are, in fact, disproportionately benefiting from the Trump administration's focus on "economic nationalism" rather than upon public sector investments and regulatory interventions—belies what I consider to be a false and persistent narrative by the progressive left. That is, blacks gaining mainstream political power by participating in liberal politics in the latter half of the 20th century would naturally feed into increased prosperity for the Black community. This has not been the case.

During some of the times when blacks faced some of the starkest legal obstacles to achievement—Jim Crow segregation—blacks were able to build economic power, and made economic gains, which while slow and steady, proved to be remarkable and enduring over time. In fact, it may have been those very social challenges that spurred growth in black economic power.

Journalist Jason Riley, who sits on the Wall Street Journal editorial board and serves as a senior fellow at the conservative Manhattan Institute, wrote about this very phenomenon in his groundbreaking book titled *False Black Power?*,[54] which came out in 2018. In the book and in television interviews, Riley argues that the focus of black leadership in the first half of the 20th century was not political power, but human capital attainment. "What was going on in the first half of the 20th century," Riley argues, was a focus on "growing Black human capital—skills, behaviors, habits, and attitudes. You saw a narrowing of Black racial gaps versus whites, in terms of educational attainment, poverty rates, and economic achievement. Slow but steady progress was occurring. In the post 1960s era, after the focus shifted to Black political power, you saw that progress slow, stall, and in some cases reverse course.

"If you go back and look at the cities where there is tremendous Black political influence—Black mayors, police chiefs, and school

---

54    Jason L. Riley, *False Black Power?* (West Conshohocken, PA, Templeton Press, 2018).
      Riley explains why the political strategy of civil rights leaders has left so many blacks behind. The key to black economic advancement today is overcoming cultural handicaps, not attaining more political power.

superintendents, and the like—the Black poor actually lost ground. By and large, because these politicians were not doing things to satisfy the interests of the low-income constituencies. Racial gaps in home ownership, employment, and poverty rates grew in the Obama era. The emphasis on seeking political saviors and using politics to pursue economic prosperity is not the way to go."

Riley is on to something. There were more black millionaires in America before 1950 than there were for the next twenty-five years[55] despite an explosion in population growth over that time.[56] These entrepreneurs included pioneering figures such as Madame CJ Walker, who revolutionized hair care for African Americans and became the first black female millionaire. There was insurance mogul A.G. Gaston who founded the first black-owned insurance company and the only black-owned bank in Alabama in the midst of the Jim Crow Era. These entrepreneurs survived primarily because of two factors: they were able to serve the African-American community at a time when many white-owned businesses refused to do so, and more importantly, because of the pro-business policies of presidents like Calvin Coolidge that promoted limited business regulation and low taxes. As a result, a culture of entrepreneurship and self-determination evolved that has in some ways gotten lost when blacks shifted their focus to political activism with the onset of the modern civil rights movement.

Many of the entrepreneurs and the society that evolved amid segregation became, by default, economic nationalists. They were focused on building economic power within the black community. But there were others such as Frederick Patterson who used their

---

55    Center for Social Policy. *A Dream Deferred: The Economic Status of Black Americans.* A Working Paper, Washington: Center for the Study of Social Policy, 1983. John Herbers, "Income Gap Between Races Wide as in 1960, Study Finds," *The New York Times,* July 18, 1983, https://www.nytimes.com/1983/07/18/us/income-gap-between-races-wide-as-in-1960-study-finds.html.

56    "2016 SCF Chartbook," SCF (Survey of Consumer Finances), https://www.federalreserve.gov/econres/files/BulletinCharts.pdf.

manufacturing skills to provide services to the broader community, and in the process, also achieved remarkable financial success.

Ironically, at the very time of the civil rights breakthrough of the 1960s, black America began a path of family breakdown that hurts economic growth and wealth creation to this day. New economic opportunities will only go so far. A culture shift will also have to occur in terms of family formation to fully achieve the potential that the current economy affords African Americans. As racial attitudes among White America shifted during the 1960s, many African Americans began to pursue opportunities in mainstream America, in major corporations, and at mainstream educational institutions. The evidence points to the fact that while a few elite blacks were able to thrive in the new environment, a majority of blacks, especially the black poor (stymied by illegitimacy and changing cultural mores), fell further behind.

## CONCLUSION

The Trump administration's focus on economic nationalism bodes well for Black America. It has already delivered in terms of record-breaking gains in black employment and business growth. For it to fully succeed, black entrepreneurs will need to pursue market-based strategies to expand and grow business and employment opportunities. A shift from a "public sector" employment strategy to a private sector strategy that focuses on skills development and entrepreneurship in health care, technology, and science will be highly beneficial for blacks and the American economy. The Trump administration's deregulatory agenda and incentives for capital deployment in black communities makes this strategy easier, and likely, even more profitable.

Economic nationalism as espoused by President Trump is not based on a person's race, color, gender, or ethnicity. It is focused on developing economic opportunities for all American citizens. A large economic door has been opened as a result. African-American prosperity, going forward, will be most effective if the community aligns itself with the president's quest to reclaim American greatness and steps through the door.

As blacks continue to see growth in economic opportunity, there is likely to be a reckoning between black Americans who feel confident about their prospects in the labor market and the Democrats, who have no market-oriented growth solutions to offer. These differences are likely to manifest in higher votes for Trump (especially among black men) who have been courted by Trump and who see some of Trump's overtures—particularly with regards to criminal justice reform and immigration reform—as especially beneficial to them.

President Trump won upwards of 13 percent of the black male vote in 2016 (as opposed to 4 percent of the Black female vote).[57] That number is likely to be far higher in 2020 as more black males enter the workforce and begin to reap the rewards of the Trump economy. Will Democrats shift from their public sector/regulatory policy directives as way to retain these voters? Time will tell.

---

57    Matthew Yglesias, "What Really Happened in 2016, in 7 Charts: Okay, Some of Them Are Tables," Vox, September 18, 2017, https://www.vox.com/ policy-and-politics/2017/9/18/16305486/what-really-happened-in-2016.

## *Chapter 3*

ᕼ

# ANOTHER BRICK IN THE WALL—WHY CURBING ILLEGAL IMMIGRATION PROMOTES FREEDOM FOR AFRICAN AMERICANS

In January 2019, after months of negative media reporting about President Trump's "zero-tolerance" illegal immigration stance, the president finally addressed the crisis at the border. He said, "America proudly welcomes millions of lawful immigrants who enrich our society and contribute to our nation. But all Americans are hurt by uncontrolled, illegal migration. It strains public resources and drives down jobs and wages. Among those hardest hit are African Americans and Hispanic Americans."[58]

The Trump administration's willingness to put in place strong measures to curb illegal immigration despite the media and political backlash actually helps black Americans. While the media has chosen to focus on a limited set of those measures, specifically detentions

---

58    "President Donald J. Trump's Address to the Nation on the Crisis at the Border," The White House, January 8, 2019, https://www.whitehouse.gov/briefings-statements/president-donald-j-trumps-address-nation-crisis-border/.

of illegal immigrants caught crossing the border and apprehensions of illegal immigrants already residing in the United States, Trump's policy initiatives go far beyond the headline-grabbing controversies.

The various ways that the administration has already begun to battle illegal immigration, such as challenging "sanctuary cities" that seek to give safe-haven to illegals, closing loopholes in federal immigration laws that make it easier for illegals to remain, and supporting federal legislation that would replace the current permanent employment visa framework with a skills-based system that rewards applicants based on their individual merits, all put the American worker at the front of the line. Trump's proposed immigration law, which would mirror the merit-based immigration systems in Canada and Australia, rewards education and English language ability, prioritizes high-paying job offers and past professional and educational achievements, and builds on entrepreneurial initiative while reducing overall immigration numbers to limit low-skilled and unskilled labor entering the United States. The basic theme is that the immigrants we should welcome to America should add to America's workforce and economy in ways that are difficult to replicate with America's existing domestic labor pool. In the economics of international trade, countries with specific "natural advantages" such as access to fertile soil or deep-water fishing, should trade with other countries who have complementary but not identical advantages, such that each party is made better off in the exchange. The same concepts hold true regarding immigration. America should import immigrants who have skill sets and resources that the American labor force cannot easily fulfill from its current labor pool. That is to say we should prioritize importing labor for skills that are rare and valuable here at home.

The Trump administration also pushed for the House's passage of Kate's Law, which increases criminal penalties against illegal immigrants who repeatedly re-enter the country after being expelled, and the No Sanctuary for Criminals Act, which restricts taxpayer grant money from cities that prevent their police from turning over dangerous criminal illegal immigrants to federal authorities.

While media analysts fail to mention this obvious fact in their coverage of the issue, illegal immigrants compete disproportionately for jobs held by black workers. Illegal immigrants also over-consume[59] community and government services at the state and local levels, which are the very services that blacks subsidize through their disproportionate contributions to local and state sales taxes in the inner city.[60] By clamping down on illegal immigration, President Trump is working to ensure black Americans will not be forced to subsidize those who have come to the U.S. illegally to compete with them in the U.S. job market and to consume public services for which blacks and many other working class Americans are eligible and have paid for with their taxes.

Fighting massive unskilled illegal immigration will help prevent long-term multigenerational poverty among U.S. minorities by giving them a competitive foothold in the labor market from which they can ultimately build strong families and communities and income security. Elevated unemployment makes black men less attractive as marriage partners and low marriage rates lead to lessened educational attainment, wealth creation, and social immobility among blacks as a whole. Trump's policies are obviating these phenomena and aiding blacks in the process.

## HISTORY OF IMMIGRATION AND BLACK LABOR

Along with the end of the Civil War came the dawn of the age of a broader racial, free enterprise system in America. Former slaves,

---

59  Steven A. Camarota, "Welfare Use by Legal and Illegal Immigrant Households: An Analysis of Medicaid, Cash, Food, and Housing Programs," Center for Immigration Studies, September 9, 2015, https://cis.org/Report/Welfare-Use-Legal-and-Illegal-Immigrant-Households.

60  Michael Leachman, Michael Mitchell, Nicholas Johnson, and Erica Williams, "Advancing Racial Equity With State Tax Policy," Center on Budget and Policy Priorities, November 15, 2018, https://www.cbpp.org/research/state-budget-and-tax/advancing-racial-equity-with-state-tax-policy.

many of whom had actual marketable skills as farmers, carpenters, farriers, wheelmakers, cotton gin mechanics, and the like, became some of the most sought-after workers in the post-bellum South. Accustomed to working in ungodly conditions, under physical bondage, they welcomed the opportunity to work and support their families as free citizens. The common aim of many black men at the time was to find children and wives who had been sold away during slavery and then seek work that enabled them to support their families. Employers, in many cases, highly valued black laborers because the newly freed people were generally regarded as skilled, industrious, and exceptionally hard working. Whereas a typical white worker might beg off after nine hours or so, black employees would typically stay on until the job was finished and/or work at wage rates lower than their white counterparts.[61]

In the first census taken in America that included black employment figures, in 1900, non-whites edged out whites for lower unemployment (at the time the census included three races: black, mulatto, and white). From the first census until 1950, black and white labor market participation and employment were roughly equal. And notably, black men were employed at higher rates than whites up through the beginning of the Great Depression.[62]

In the immediate aftermath of the Civil War, America became a net importer of labor once again. This time, instead of slaves brought over in the cargo holds, it was free labor coming by boat from Europe, mostly by way of Ireland. Blacks felt the competition from foreign immigrant labor at the time and complained bitterly about it. Frederick Douglass, the famous humanitarian and civic leader, once

---

61    Horace Cooper, "The Untold, Racist Origins of 'Progressive' Labor Laws: Protecting 'White Jobs' Was the Purpose of Union-Backed Legislation," Capital Research Center, June 17, 2014, https://capitalresearch.org/article/the-untold-racist-origins-of-progressive-labor-laws-protecting-white-jobs-was-the-purpose-of-union-backed-legislation/.

62    Dr. Tomas Sowell, "Ruinous 'Compassion,' " Creators, March 17, 2015, https://www.creators.com/read/thomas-sowell/03/15/ruinous-compassion.

complained that employers should hire blacks, who were native-born Americans, rather than newly arrived immigrants from Ireland and other parts of Europe. In a speech before the American Anti-Slavery Society in 1853, Douglass explained his position in detail:

> "The Irish people, warm-hearted, generous, and sympathizing with the oppressed everywhere, when they stand upon their own green island, are instantly taught, on arriving in this Christian country, to hate and despise the colored people. They are taught to believe that we eat the bread which of right belongs to them. The cruel lie is told the Irish, that our adversity is essential to their prosperity...The old employments by which we have heretofore gained our livelihood, are gradually, and it may be inevitably, passing into other hands. Every hour sees us elbowed out of some employment to make room perhaps for some newly-arrived emigrants, whose hunger and color are thought to give them a title to especial favor....the colored people are thus elbowed out of employment; while the enmity of emigrants is being excited against us!"

Three things stand out about Douglass' speech a century and a half ago that are especially apropos today:

First, Douglass did not direct his ire against the immigrants themselves. In fact, he honored their culture and character, and empathized with the poverty and deprivation that drove them from their homes in Ireland, seeking opportunities here in America. He, in fact, identified with their plight as marginalized minorities in their own country, and went on to form solid bonds with the Irish independence movement, traveling to Ireland on several occasions to speak in support of their cause. While Douglass was a staunch advocate for native-born American labor, he also saw his role as an abolitionist within the broader context of a global struggle for human dignity and freedom.

Second, Douglass acknowledged back in 1853 that the principal occupations of blacks (outside of agriculture) were concentrated in the lower-skilled service trades—cooks, stewards, common laborers. The same is remarkably true today. It is also true that illegal immigration both then and now is driven primarily by the demand for lower-skilled service and manufacturing jobs. These are jobs that many African Americans have traditionally occupied and now find themselves "elbowed" out of.

Third, and most presciently, Douglass argued that newly arrived immigrants were being used by those in power to form a political wedge against African Americans. Douglas implied that the plight of African Americans was being marginalized because the political establishment favored the newly arrived immigrants over the resident black population. We see the same thing happening today within the Democratic Party. The Democratic Party leadership has gone out of its way to develop programs (sanctuary cities, DACA, and the like) to attract Latino votes, literally at the expense of opportunities for African Americans.

But despite their rather blatant racial appeals to Latinos, Democrats are currently attracting only about two-thirds of the Latino vote—even in border states where immigration issues figure most prominently. Blacks, on the other hand, overwhelmingly vote for Democrats on almost a nine-to-one basis. The reasons for this disparity are several, but are rooted in two core factors. First, Latinos are far from a racial monolith. Nearly seven out of ten Puerto Rican voters, for example, self-identify as white. Moreover, the further along in the generational line since immigration (i.e., by the fourth and fifth generations), the more likely Latino Americans in general are to self-identify as "white." Latinos tend to assimilate into white culture at a far more rapid rate than African Americans. The other factor is that Latino Americans themselves are also disproportionately represented at the lower rungs of the labor market. They, too, feel the crowding-out effects of cheaper illegal immigrant labor on their efforts to obtain an economic foothold in America.

Curiously, despite the cynical racial calculus by the Democratic Party to forsake blacks for Latinos, the political coalition that has held blacks and liberals together since the civil rights movement continues to provide the governing framework for black political organization in the United States. But the overconcentration of support for the Democratic Party seems particularly harmful given blacks' declining importance as an electorally decisive minority group, and the Democratic Party's transparent strategy to shift its appeal to Hispanics rather than blacks. In 2020, Hispanics will eclipse blacks as the electorate's largest minority group.[63] Blacks need to take a hard look at this situation and develop a better organizational strategy vis-a-vis national politics and party allegiance.

The difference in what Democrats offer blacks and Hispanics is stark. Blacks are promised a "study" for reparations, and new national police training for inner city law enforcement, while Hispanics are offered legalization, work permits, free health care[64,] and access to earned income tax credits, as well the abolition of ICE (Immigrations and Customs Enforcement).[65]

63    Stef W. Kight, "The demographic shifts disrupting the political world," *Axios*, February 2, 2020, https://www.axios.com/demographic-shifts-what-matters-2020-424161bf-1e6e-4da9-b2b2-9a6b2b2099fa.html.

64    Tami Luhby, "Democrats want to offer health care to undocumented immigrants. Here's what that means," CNN, September 11, 2019, https://www.cnn.com/2019/09/11/politics/undocumented-immigrants-health-care-democrats/index.html.

65    Elaine Godfrey, "What 'Abolish ICE' Actually Means," *The Atlantic*, July 11, 2018, https://www.theatlantic.com/politics/archive/2018/07/what-abolish-ice-actually-means/564752/.

# TRUMP'S IMMIGRATION POLICIES ARE REDUCING BARRIERS TO BLACK EMPLOYMENT

By clamping down on illegal immigration, President Trump has signaled to black Americans now that they will no longer be forced to subsidize those who have come illegally to compete with them for jobs. Reducing illegal immigration helps to prevent long-term, multigenerational poverty among African Americans.

## The RAISE ACT Helps to Curb Incentives for Illegal Immigration and Protects Black Workers

The Reforming American Immigration for Strong Employment (RAISE) Act—initially proposed by Congressional Republicans in 2017, and then reintroduced in 2019—proposed to reduce immigration by half by changing the way the U.S. issues green cards to nationals from other countries. For decades, the U.S. has operated a low-skilled immigration system, issuing millions of green cards to low-wage immigrants. This policy of unregulated labor insourcing has placed unfair economic hardships on American taxpayers, community resources, and workers, and especially minority workers competing for low-skill jobs against new arrivals. The RAISE Act, as proposed, also ends chain migration by limiting the family members allowed to emigrate under family status to spouses and minor children, and replaces a system dominated by emigres with low skills, with a new points-based system for receiving a green card.

The competitive application process proposed under the RAISE Act favors applicants who can speak English, have the means to support their families, and demonstrate skills that will contribute to our economy. The RAISE ACT prevents migrants and new immigrants from collecting welfare—a key provision—and protects U.S. workers from being displaced by foreigners. Crucially, the green card reforms in the RAISE Act give American workers a pay raise by reducing unskilled labor immigration, which artificially lowers the wage-earning power of working class Americans, whether they are of black, white, or Hispanic origin.

## Black Males Have Been the Primary Victims of Policies Encouraging Low-Skill Immigrant Labor

Black men have been, by far, the biggest victims of the crowding-out effects of low-wage illegal labor.[66] Illegal immigration has had a truly devastating impact on wage and employment levels in the black community. It really comes down to economics 101. When there is an oversupply of low-skilled labor, the price of labor is going to be depressed. The bulk of our (both legal and illegal) immigration takes place on the low-skilled labor side. This has a particularly magnifying effect on black males, who are concentrated in the low-skill labor market. It is also beginning to have trickle-up effects on middle-class Americans.

A U.S. Commission on Civil Rights analysis indicates that nearly half of the 18 percent decline in black labor force participation rates among black males over the past thirty years is due to an oversupply of competing illegal immigrant labor. This translates to between five hundred thousand and 1.2 million blacks losing out on job opportunities, the loss of which has a significant and pernicious impact on the black community. Black unemployment—especially among black males—produces profound sociological effects that cascade throughout the black community and American society. It tends to suppress family formation, reduces intergenerational wealth creation and transfers, associates with increased incarceration rates, exacerbates addiction and mental health problems, and produces a whole host of other social pathologies associated with reduced labor market participation.

---

66    "The Impact of Illegal Immigration on the Wages and Employment Opportunities of Black Workers," A Briefing Before The United States Commission on Civil Rights, Washington, DC, April 4, 2008, https://www.usccr.gov/pubs/docs/IllegImmig_10-14-10_430pm.pdf.

While under the Trump economy, black unemployment has reached its lowest point in over forty years, black labor force participation remains relatively low at 61.8 percent, compared to around 66 percent for whites.[67] Family formation among African Americans (that is, children born to wedded parents) is at its lowest point in history. Roughly three-quarters of black children are born to single mothers. Incarceration rates among black males are abysmally high. All of these are both causes and effects of low labor market participation and systemically high relative unemployment rates, and the related social ills of ill-education, crime, and illegitimacy are negatively impacted by the "crowding out" effect of an oversupply of low-skilled illegal labor.

While some may view this state of play as the "status quo" for the black community, it has not been the case historically. As late as 1932, being a black male was the least likely racial characteristic of a person in federal prison.[68] Note, this period was before the civil rights era of the 1960s. Prosperity in the 1950s, like that in the pre-Great Depression Era, correlated with strong black family formation.[69] In 1954, black family formation and births within marriage roughly equaled the national average, and in fact were slightly higher than that of whites.

Trump's immigration policies have the potential to help restore Black America to the degree of economic prosperity they enjoyed

---

67     Sharon Nunn, "After 40 Years, the Black-White Labor Force Participation Gap Has All But Closed: Fields with High Concentrations of African-Americans Add Jobs Quickly, Though Economic Disparities Persist," *The Wall Street Journal*, March 11, 2018, https://www.wsj.com/articles/after-40-years-the-black-white-labor-force-participation-gap-has-all-but-closed-1520780610.

68     Langan, Patrick A., Ph.D., BJS Statistician, "Race of Prisoners Admitted to State and Federal Institutions, 1926-86." U.S. Department of Justice/Office of Justice Programs/Bureau of Justice Statistics, May 1991, NCJ-125618, https://www.ncjrs.gov/pdffiles1/nij/125618.pdf.

69     R. Kelly Raley, Megan M. Sweeney, and Danielle Wondra, "The Growing Racial and Ethnic Divide in U.S. Marriage Patterns," PMC (PubMed Central), April 29, 2016, https://www.ncbi.nlm.nih.gov/pmc/articles/PMC4850739/.

in the period immediately pre-dating the civil rights era or the early 20th century, and even increase it given that legal and policy obstacles to the hiring of blacks have subsequently been removed by civil rights legislation.

Another point bears introduction here. That is, the call to "Make Black America Great Again" is a not a revisionist dream about an idyllic past where blacks once prospered without problems associated with race and racism. Certainly racism, especially as endorsed by the KKK in the late 19th and early 20th centuries, along with trade unionist Democrats of the 1930s and '40s, posed significant barriers to black achievement in the past.

Efforts by blacks to achieve equality of opportunity, even under conditions of strong family formation and full employment during the Jim Crow era were necessary and well worth it. But a major point that has been lost in the narrative of ending racial injustice is that the struggle was not just about voting and public facilities discrimination, but that, in fact, it was the struggle to obtain equal access to jobs and economic prosperity that was the principle driver of the civil rights movement.

Martin Luther King's famous "I Have a Dream" speech at the March on Washington in 1963 was a call for freedom and equality for all Americans. But the major way in which King and others in the civil rights movement envisioned such "freedom" occurring is through greater access on the part of blacks to jobs and economic opportunities.[70] Black Americans (and others) converged on the Lincoln memorial in the hundreds of thousands because they were concerned that there was not a lot of economic opportunity. The essence of the civil rights movement was about letting people get control over their own lives through the strength of their labor and skills—not the model of social subsidies and quotas that currently characterizes the conversation over civil rights in America.

---

70    "March on Washington," History.com, October 29, 2009, updated December 4, 2019, https://www.history.com/topics/black-history/march-on-washington.

In fact, the march itself was billed as the "March on Washington for Jobs and Freedom." The march's chief organizer and visionary was A. Phillip Randolph, a long-time labor organizer and then-President of the Brotherhood of Sleeping Car Porters, which was the first predominately black labor union in America. Throughout his entire career, Randolph continuously fought against what he saw were unfair labor practices in relation to blacks. He was instrumental in persuading President Harry Truman to end segregation in the U.S. military in 1948. Randolph was also a huge proponent of immigration restriction, and opposed the fact that African Americans were having to compete with immigrants who were willing to work for lower wages. He firmly believed in the dignity of the American workers and strove to remove impediments—including illegal labor—that stood in the way of workers getting their fair share.

Martin Luther King, despite the media slander against him, was never a communist or a socialist. He never envisioned nor advocated for a welfare state in which the government would assume financial responsibility for the poor. When he spoke in his famous "I Have a Dream Speech" about coming to Washington to "cash a check," he was not referring to a welfare check. Rather, he was referring to the basic constitutional rights that all Americans are guaranteed. The constitutional "promissory note" was, in King's words, "a promise that all men, yes, black men as well as white men, would be guaranteed the 'unalienable Rights' of 'Life, Liberty and the pursuit of Happiness.'" He was not demanding Washington give blacks handouts, but merely that America honor the promise it had made in the Constitution to provide all of its citizens "upon demand the riches of freedom and the security of justice."

# TRUMP ADMINISTRATION POLICIES ARE REDUCING THE DISPROPORTIONATE BURDEN OF REGRESSIVE GOVERNMENT SUBSIDIES OF ILLEGAL IMMIGRATION BORN BY BLACK AMERICANS

### The "Real" Ferguson Effect

On August 19, 2014, twenty-eight-year-old Ferguson, Missouri, Police Officer Darren Wilson shot and killed a black teenager named Michael Brown. Brown, who had earlier that day stolen a pack of cigars from a local convenience store, had been detained by investigating officer Wilson as a suspect. In the ensuing encounter, Brown assaulted Officer Wilson, who, believing his life was in danger, shot and killed Brown in self-defense. A rumor quickly spread around the local community that Officer Wilson had shot Brown while Brown was surrendering with his "hands up." But when the evidence eventually went to a grand jury months later, eyewitness accounts disputed this narrative. The grand jury ultimately decided that Officer Wilson had indeed been under attack by Brown and was justified in using deadly force.

In the aftermath of the shooting, protesters from around the country descended upon the small Missouri city and rioted, destroying property and looting with abandon. One of the rioters' principle demands was to increase police accountability in an effort to stop what they characterized as a nationwide epidemic of police violence against unarmed black people. Tellingly, one of the young leaders of the protest, Taurean Russel, when asked when he thought the chaos would die down, responded candidly, "They don't want to employ us, so we have nothing but time on our hands." A grassroots movement formed in 2013[71] called *Black Lives Matter* highlighted the town of Ferguson in the aftermath of the Brown incident to demand greater scrutiny and accountability for law enforcement.

---

71    "Herstory," Black Lives Matter, https://blacklivesmatter.com/herstory/.

Then-FBI Director James Comey pointed out that increased scrutiny of police following the controversial shooting and verdict had caused police to become more hesitant in making arrests, which in turn led to an increase in crime nationwide. He called this phenomenon the "Ferguson effect."

The FBI director's off-the-cuff assessment hits the mark in several respects. First, in the aftermath of the Michael Brown shooting, there was significant evidence that police in certain jurisdictions had begun making fewer arrests than usual. Furthermore, there have been actual spikes in crime in certain cities with high concentrations of African Americans—namely in Baltimore and Chicago, which have set records over the ensuing years for violent crime. Both Baltimore and Ferguson were sued by the Obama administration and entered consent decrees which placed heightened scrutiny on the police departments of those cities.

But there is another so-called Ferguson effect that did not receive the same level of attention. One of the common misconceptions about the conflagration that erupted in Ferguson is that it stemmed primarily from the shooting of Michael Brown. A U.S. Department of Justice study commissioned in the aftermath of the shooting revealed a conclusion that belies this prevailing misconception. One of the DOJ study's key findings is that in the years leading up to the Michael Brown incident, the City of Ferguson directed the Ferguson Police Department to "aggressively enforce the municipal code."[72] It further found significant evidence that "the code enforcement system had been honed to produce more revenue."[73] The report goes on to

---

72    Langan, Patrick A., Ph.D., BJS Statistician, "Race of Prisoners Admitted to State and Federal Institutions, 1926-86," U.S. Department of Justice, Office of Justice Programs, Bureau of Justice Statistics, May 1991, NCJ-125618: 9–12. https://www.ncjrs.gov/pdffiles1/nij/125618.pdf.

73    Langan, Patrick A., Ph.D., BJS Statistician, "Race of Prisoners Admitted to State and Federal Institutions, 1926-86," U.S. Department of Justice, Office of Justice Programs, Bureau of Justice Statistics, May 1991, NCJ-125618: 9–12. https://www.ncjrs.gov/pdffiles1/nij/125618.pdf.

cite both statistical and anecdotal evidence proving that aggressive code enforcement disproportionately ensnared African Americans, putting them on the hook for fines, imprisonment for minor traffic offenses, license suspensions, and asset seizures in lieu of fines (car towing, etc.).

This backdoor method of revenue generation effectively acted as an onerous and regressive tax on an already vulnerable population who could ill afford to be further financially burdened. It also placed blacks in increasingly dangerous confrontations with law enforcement for relatively minor infractions. The tensions arising between police and the citizens of Ferguson had been mounting long before the shooting of Michael Brown. That incident merely proved to be the straw that broke the proverbial camel's back.

The importance of the DOJ finding in Ferguson is difficult to overstate. In fact, if there really is a "Ferguson effect," it is that increased code enforcement for the explicit purpose of raising revenue for state and municipal government services rather than for safety or security has generated a high level of hostility between inner city blacks and law enforcement that is somewhat akin to the way in which increased tax audit rates heighten antipathy towards the IRS among taxpayers of all races.

Here's the quandary. If blacks believe they are being unfairly targeted by law enforcement, why then do their so-called leaders align with the "taxation" liberals who have implemented a host of "safety" regulations and laws that grant law enforcement wide discretion to interfere with citizens as they go about their daily lives? These include seatbelt laws (how many black motorists' encounters with police start out as seat-belt violations?), requiring parking lights to be operational on vehicles, predatory parking enforcement, automated traffic enforcement fines, and automobile-usage related fines—the list goes on and on. We live in such a heavily regulated society that we have essentially weaponized law enforcement to be able to interfere with almost any aspect of daily life of any person they encounter. This is doubly so in many "blue" jurisdictions where these regulations are an alternative to straightforward taxation. All too often in the inner city, with high minority populations, this problem manifests itself disproportionately against blacks.

Consider this: most prosperous Americans rarely encounter law enforcement. They live in safer communities.[74] They have access to private security. On the occasions when they do encounter police officers, it is most often when those officers are carrying out "traditional" law enforcement responsibilities.[75] On the contrary, many inner city residents prepare daily for encounters with a "revenuer" carrying a gun. This attitude often surprises mainstream America.

But to get a sense of how people respond when they view law enforcement as the adversary rather than the aid, perhaps it would be useful to look back at the 1970s, when police enforced the hated 55-mph speed limit. Americans of all stripes rebelled and engaged in avoidance techniques, and even engaged in nationwide protests.[76] Even though it was the federal law, local law enforcement bore the brunt of this unpopular initiative. Eventually, the federal law was repealed and speed limits across the country have risen. At least one state today has a maximum limit of 85 mph.[77]

If we truly want to see a renaissance in the cordial relationship between inner city blacks and law enforcement, let's end the "revenue" collection role for cops and let them go back to the crime fighting roles that all Americans support.

---

74      Ronald E. Wilson, Timothy H. Brown, and Beth Schuster, "Preventing Neighborhood Crime: Geography Matters," NIJ (National Institute of Justice), June 14, 2009, https://nij.ojp.gov/topics/articles/preventing-neighborhood-crime-geography-matters.

75      Donovan X. Ramsey, "White America's Unshakeable Confidence in the Police," The Marshall Project, July 19, 2017, https://www.themarshallproject.org/2017/07/19/white-america-s-unshakeable-confidence-in-the-police.

76      Lindsey Gruson, "Issue and Debate; Threat To Highway Money Enlivens Speed Law Fight," The New York Times, January 30, 1983, https://www.nytimes.com/1983/01/30/automobiles/issue-and-debate-threat-to-highway-money-enlivens-speed-law-fight.html.

77      IIHS (Insurance Institute for Highway Safety), https://www.iihs.org/topics/speed/speed-limit-laws.

## Blacks Bear the Brunt of the Resource Constraints Imposed by Government Services for Illegal Immigrants

Poor blacks and the working class shouldn't be taxed to pay for government services to illegal immigrants. The millions of people staying in our country illegally causes a significant strain on public services, especially at the state and local level. Our neediest Americans, particularly blacks in urban communities, must compete for education and health programs with those who shouldn't even be here. Furthermore, much of the funding for these local programs comes from regressive taxes that hit poor and working class blacks the hardest. This means they must pay for the privilege of having unlawful immigrants in their neighborhoods. This is unfair, and it should end.[78]

This influx of illegal immigrants strains public services and disproportionately burdens black communities. Black students are more likely to suffer the consequences of expanding class sizes to accommodate immigrants than their white counterparts. In eighty-three of the largest one hundred cities, black and Hispanic students attended schools with majority non-white populations. In many of these cities, including sanctuary cities like Los Angeles, San Francisco, Chicago, and New York, the schools that black students attend have been increasingly populated by non-English speaking illegal immigrants. Resources for reading and mathematics are diluted by English as a Second Language (ESL) activities, likely limiting opportunities for all.

Illegal immigration costs taxpayers about $113 billion a year at the federal, state, and local levels, according to the Federation for American Immigration Reform. About $84 billion of that cost is being absorbed by state and local governments, which mostly derive

---

78    Paul Bedard, "Report: Illegal Immigration Harms Blacks, Robs Social Services From Legal Americans," Washington Secrets, *Washington Examiner*, June 19, 2018, https://www.washingtonexaminer.com/washington-secrets/report-illegal-immigration-harms-blacks-robs-social-services-from-legal-americans.

funding through property, sales, and income taxes. Black citizens have paid their share of these taxes since birth, yet the government programs funded through these taxes are then reduced or stretched to capacity for black Americans in too many communities because of the diluting effect of providing for increasingly larger numbers of newly arrived illegal residents.

## The Tragic Case of Jamiel Shaw

On March 2, 2008, Jamiel Shaw, Jr., a seventeen-year-old teenager living in Los Angeles, was shot and killed on the very street where he had been born and had lived his entire life. His killer was an illegal immigrant gang member named Pedro Espinoza. Jamiel, who had just graduated from high school, was a three-time MVP football player and had been recruited by Stanford, Rutgers, and a host of other top-tier colleges and universities. Jamiel had no criminal record, and by all accounts was destined for greatness. His mother, Army Sgt. Anita Shaw, was on her way back from serving her second tour in Iraq at the time of his death.

Twenty-three-year old Pedro Espinoza could not have been more opposite from Jamiel. A confirmed gang member, Espinoza had just been released from the LA County Jail after being granted parole on his third gun conviction, on the day he killed Jamiel. Had there been regulations in place to discourage sanctuary cities from protecting illegal immigrants, Espinoza's prior criminal history would have qualified him for immediate deportation. However, he was protected from federal immigration detection by the city of Los Angeles, which bills itself as a "sanctuary city" for illegal immigrants.

According to Espinoza's prison gang code, he was required to go out on the streets the day he was released and kill a black gang member. While there is no evidence Jamiel had any gang affiliation whatsoever, apparently Espinoza killed Shaw because he mistook the color of Jamiel's skin and the color of the backpack he was wearing for that of a black gang member. Jamiel's father heard the shots from inside his home and rushed out to provide aid to his son, who died in his arms at the scene of the shooting.

Why is this otherwise tragic death a "curious" case? Well, because of the notable silence about it among mainstream Black political leadership. In fact, most of California's black state and congressional leadership were and are vocal supporters of both sanctuary cities and the DREAM Act. This has been a core plank of the Democratic Party for over a decade, and the African American leadership—particularly those in Los Angeles, like Congresswoman Maxine Waters—has walked in lockstep with the Party on this issue.

Imagine for a moment that this was Ferguson, Missouri, and instead of an illegal immigrant, Jamiel's killer had been a white police officer. In fact, we do not have to imagine. We know that this would be a national outrage. Curiously, in Los Angeles, the murder of Jamiel Shaw barely made the news. His grieving father, Jamiel Shaw, Sr., has gone all over the country trying to raise awareness about the issue of sanctuary cities shielding illegal immigrants who have committed crimes from deportation. He traveled to the state capitol in Sacramento and to Washington, DC, where he tried to meet with members of the Congressional Black Caucus. Not only were his pleas to do something about sanctuary cities dismissed, he was derided in the media by black elites as a racist and a sellout. Imagine that. A father who was merely fighting for his son, a son whose bright future was senselessly snuffed out by an illegal alien, called a racist by the very leaders who were supposed to protect him. What would you do if something like this happened to you?


## THE RIGHT WAY TO PUT HEAT ON ILLEGALS

The debate over illegal immigration has managed to conflate two separate issues: American immigrant citizenship status (and related requirements) on the one hand, and the economic consequences of having limited access to unskilled workers in the domestic labor pool on the other. The two issues are not one and the same. Resolving the complex choices associated with each will be easier when they are treated separately.

On the one hand, U.S. immigrant citizenship policy as modified in 1986 by the Immigration Reform and Control Act—which attempted to address seasonal temporary workers—has been an abysmal failure. The act made it unlawful to knowingly hire an undocumented worker, and provided for a one-year amnesty for illegal aliens who had already worked and lived in the U.S. since January 1982. Although at the time there were less than three million illegal aliens in the U.S., the grant of amnesty sent a signal to the world that the U.S. would no longer be serious about its border. Combined with a phasing out of employer sanctions, predictably, the 1986 "reforms" caused the number of illegals to swell nearly four times to more than twelve million today.

To deal effectively with illegal immigration, we need to adopt a policy that separates those aliens seeking permanent status from those only interested in temporary employment opportunities. Unfortunately, much of the present debate treats the groups as if they are one and the same. By failing to make this distinction, we risk going forward with an updated but incoherent program.

U.S. policy for temporary employment should expressly include provisions making it easier for foreigners with skills that are domestically scarce to find to obtain work permits, and specifically limit entry of temporary workers who are unskilled. Employers of those temporary workers should be required to indemnify the local communities for the costs of social services that these immigrants use. With regard to long-term residency and citizenship reform, we should prioritize highly educated and economically self-sufficient applicants over the existing family-based immigration pathways.

## THE TRUMP ADMINISTRATION HAS CHAMPIONED POLICIES THAT PROTECT BLACK FAMILIES FROM CRIME COMMITTED BY ILLEGAL IMMIGRANTS

The Trump administration cheered House of Representative's passage of Kate's Law,[79] which increases criminal penalties for illegal immigrants who repeatedly re-enter the country, and the No Sanctuary for Criminals Act, which restricts taxpayer grant money from cities that prevent their police from turning over dangerous criminal illegal immigrants to federal authorities.

Kate's Law is named for Kate Steinle, a woman who was killed by an illegal immigrant from Mexico who had been repeatedly deported from the United States, only to return to the sanctuary protection of San Francisco. Her tragic case highlights the pernicious problem of porous borders and the perverse incentives built into the current immigration system. Entering the country illegally is a crime. Deportation has traditionally been the only remedy, but it is not necessarily a deterrent to re-entrance. Under the current policy regime, immigrants are usually given a free ride home and a free chance at another attempt at illegal entry.

It certainly costs the prospective illegal immigrant to travel to the border; border crossing for illegals is a struggle often rife with expense, danger, violence, and almost unspeakable horrors. When President Trump spoke about illegal immigrants from south of the border being "rapists," he was not, as many in the media and on the left have implied, calling out any specific race for being especially likely to rape. Rather, he was noting the extremely high levels of rape committed against women and children attempting to cross the border. Trump has committed both in word and action to

---

79    No Sanctuary for Criminals, H.R. 3003, 115[TH] Congress. (2017–2018). https://www.congress.gov/bill/115th-congress/house-bill/3003.
      Kate's Law, H.R. 3004, 115th Congress. (2017–2018). https://www.congress.gov/bill/115th-congress/house-bill/3004.

preventing the criminal element coming into our country to commit rapes against Americans (or even illegals) here. Because of the heightened dangers that illegal immigration poses to American citizens, a bigger disincentive than mere deportation must be implemented to stem the tide. Imagine if one had not only to compute the monetary and physical risk of the border crossing itself, but also faced potential criminal penalties, including prison and fines once arriving in the U.S. That creates a whole different cost-benefit analysis for the potential illegal immigrant.

The No Sanctuary for Criminals Act, which was passed by the U.S. House of Representatives in 2017, and reintroduced by Congressman Guy Reschenthaler in April 2019, penalizes "sanctuary cities" that claim to give safe haven to illegals by withholding federal funding from jurisdictions that frustrate federal law by prohibiting their officers from communicating with U.S. Immigration and Customs Enforcement (ICE). This law has the potential dual impact of reducing government expenditure on services for illegal immigrants (which, as discussed above, are largely funded on the state and local level through regressive taxes that are born disproportionately by African Americans) and reducing the number of potential criminals targeting American citizens, including African Americans.

## ECONOMIC REFUGEES, LABOR FLEXIBILITY, AND THE BENEFITS OF LEGAL IMMIGRATION

While on a social and political level immigration raises concerns about the boundaries of citizenship, there can be some economic disadvantages to allowing geographical barriers to determine wages, particularly in the context of low-skilled workers. Every American household pays an arbitrarily (and therefore wasteful) higher price for goods and services when they are denied the benefit of competition simply because of where they live. Although often mentioned in the context of goods, the principle is no less true of labor costs. Therefore, a rational temporary worker plan which recognizes that we exist in a global economy that requires "labor flexibility" and allows honest workers interested in coming to America to provide for their families while respecting our laws could be beneficial to Americans overall in carefully controlled amounts.

However, the vast majority of low-skilled laborers seeking to enter the U.S. are economic refugees plagued by the corrupt and chaotic political regimes and attendant policies of Mexico and other Latin American nations. The problems faced by the citizens of these countries are not America's fault or responsibility. And arguably, were it not for the fact that they have a ready escape valve at the northern border—the United States—many of these workers would likely challenge their own governments to implement fair and legitimate laws that benefit all of their citizens.

In fact, in the aftermath of President Trump's virtual shutdown of the flow of immigrants entering the United States at the southern border, we are seeing some of this happening. In Bolivia, for example, citizens and police effectively protested the fraudulent re-election of socialist leader Evo Morales and forced him to step down and hold new elections.[80] While Morales' abdication has been characterized as a "coup" by the American left, the evidence thus far suggests it was a popular uprising against Morales' illegal power grab—he engineered an unlimited term in office for himself despite the Bolivian Constitution limiting presidential terms to two. These types of popular uprisings in Central America were virtually unheard of before Trump closed the outlet valve—that is, illegal immigration to the U.S.—and thereby cut off the road of retreat and forced a reckoning among Bolivia's citizens.

Candidly, introducing a large number of new immigrant workers increases labor supply and tends to drive down prices for domestic low-skilled labor, this harm may be at least partially offset by the benefit to American consumers of lower priced goods and services.

---

80    Yascha Mounk, "Evo Morales Finally Went Too Far For Bolivia," *The Atlantic*, November 11, 2019, https://www.congress.gov/bill/115th-congress/house-bill/3004.

According to several studies, immigrant labor effectively raises Americans' incomes by upwards of $12 billion a year. In a study he conducted for the U.S. Council of Foreign Relations, titled "The Economic Logic of Illegal Immigration," U.C. San Diego Economist Gordon Hanson puts the issue succinctly:

> "From a purely economic perspective, the optimal immigration policy would admit individuals whose skills are in shortest supply and whose tax contributions, net of the cost of public services they receive, are as large as possible. Admitting immigrants in scarce occupations would yield the greatest increase in U.S. incomes, regardless of the skill level of those immigrants. In the United States, scarce workers would include not only highly educated individuals, such as the software programmers and engineers employed by rapidly expanding technology industries, but also low-skilled workers in construction, food preparation, and cleaning services, for which the supply of U.S. native labor has been falling."[81]

But the nexus between migrant workers and long-term residency must absolutely be broken. A rational "temporary" worker program would allow us to match foreign workers with American employers, but would not require that we throw in citizenship as part of the deal. It also would not entitle immigrants to receive government social services, including medical care or education, nor would it entitle children born to guest workers in the United States to automatically receive U.S. citizenship. All costs of employing and caring for these

---

81    Hanson, Gordon, H. "The Economic Logic of Illegal Immigration," The Bernard and Irene Schwartz Series on American Competitiveness, CSR no. 26, Council on Foreign Relations, April 2007, https://cdn.cfr.org/sites/default/files/pdf/2007/04/ImmigrationCSR26.pdf.

immigrant workers and any families under their care should be born directly by the immigrants and/or their employers. There would be less school crowding, hospital swarms, and overutilization of social services if new arrivals and/or their employers were required to pay for them.

The last time an immigration deal was struck came in the form of the Immigration Reform Act of 1986, a bipartisan piece of legislation signed into law by President Reagan. Unfortunately, provisions of the 1986 act that criminalized illegal entry into the country had the unintended effect of turning the informal, flexible, and largely seasonal migration of undocumented workers into long-term permanent residents. Penalties imposed under the law for crossing the border interrupted immigrants' natural migration cycles by making it harder to re-enter the U.S. when seasonal or other temporary opportunities were available. A "temporary" legal status granted under any future immigration reform legislation would alleviate much of the pressure for illegals to seek permanent status since they would be permitted to come and go across the border more freely. Additionally, requiring these workers or their employers to pay for their receipt of any public services would shift the makeup of the type of economic migrants seeking entry to the U.S. and reduce the economic externality (that is uncompensated cost) incurred by their employment.

Under the rules in place today, both companies and immigrant laborers have the opposite incentive. They are incentivized to make a permanent residence of America—including resorting to having "anchor babies" (children born by illegal aliens in the U.S. that automatically become citizens)—as well as to use local and state government funded social services that immigrants can't easily go home to obtain.

Since the primary motivation for the new temporary workers is not to receive citizenship, there should be no easy footpath to citizenship built into the program. Working in America is an economic opportunity of a lifetime. In other words, getting the work permit is its own reward. With a new temporary worker program, economic migrants would be given a chance to obtain wealth and related economic sustenance they can't get in their home country, while presenting little to no financial burden on the communities where they reside. There is no need to offer citizenship as an added inducement.

Once a robust temporary work authorization program for immigrants becomes operational, those individuals here in America illegally will face a choice: either return to their home country and apply for the program and wait their turn, or watch as others do exactly that while they miss out on the benefits of legal status.

Faced with such a choice, would-be employers will quickly demonstrate that they far more prefer a steady and reliable supply of legal unskilled workers (who have all passed background checks) along with actual Americans they employ who can, along with their families, receive social service assistance, to the outlaw labor force they rely on today. Ironically, it will be the illegal aliens who will feel the heat of competition most, because when the program is up and running and operating on a first-come-first-served basis, those who join in first will see the benefits sooner. (And by charging a fee for this, a temporary worker program could likely be used as a revenue source to pay for itself as well as to provide additional border enforcement resources.)

Ideally, the program would have a fluctuating fee level which would rise and fall depending on demand. Starting at around $1,500 (the going rate for smugglers) and rising to a maximum of $25,000 per applicant annually, potential workers and their employers could decide for themselves what the ultimate level should be. On the other hand, with a floor of $8 billion and a ceiling of nearly $150 billion in revenue (and the substantial reduction in social services utilization), even if only a quarter of the existing undocumented workers in the U.S. joined the program, the American taxpayer would easily come out ahead.

Fundamentally, any new immigration plan should have two features. First, it would require potential employers or the workers themselves to be responsible for the social services they consume. Employers could provide health insurance if they chose. If not, whenever the temporary workers receive public assistance, hospitals and other government service providers could seek reimbursement from the employers instead of sending the bill to the American taxpayer. A second feature would be that participants in the program would agree that their participation in the program in no way may be used to advance or assist them or their children in seeking citizenship status.

The program would have other benefits as well, such as being attractive to fathers and older sons and single women who generally prefer to work seasonally or annually and then return to their home country. In a return to the practice prior to the 1986 act, participation in the new program would provide little incentive for migrant workers to uproot their entire family or to have "anchor babies" in order to protect their ability to maintain their presence in the U.S. Employers would also realign their hiring expectations to compare the trade-offs of paying more directly to American workers (including blacks) or making payments into federal and state coffers to get access to foreign labor.

## Border Security

For those individuals uninterested in employment opportunities in the immigration areas open for migrants, the U.S. should signal a reinvigorated commitment to strong border security. The U.S. has every right to restrict who it will invite to become an American, and to set the terms. Indeed, any policy that rewards those who enter the country illegally is a poor one and undermines our nation's sovereignty.

In fact, knowing who is crossing our borders has taken on a greater urgency, particularly after the terrorist attacks on 9/11 and the U.S. global war on terror that has ensued in the intervening two decades. To discourage employers and illegal immigrants from attempting to game the system, the U.S. should commit itself to a policy of immediately returning every illegal alien caught crossing the border, without exception. New approaches, such as interior repatriation for Mexican nationals (which transports illegals to interior portions of Mexico instead of simply escorting them back across the border), should be employed, and greater use of electronic surveillance at border sites should be undertaken.

The completely unworkable policy of "catch and release" should be ended. Under this practice, if non-Mexican illegal aliens are apprehended, they are released and told to return later for an immigration status hearing. As you might imagine, a significant number of these persons simply fail to ever show up for their day in court.[82]

Also, the U.S. should commit the resources to allow expedited hearings and new detention facilities so that once illegal aliens are caught by border patrol, they aren't allowed a chance to escape deportation, and instead are required to appear in court. As illegal border crossings of economic migrants begin to decline, interdiction of drug smugglers and related criminals will be much easier to accomplish. Furthermore, processing individual immigrants by requiring formal adjudicative proceedings would require them to be "documented," and repeat offenders could be easily identified and punished more severely.

Ultimately, by separating immigrant citizenship policy from a temporary unskilled labor program, America will be living up to its own ideals—keeping our borders open to legal travel and honest trade while securing them from exploitation by criminals, terrorists, and drug traffickers. And by ensuring that citizenship is granted solely to those who understand and value the benefits of being an American, we'll protect our culture and the American way of life.

---

82   John Kruzel, "Majority of Undocumented Immigrants Show Up For Court, Data Shows," PunditFact, Politifact, June 26, 2018, https://www.politifact.com/punditfact/statements/2018/jun/26/wolf-blitzer/majority-undocumented-immigrants-show-court-data-s/.

# CONCLUSION

The effects of immigration on black labor are not new in America. Even the great abolitionist and humanitarian Frederick Douglass complained about the "crowding out" effects immigrant labor was having on lower-skilled jobs available to black Americans. Today, blacks face a similar situation with immigrant labor coming across the southern border of the U.S. A significant portion of the decades-long decline in black male labor force participation has been caused by the oversupply of cheap illegal (and some legal) immigrant labor.

The Trump administration's policies reduce illegal immigration through a variety of means, particularly restricting the flow of low-skilled immigrants who can come to this country. This helps black Americans by making more of those jobs available to them.

Blacks also disproportionately bear the burden of government services provided to illegal immigrants, which is estimated to be more than $118 billion annually. By advocating laws that would penalize sanctuary cities that provide these services, the Trump administration is helping ensure blacks receive more of the government services, particularly in health care and education, that should go to them and that they have spent their entire lives paying for.

Finally, Trump administration policies, such as the criminalization of re-entry by illegal immigrants, helps reduce net immigration and protects African Americans from crime committed by violent criminal immigrants and terrorists. Trump's immigration strategy is pro-black and pro-America.

# Chapter 4

~

# STOP OR I'LL SHOOT!

In an uncharacteristic moment of candor on the campaign trail in 2008, then-candidate Barack Obama let slip his deep contempt for the poor rural voters whom he had tried to enlist, unconvincingly, to join his movement for "hope and change." They wouldn't get it anyway, he implied, "because they get bitter, they cling to guns or religion or antipathy to people who aren't like them, or anti-immigrant sentiment or anti-trade sentiment as a way to explain their frustrations." Seizing upon the moment, his Democratic primary challenger Hillary Clinton voiced her supposed solidarity with the rural poor, declaring, "I was taken aback by the demeaning remarks Senator Obama made about people in small-town America. His remarks are elitist and out of touch."

Hillary would betray her own liberal elitism eight years later, when in a similarly unscripted moment of candor, she said, "You know, to just be grossly generalistic, you could put half of Trump's supporters into what I call the basket of deplorables. Right? The racist, sexist, homophobic, xenophobic, Islamophobic—you name it. And unfortunately, there are people like that. And he has lifted them up."

The fact that Hillary failed to heed her own message and repeated the mistake Obama made in 2008, of dismissing such a wide swath of the American electorate as backwards and out of touch, seemed to pave the way for Donald Trump's 21st century populist campaign in 2016.

Are blacks the new deplorables? Are their interests, which align more readily with main street America, rather than the plans and schemes of the academic elites that set policy for progressives, setting them on an obstacle course with the next Democrat running for the presidency?

Trump set out to be everything the Obamas and Clintons were not. They were consummate insiders, and he was the resolute outsider come to toss the Pharisees from the temple and restore American democracy.

Gun ownership is a clear issue that separates the elites from main street America. Obama and Clinton hated the Second Amendment, and Trump would not only defend the right to bear arms, but celebrate it, becoming the first president to address the NRA in thirty-four years when he spoke at its annual convention in 2017.

In taking such a strong stand in support of the Second Amendment, Trump not only stood up for the forgotten "deplorables," but also for the constitutional rights of African Americans to keep and bear arms. With his advocacy, Trump supports the right of self-defense—a right of particular importance to black Americans. Both historical precedent and current dynamics within the African-American community make it imperative that blacks maintain their Second Amendment rights, and make them also especially positioned to benefit from President Trump's efforts to defend and expand gun rights for all Americans.

## DONALD TRUMP HAS DEMONSTRATED STRONG SUPPORT FOR THE SECOND AMENDMENT

During the 2016 election primaries, Donald Trump was the only candidate who directly addressed the NRA. His decision to address the NRA Convention in May 2016 was considered by most political analysts to be an extremely risky move. While much of the country, as well as the Republican base, support gun rights, publicly promoting Second Amendment rights has been considered a politically perilous proposition by some mainstream politicians, lest they be seen as too closely aligned with the NRA's "special interest" agenda. The term "special interest," however, is probably misapplied when it comes to an organization dedicated to upholding a constitutional right. It is true—our rights are "special," and we hold them dearly. But they are not specially reserved for one class of Americans while being denied to another; they are rights enjoyed by all.

While gun rights were once an issue that received broad bipartisan support—with only radical leftists opposing them—the number of congressional Democrats who received an A-rating from the NRA declined from fifty-eight in 2008 to just twelve in 2018. The NRA also lost support among swing-state Republicans. Eight Republicans had their grades reduced in 2018. House Republicans Brian Mast of Florida, Peter King of New York, and Brian Fitzpatrick of Pennsylvania all now have F-ratings, and all three were re-elected in 2018. In 2019, Republican representatives Michael R. Turner of Ohio and Adam Kinzinger of Illinois came out in support of gun regulations, mostly in response to the public uproar over the deadly shootings in El Paso and Dayton. The point here is that Americans need a courageous champion to stand up for our constitutional rights, even in the face of popular opposition.

President Trump, though, defied critics and gave a rousing speech at the NRA Annual Convention, in which he laid down a stark choice for its members: elect Hillary Clinton and see your Second Amendment rights disappear into a maze of new regulations restricting firearm ownership, or elect me and be assured that your right to bear arms will be preserved and even strengthened by my pro-Second Amendment picks for the Supreme Court.

Candidate Trump's speech earned a standing ovation from the NRA members in attendance, and they and their friends went out and voted, not just at the election booth, but also with their pocket-books. The NRA spent an unprecedented $30 million in support of the Trump presidential campaign, including over $6 million in the critical battleground state of North Carolina—a state Trump won by a margin of only 3.7 percent. The NRA's mobilization of both voters and campaign resources proved to be an essential factor in securing Trump's winning North Carolina in the general election. Clearly, Trump's strong and early stand for the Second Amendment paid off handsomely.

Since coming into office, President Trump has continued to de-monstrate a strong support for the Second Amendment, as reflected by his two Supreme Court picks. Both Justices Gorsuch and Kava-naugh are staunch supporters of Second Amendment rights. At the NRA's Annual Convention in April 2017, Chris Cox, Executive Director of the NRA Institute for Legislative Action, called Trump "the most proudly pro-gun presidential candidate" in U.S. history.

## President Trump Has Appointed Two Conservative Supreme Court Justices Who Are Likely to Strongly Defend the Second Amendment

Justice Neil Gorsuch, who was picked to replace Justice Scalia's seat on the Supreme Court, is a prominent proponent of textualism and originalism[83] in the interpretation of the U.S. Constitution. Notably, during his confirmation hearings before the Senate, he verbally sparred with Democratic Senator Diane Feinstein over whether he agreed with Justice Scalia's concurring opinion in the case of *Heller v. District of Columbia*.[84] In that case, the court decided by a five-

---

83    Former Supreme Court Justice Antonin Scalia called his judicial approach to the Constitution "originalism" or "textualism." The idea of Originalism/Textualism is that the Constitution means no more or less than what it meant to those who originally wrote and ratified it. This is seen as a counter-approach to the "living Constitution" idea where the text is interpreted in light of current times, culture and society.

84    "District of Columbia v. Heller," *Wikipedia*, last modified January 11, 2020, https://en.wikipedia.org/wiki/District_of_Columbia_v._Heller.

to-four margin that provisions of Washington, D.C.'s handgun ban were unconstitutional. Justice Scalia, who voted for the majority, reasoned that some guns—notably those most useful for military service—could be regulated under the firearm, ban but that others—namely those in common use for self-defense—should not be regulated. Senator Feinstein grilled the nominee in the confirmation hearing before the Senate Judiciary Committee about whether he agreed with Scalia's reasoning in the Heller case. But Gorsuch stood his ground. He said, "Heller is the law. It is not a matter of agreeing or disagreeing, it's a matter of if it's the law."

Gorsuch and other originalists rightly interpret the Second Amendment not as a "grant" of rights to citizens, but a restriction on the government's authority to prevent citizens from enjoying a preor-dained right to bear arms for self and community protection. This is a unique feature of the U.S. Constitution that has been miscast by liberals as a bug. It is not. The framers saw the Second Amendment as a necessary safeguard against the perils of both domestic tyranny and foreign invasion, and specifically vested the power to exercise the safeguard in the hands of American citizens.

After his arrival to the Court, Gorsuch joined Justice Clarence Thomas in writing a dissent from the denial of certiorari (basically declining to take the case) of a 9th Circuit ruling on gun rights that upheld California's restrictive concealed carry regulations. The dissent was important because it reflected a potential tilt of the court towards selecting gun rights cases for review in the future. Thomas, joined by Gorsuch, noted that, "the time has come for the Court to answer this important question definitively. Twenty-six States have asked us to resolve the question presented."

The justices saw the refusal of the court to grant certiorari in the case as part of a "distressing trend," namely "the treatment of the Second Amendment as a disfavored right." The Constitution does not rank certain rights above others, but the Supreme Court can sometimes impose such a hierarchy by selectively enforcing its preferred rights. The court has not heard argument in a Second

Amendment case in over seven years, while taking roughly thirty-five First Amendment cases and twenty-five Fourth Amendment cases. This discrepancy is notable, especially given how much less developed the jurisprudence is with respect to the Second Amendment as compared to the First and Fourth Amendments.

The biggest Second Amendment case to come before the court in a decade was announced in January 2019, when the court agreed to hear the case of *New York State Rifle & Pistol Association Inc. v. City of New York*. The plaintiffs in the case are challenging New York City's restrictive gun regulation which makes it, in effect, unlawful for legal gun owners to transport their guns out of the city. The nonsensical legislation was eventually rescinded and superseded by subsequent New York State legislation in an effort by Democrat politicians to render the issue moot and prevent the Supreme Court's review. The Supreme Court rejected New York's argument and ruled in October 2019 that the case would proceed to oral argument in early 2020. In other words, the court seems to be signaling that it is now eager to take on Second Amendment cases after over a decade of de-emphasizing them.

Trump's second appointment to the court of Justice Kavanaugh, who replaces the more centrist Justice Kennedy, increases the likelihood that more Second Amendment cases will be heard by the court and decided in favor of the right to keep and bear arms. In fact, Justice Kavanaugh's record on gun rights as a D.C. circuit judge confirms this. After the Supreme Court struck down D.C.'s gun ban in the Heller case, D.C. issued new regulations that imposed strict registration requirements on gun owners, and also banned most automatic weapons. Mr. Heller, the original plaintiff, then brought another case before the D.C. Circuit (Heller II) contesting the new regulations as also unconstitutional. Writing in dissent from the ruling of the three-judge panel on the D.C. circuit that upheld the district's new regulations, then-Circuit Court Judge Kavanaugh wrote, "both

D.C.'s ban on semi-automatic rifles and its gun registration requirement are unconstitutional under Heller."[85]

Kavanaugh believes that some gun regulations are permitted under the Constitution, but not based on whether the government finds that changing attitudes in big cities lead to more gun restrictions. He believes that history, constitutional text, and tradition should guide any proposed regulations. Similarly, Kavanaugh did not express disdain for gun owner "licensing" that could provide for the safe use of firearms. Rather, he objected to the district's unusual requirement that each gun be "registered" with the government, as that was never contemplated by either the framers of the Constitution, nor by most other gun laws around the country. In other words, Justice Kavanaugh believes the Constitution and its historical underpinnings, not legal balancing tests, directly govern the application of enumerated rights, like the right to keep and bear arms.

### The President Has Explicitly Refused to Use Mass Shootings to Call for More Restrictions on Gun Owners.

Perhaps in keeping with his overall character, President Trump has proven implacable in refusing to retreat from his commitment to preserving Second Amendment rights despite media pressure to do so in the aftermath of recent highly publicized mass shootings.

Since President Trump took office, there have been roughly six or seven dozen mass shootings in the country. In the cases where the president has responded to the shootings, he has expressed comfort and condolences to the victims, but either refused to answer questions about calling for more gun regulations, or explicitly stated that

---

85    Dick Anthony Heller, et al., Appellants v. District of Columbia, et al., Appellees, no. 10-7036 (Argued: November 15, 2010, Decided: October 4, 2011). Appeal from the United States District Court for the District of Columbia no. 1:08-cv-01289. https://www.cadc.uscourts.gov/internet/opinions.nsf/ DECA496973477C748525791F004D84F9/$file/10-7036-1333156.pdf.

he would not talk about gun regulations in that context. However, Trump has alluded to specific policy recommendations for dealing with mass shootings in schools, including stating that "Armed Educators (and trusted people who work within a school) love our students and will protect them."[86]

President Trump's record on refusing to use mass shootings as a platform to call for more gun regulation contrasts favorably with that of President Obama, who often used mass tragedies as a bully pulpit to try to force through stricter regulations on firearm ownership. In the aftermath of the Pulse nightclub shooting in Orlando, Florida, in 2016, then-President Obama said, "this massacre is therefore a further reminder of how easy it is for someone to get their hands on a weapon....we have to decide if that's the kind of country we want to be. And to actively do nothing is a decision as well." Obama was right, of course. By actively refusing to impose more regulations in response to tragedies of these kinds, President Trump is making an affirmative choice in favor of upholding the Second Amendment. In the aftermath of the shooting at Parkland High School in 2018, President Trump emphasized working "together to create a culture in our country that embraces the dignity of life.... that creates deep and meaningful human connections, and that turns classmates and colleagues into friends and neighbors."[87] He did not mention firearms.

---

86    Jacob Shamsian, "Here's What Trump Tweeted About Each of the 62 Mass Shooting of His Presidency," Insider, June 28, 2018, https://www.insider.com/what-trump-tweeted-after-mass-shooting-president-2018-5.

87    Patrick May, "Another Mass Shooting, Another President Trying to Comfort the Nation: Trump Speaks After News of High-School Massacre in Texas," *The Mercury News*, May 18, 2018, https://www.mercurynews.com/2018/05/18/another-mass-shooting-another-president-trying-to-comfort-the-nation/.

# THE RIGHT TO BEAR ARMS IS CRITICALLY IMPORTANT TO AFRICAN AMERICANS

The Second Amendment is a vital way for any people to maintain autonomy and freedom. Keeping and bearing firearms are essential to everyday citizens' ability protect their God-given (and Constitutionally enumerated) rights. While it would be great if the government could provide every citizen with an armed guard to protect them, that would not be economically feasible. And contrary to popular belief, it is neither the government's obligation, nor in its capability, to protect citizens from violent crime.[88] Furthermore, keeping and bearing arms has traditionally served as a primary means by which African Americans have sought to protect themselves against racially motivated violence. In today's America, blacks are more likely to live in communities that are under-policed, and thus the right to bear arms and use them for self-defense may be the first (and sometimes only) line of defense they have against the epidemic of violent crime in their own neighborhoods, committed overwhelmingly by people who look like them.

### Having Access to Firearms Helps African Americans in Communities Plagued by Violent Crime

The individual right to bear arms is important to black Americans—and especially black women—who tend to live in areas plagued by higher violent crime. High crime areas must either be policed more heavily by local and state police forces, or they must be defended by the men and women who live there. Thanks to the efforts by anti-law enforcement activism, a redirection of police funding, and a perception that the officers themselves will be scrutinized more when they

---

88    DeShaney v. Winnebago County Department of Social Services, no. 87-154, 489 U.S. 189 (Argued: November 2, 1988, Decided: February 22, 1989). Cornell Law School, https://www.law.cornell.edu/supremecourt/text/489/189. Castle Rock v. Gonzales, no. 04-278, 545 U.S. 748 (2005).

interact with minorities, police have already shown themselves to be unwilling or unable to adequately defend black neighborhoods.

The ACLU found that in Chicago, "African American and Latino neighborhoods wait much longer for a police officer to be dispatched after an emergency 911 call, have fewer officers assigned to minority districts for each emergency call than predominantly white neighborhoods, and that minority neighborhoods continue to have more violent crimes per officer than white neighborhoods."[89] As a result, in 2014, the ACLU and the Central Austin Neighborhood Association (CANA) sued the city of Chicago on the basis of inadequate and disparate police and emergency services deployment in minority communities. The ACLU found that the average response time to Priority 1 Emergency calls (those relating to violent crime or accidental injury) was four times longer in black neighborhoods in Chicago than white neighborhoods.

This is an outrageous statistic in a city like Chicago, which, in 2019, and during the previous six years, led the nation in gun-related homicides. Most of those murders are occurring in communities of color, where police services are more critically needed than anywhere else. Ironically, the self-appointed leaders of Black America continue to claim that the problem is law enforcement, not criminals.

Chicago Mayor-Elect Lori Lightfoot, the day after her historic election in April 2019 (she is Chicago's first black female mayor) blamed the "fractured relationship" between police and the black community for Chicago's crime problem. She argued that the Chicago PD "ha[d] not adequately taken into account the segregation in our city and that race does matter," and that the gulf between police and the community, "…has left many people feeling like the police are an illegitimate occupying force." Lightfoot, a former federal

89    "Newly-Released Data Shows City Continues to Deny Equitable Police Services to South and West Side Neighborhoods," ACLU of Illinois, March 31, 2014, https://www.aclu-il.org/en/press-releases/newly-released-data-shows-city-continues-deny-equitable-police-services-south-and.

prosecutor, then urged the U.S. Attorney's Office to reopen a grand jury investigation into the shooting of black teen Laquan McDonald by a white officer. It seemed she was grandstanding, because this was a case in which a state trial had already been convened. A Chicago jury would ultimately convict the offending officer, Jason Van Dyke, of second degree murder and sixteen counts of aggravated battery with a firearm, and sentence him to six years in prison.

Liberal black leaders like Lightfoot tend to express the issue of crime and policing in black neighborhoods in starkly Marxist terms. Lightfoot believes that economic disparities and the lack of opportunity for blacks is the primary cause of crime in black communities. Notably, however, Lightfoot oversees one of the least business-friendly regulatory and tax regimes in the nation. Chicago is also a sanctuary city in which the taxpayers pay hundreds of millions of dollars in public services for illegal immigrants. Perhaps if black liberal leaders focused on the needs of their citizens instead of adopting the policy prescriptions of big government and open borders, economic opportunities might increase for black residents.

The fact is that black communities suffer far more from the under-policing of violent crime than over-policing. The homicide rate in Chicago has nothing to do with police committing murders, but is largely due to underfunding law enforcement leading to elevated response times in emergencies, and the mounting list of unsolved murders resulting from under-policing.

Under-policing leaves black neighborhoods and their residents with no real alternative but to arm and defend themselves. Incredulously, while Chicago has some of the highest rates of violent gun crimes, it also has one of the most restrictive set of firearms regulations in the country.

Illinois was the last state in the nation to allow concealed carry permits, after a 2012 7th Circuit Court of Appeals ruling that the state's prohibition was unconstitutional under the Second Amendment right to bear arms. In the wake of the ruling, state lawmakers then enacted the Firearm Concealed Carry Act to regulate concealed carry licenses. The process for obtaining a concealed carry license in Chicago is unduly onerous and monstrously opaque. There is a training requirement and a host of expensive fees and background checks. The Concealed Carry Licensing Review Board—seemingly named in honor of a Soviet-era bureaucratic relic—has denied over 800 people who passed all the tests and background checks and paid fees for the right to carry a concealed weapon.

Michael Thomas, an African-American Chicago resident and a U.S. Air Force Reservist who routinely carried a gun during military service and has never had a run-in with the law, was nonetheless turned down for a concealed carry license. When he asked for a reason from the review board, he was told by the Illinois State Police that the reasons for the board's findings were secret and would not be explained to him, even though the law does not afford police the discretion to deny permits to those who meet the prerequisites. Thomas was told that he would have to petition a court in order to appeal his denial. So that's what he did. He joined 193 other Illinoisans—many of whom happen to be African Americans—in filing lawsuits against the state police.

In response to the class action lawsuit filed on their behalf, Illinois State Police reversed course and published a set of emergency rules that purported to address the issues of notice and opportunity to be heard. Thomas, who was the lead plaintiff, was able to obtain additional information about his denial and provide a response. His application was subsequently approved.[90] Should it have taken a full-out bureaucratic battle merely to exercise one's constitutional right to bear arms?

Despite having been repeatedly corrected by federal courts, the state of Illinois appears to remain hell-bent on keeping guns out of the hands of law-abiding black citizens and putting them at the

---

90    "NRA Supports Two Concealed Carry Cases in Illinois," NRA-ILA (National Rifle Association-Institute for Legislative Action), November 6, 2014, https://www. nraila.org/articles/20141106/nra-supports-two-concealed-carry-cases-in-illinois.

mercy of violent criminals. And it does all this while affording far less police protection to black communities than white communities. The vast majority of Illinois's 73,714 active concealed carry licenses—90 percent—have been issued to whites, demographic data shows. Only 8 percent of the licenses have been awarded to African Americans. Within Cook County, the top five concealed carry ZIP codes per capita are all predominately white, middle class, and are in areas that have low crime rates. However, the most violent neighborhoods within the county—all of which are on the South Side of Chicago—are predominately black, where residents hold the fewest concealed carry licenses.

Every government hurdle placed on legal gun ownership renders citizens—and especially blacks in police-less, high-crime neighborhoods—more dependent upon the state for their own protection. By not only declining to put more hurdles in their way, but actively promoting the Second Amendment, President Trump has already helped black Americans. The 2nd amendment and gun ownership is a vital tool for the safety and security of all Americans, including blacks. Additionally, his support for H.R. 38, the Concealed Carry Reciprocity Act, which would allow Americans who get a concealed carry license from any state to be able to use it in any other state that allows conceal carry, would be a great aid for black America and any American trapped in a dangerous community.[91]

## Courts Have Declared That It Is Not the Government's Responsibility to Protect Individual Citizens from Violent Crime.

The police have no duty to protect you, the individual citizen. Yes, that's right. It may come as a surprise to some people, but the courts have repeatedly said that private citizens have no constitutional right to police protection.

---

91    Concealed Carry Reciprocity Act of 2019, H.R. 38, 116TH Congress. (2019–2020). https://www.congress.gov/bill/116th-congress/house-bill/38.

The tragic case of Carolyn Warren and her housemates clearly illustrates the problem. In the early morning hours of March 16, 1975, Carolyn Warren, Joan Taliaferro, and Miriam Douglas were asleep in their rooming house in northwest Washington, D.C., when they were awakened by the sound of the back door being broken down. Two men entered Douglas' second floor room and sodomized and raped her.

Warren and Taliaferro heard Douglas' screams from the floor below. Warren telephoned the police, told the officer on duty that the house was being burglarized, and requested immediate assistance. The department employee told her to remain quiet and assured her that police assistance would be dispatched promptly. Meanwhile, Warren and Taliaferro crawled from their window onto an adjoining roof and waited for the police to arrive. While there, they saw one policeman drive through the alley behind their house and proceed to the front of the residence without stopping, leaning out the window, or getting out of the car to check the back entrance of the house. A second officer apparently knocked on the door in front of the residence, but left when he received no answer.

Warren and Taliaferro crawled back inside their room. They again heard Douglas' continuing screams. They called the police emergency line a second time and again told the dispatcher that the intruders had entered the home, and requested immediate assistance. Once again, a police officer assured them that help was on the way. This second call was recorded merely as "investigate the trouble," and it was never dispatched to any police officers.

Believing the police might be in the house, Warren and Taliaferro called down to Douglas, their voices alerting the assailants, who were still in the home, to their presence. The assailants then forced all three women, at knifepoint, to accompany them to one of the assailant's apartments, where, for the next fourteen hours, the women were held captive, raped, robbed, and beaten.

The women subsequently sued the Metropolitan Police Department for negligence, alleging that their failure to properly investigate the emergency call caused the women to be injured. The D.C. Circuit Court of Appeals ultimately ruled against the women, stating that such a ruling would violate the "the fundamental principle that a government and its agents are under no general duty to provide public services, such as police protection, to any particular individual citizen." The duty to provide public services is owed to the public at large, the court said, and absent a special relationship between the police and an individual, no specific legal duty to protect an individual exists.

The Supreme Court declined to take the case on appeal, essentially making Warren the law of the land.[92] Given the government's niggardly stance about protecting individuals, it seems incongruous with any notion of law and justice that we should have a policy of removing from citizens the ability to protect themselves by taking away their right to keep and bear arms. When the government has no duty to protect an enumerated right—the right to life and liberty in this case—then it seems only logical that the ability to protect those rights should vest with the individual.

## Gun Rights for African Americans in Context of Historical Racial Violence

One vital root cause for protecting firearm rights is strangely absent from public discussion: violent white racist ideology. From the advent of the Civil War, and well through the 1960s, white supremacist terrorists engaged in a campaign of murder, property destruction, and intimidation against blacks. Lest you think this problem is overstated, lynching and other racist murders of blacks were so prevalent in the early 20th century that Congress voted several times to try

---

92    DeShaney v. Winnebago County Department of Social Services, no. 87-154, 489 U.S. 189 (Argued: November 2, 1988, Decided: February 22, 1989). Cornell Law School, https://www.law.cornell.edu/supremecourt/text/489/189.
Castle Rock v. Gonzales, no. 04-278, 545 U.S. 748 (2005)

to adopt a federal law explicitly banning lynching.[93] Although some states have more recently enacted anti-lynching legislation, blacks lived for decades under conditions of widespread racial terror.

How would blacks defend themselves in the absence of government protection against domestic terror? African Americans began to develop one of the richest traditions of gun rights advocacy among all groups, despite (or even perhaps because of) being targeted by and resisting local, state, and federal gun control measures since before America's founding. The 1792 Uniform Military Act restricted militia service by excluding black men from joining. The sale of firearms to enslaved people was for obvious reasons made unlawful in Florida. In 1825, Florida was merely a U.S. territory (before statehood) when it adopted a gun control law aimed at disarming free blacks. The law authorized white citizen patrols to search and seize arms and other weapons in "all Negro houses" and mandated that blacks could only use a firearm "in the presence of a white person." After Florida became a state 1861, it permitted white patrols to summarily punish any blacks—free or enslaved—in possession of a firearm.[94]

The history of blacks and gun ownership continues after the end of slavery, where, in the South, blacks had to use firearms to protect their lives and property from racial violence. They had to do this because the government, in many cases, refused to protect rights of African Americans at the expense of white citizens. Ironically, given this history of failure by the government to protect their rights, blacks as a group consider themselves more pro-government than any other ethnic group. By their actions, in voting for candidates promising government welfare and enhanced governmental intervention in the

93    "NAACP History: Charles Hamilton Houston," NAACP, Accessed on February 12, 2020, https://www.naacp.org/naacp-history-charles-hamilton-houston/.

94    Jeremy Levitt, "African-Americans for Gun Rights: Blacks Embrace Second Amendment," *Orlando Sentinel*, February 28, 2018, https://www.orlandosentinel.com/opinion/os-ed-blacks-embrace-second-amendment-20180228-story.html.

marketplace, they tend to subject themselves to state power more readily than others.

Surveying the political landscape in the summer of 1892, African-American journalist, civil rights leader, and anti-lynching activist Ida B. Wells advised that "the Winchester rifle deserved a place of honor in every black home." She wasn't kidding. She was advancing a well-considered personal security policy, and specifically referencing two recent episodes in which armed blacks had saved their neighbors from white lynch mobs.

Twice within one month, lynch mobs formed, one in Paducah, Kentucky, another in Jacksonville, Florida, for the explicit purpose of finding some hapless black person to lynch—ostensibly over unfounded rumors of a crime committed by a "negro." In both cases, however, armed blacks thwarted the mob. These episodes confirmed for Ida Wells the importance of armed self-defense in an environment where the idea of relying on the state for personal security was an increasingly absurd proposition.

In the 1890s, Wells documented lynching in the United States. She showed that lynching was often used in the South as a way to control or punish black people who competed with whites, rather than as an extra-judicial punishment for crimes allegedly committed by black people. Lynching "criminals" was usually just an excuse claimed by whites for a cruel and barbaric form of domestic terrorism against blacks.

In retaliation for her reporting, which was carried nationwide in black newspapers, her newspaper presses were destroyed by a mob of white men. For Wells and for many of her contemporaries, the Winchesters became a common rhetorical theme. At a meeting of the Afro-American Press Association, editor of the *New York Age*, T. Thomas Fortune, incensed by a recent wave of lynching in the South, exclaimed, "We have cringed and crawled long enough. I don't want any more 'good niggers.' I want 'bad niggers.' It's the 'bad nigger' with the Winchester who can defend his home and child and wife." Another journalist followed Fortune on the dais and affirmed the sentiments of the group that racist thugs were "afraid to lynch us where they know the Black man is standing behind the door with a Winchester."[95]

Well into the 20th century and up until present times, the ability to have access to firearms was crucial to black Americans' survival. But for the willingness of blacks to use firearms to protect their property and their lives, the post-Civil War era may well have ended quite differently for blacks in the South.

This history of bigotry and guns is often ignored or obscured. Consider the Charleston church shooting of 2015. Several alarming facts came to light in the aftermath of the Charleston, South Carolina, church shooting in which a young white man attended a prayer meeting at a historic black church and killed nine of the parishioners, including the beloved pastor. The first and most alarming is that the shooter, Dylan Roof, had intended to kill the church members in revenge for black men dating white women.

Notably, his angst was not directed against any named black person, but against the general concept of sexual competition between black men and white men for white women. Secondly, according to his friends, he also hoped to use the event to spark a race war.[96] At the federal trial for his crime, FBI Agent Joseph Hamski read for the court excerpts of a journal found in Roof's jail cell, where Roof proclaimed that white women who date black men are "race-traitors," and complained that more white people would not join him in taking violent action.[97]

---

95    Professor Nicholas Johnson, "Negroes and the Gun: A Winchester in Every Black Home," The Volokh Conspiracy, The Washington Post, January 29, 2014, https://www.washingtonpost.com/news/volokh-conspiracy/wp/2014/01/29/negroes-and-the-gun-a-winchester-in-every-black-home/.

96    Janell Ross, "Dylann Roof Reportedly Wanted a Race War. How Many Americans Sympathize?" The Fix, The Washington Post, June 19, 2015, https://www.washingtonpost.com/news/the-fix/wp/2015/06/19/dylann-roof-reportedly-wanted-a-race-war-how-many-americans-feel-like-he-supposedly-does/

97    Matt Zapotosky, Jury in Dylann Roof Death Penalty Trial Expected to Start Deliberations Tuesday," The Washington Post, January 6, 2017, https://www.washingtonpost.com/world/national-security/deliberations-in-dylann-roof-death-penalty-trial-expected-to-start-tuesday/2017/01/06/1338a482-d412-11e6-a783-cd3fa950f2fd_story.html.

These racial tropes—the hyper-sexualization of black males as a pretext for racial violence and the instigation of racial war—are both familiar and highly alarming to blacks and whites alike. In the aftermath of the church shooting, blacks, particularly in the South, began to arm themselves. The National African-American Gun Association, with about twenty thousand members, grew from four chapters in 2016, to more than thirty chapters in 2017. Gun sales among African Americans have also increased since the 2016 election, while overall gun sales in the country declined.[98]

## THE KKK: The Democrat's Military Wing

While most Americans are aware of the odious history of the Ku Klux Klan, most are not aware of the group's close ties to the Democratic Party. Eric Foner, a Columbia University history professor, himself a Democrat, noted the Klan was a "military force." He states, "In effect, the Klan was a military force serving the interests of the Democratic Party, the planter class, and all those who desired restoration of white supremacy. Its purposes were political, but political in the broadest sense, for it sought to affect power relations, both public and private, throughout Southern society."

It is somewhat strange that today when most people think of the push for racial equality in the United States, they think of Presidents John Kennedy, Lyndon Johnson, and the Democratic Party. But the history of the Democratic Party reveals quite a different, and far more sordid, story. Since its founding in 1829, the DNC fought against every civil rights initiative proposed in the U.S. The Democratic Party defended slavery, started the Civil War, opposed

---

98    Max Blau, "The NRA's Struggle to Prove Black Guns Matter," *Politico*, April 30, 2017, https://www.politico.com/magazine/story/2017/04/30/the-nras-struggle-to-prove-black-guns-matter-215084.
In the first three months of this year, gun purchases have gone down nationally by 14 percent compared with the same period in 2016, according to federal background check data, but gun store owners report an increase in sales to blacks, Hispanics, and members of the LGBT community.

Reconstruction, provided the foot soldiers for the KKK, imposed segregation, perpetrated lynching throughout the country, imposed labor policies intended to hurt blacks, and fought against most of the civil rights acts of the 20th century.

After Reconstruction ended, and when the federal troops who had stayed behind to protect newly freed blacks went home, Democrats came back into power in the South. They quickly reestablished white supremacy across the region with measures like black codes—laws that restricted the ability of blacks to own property and start businesses. They imposed poll taxes and literacy tests used to subvert black citizens' voting rights. These laws were enforced by terror, much of it instigated by the KKK, which was founded by Democrat Nathan Bedford Forrest. President Woodrow Wilson, a Democrat, re-segregated several federal agencies and screened the first movie ever shown at the White House, the racist movie *Birth of A Nation*, originally titled *The Klansman*.

Democratic Senator Robert Byrd, who ultimately became known as a mainstream Democratic leader in the 1970s and 1980s, and served as a mentor to Hillary Clinton, was an "exalted cyclops" of the Ku Klux Klan. Although he apologized numerous times for what he considered a youthful indiscretion, his early votes in Congress—notably a filibuster against the 1964 Civil Rights Act—reflected racially separatist views.

In several interviews, Byrd acknowledged that he had "briefly" been a member of the KKK, and blamed it on "youthful indiscretion." In fact, his involvement in the KKK was far more extensive than he ever admitted. In the early 1940s, Byrd recruited 150 of his friends and associates to form a chapter of the Ku Klux Klan in Crab Orchard, West Virginia. After Byrd had collected the ten-dollar joining fee and three-dollar charge for a robe and hood from every applicant, the "Grand Dragon" for the mid-Atlantic states came down to officially organize the chapter. Despite Byrd's claims that he had only been a member between 1942 and 1943, a handwritten letter from Byrd to the KKK Imperial Wizard, dated 1946, stated,

"The Klan is needed today as never before, and I am anxious to see its rebirth here in West Virginia."

Robert Byrd is the only senator to have the distinction of voting against both black nominees to the United States Supreme Court, Thurgood Marshall and Clarence Thomas.[99]

Supreme Court Justice Hugo Black, another powerful Democratic leader, was known as a defender of civil rights during his three decades on the Supreme Court. But what many do not know is that Justice Black was a prominent and secretive member of the KKK. He supposedly resigned membership in 1925, but it was later discovered that he was subsequently welcomed back into the Klan and given a lifetime membership. When he was a United States senator, he introduced and successfully shepherded through Congress the Fair Labor Standards Act, which along with the creation of the National Recovery Administration and the National Labor Relations Act, were opposed by blacks at the time for their deleterious effects on the black male workforce, which many at the time believed was intentional.

Senator Theodore Bilbo, another Democratic leader in the 1930s and 1940s who was known as a prominent white supremacist, actually stated in an interview for *Meet The Press*, that "No man can leave the Klan. He takes an oath not to do that. Once a Ku Klux, always a Ku Klux." Bilbo's name is synonymous with the filibuster, as he led the Democrats filibuster of the 1938 anti-lynching bill. In opposing the anti-lynching legislation along with Senator Hugo Black, he stated:

> "If you succeed in the passage of this bill, you
> will open the floodgates of hell in the South.
> Raping, mobbing, lynching, race riots, and crime
> will be increased a thousand-fold; and upon your
> garments and the garments of those who are

---

99    Theo Lippman, Jr., "One Senator Who in 1967 Voted Against…" *The Baltimore Sun*, October 19, 1991, https://www.baltimoresun.com/news/bs-xpm-1991-10-19-1991292020-story.html.

> responsible for the passage of the measure will be
> the blood of the raped and outraged daughters of
> Dixie, as well as the blood of the perpetrators of
> these crimes that the red-blooded Anglo-Saxon
> White Southern men will not tolerate."

Bilbo was unabashed in his insistence that blacks should not be allowed to vote anywhere in the United States, despite their constitutional right to do so.

Another Democrat and prominent early member of the KKK, Edward Douglas White, served as the ninth Chief Justice of the Supreme Court and sided with the Supreme Court majority in *Plessy v. Ferguson*, which upheld the legality of state-sponsored segregation.

The Democrat Party leadership was in fact replete with members of the KKK, ranging from senators to governors, to mayors, judges, and police chiefs. In fact, it was an unwritten rule that in order to be elected to a major leadership position in the Democratic Party, one had to have the blessing of the Ku Klux Klan.

When faced with a military force, is it any surprise that in the 19th century and the early 20th century, black Americans embraced gun ownership? Today the KKK is not even a shadow of the force it once was. Blacks face physical dangers in their communities of a different stripe—one just as predatory but not philosophically motivated. Shouldn't the successful strategy of gun ownership in the past be employed today?

## BLACKS, LAW ENFORCEMENT, AND PRESIDENT TRUMP

When talking about blacks and the Second Amendment, we must include within the discussion recent dynamics in the relationship between blacks and law enforcement.

By tolerating elevated levels of crime in their communities, Blacks in America seem to betray a deep ambivalence towards law enforcement. This comes across in the culture we see broadcast by the media. The "no snitching" movement that arose in the "hip hop" culture in the early to mid-2000s was perhaps the height of absurdity in terms of the extent to which black culture was willing to side with the criminal element and oppose law enforcement.

When Fox News Commentator Bill O'Reilly interviewed popular, multiplatinum-album-selling rapper Cam'ron in 2003 about whether he would report to police if a known serial killer moved in next door to him, the rapper replied, "I wouldn't snitch. I might move though." According to Cam'ron, "snitches get stiches."

The real danger of taking such a stance towards law enforcement is that if adopted, it aligns blacks psychologically with criminal interests and subjugates the overwhelming majority of black citizens who are law-abiding to the nonsensical whims of the criminal "code."

A recent case illustrative of this entrenched criminal psychology in black communities occurred in Miami in 2016, when nineteen-year old teen Trevon Johnson was shot and killed by fifty-four-year-old, black homeowner, Gwendolyn Jenrette, who encountered Johnson one evening as he was burglarizing her home. In the aftermath of Johnson's death, the media and Johnson's family voiced outrage over the fact that Jenrette had shot Johnson in the chest, ostensibly as he was fleeing her home. Johnson's cousin Naukita Harris even went as far as to argue that Johnson should not have been killed because he was acting in accordance with "hood" values. "You have to look at it from every child's point of view that was raised in the hood," said Harris, in a televised interview. "You have to understand…how he gonna get his money to have clothes to go to school? You have to look at it from his point-of-view."[100] This is a shocking admission— that some black adults believe children from poor black communities

---

100    Michael E. Miller, "A Miami Woman Killed a Teen Burglar As he Fled Her Home. Should She Be Charged?" Morning Mix, *The Washington Post*, March, 15, 2016, https://www.washingtonpost.com/news/morning-mix/wp/2016/03/15/a-miami-woman-killed-a-teen-burglar-as-he-fled-her-home-should-she-be-charged/.

are justified in committing crimes—even against their own neighbors—in order to fulfill personal needs.

And yet despite sympathizing with the "needs" of criminals, the media and Johnson's family ignored Ms. Jenrette's obvious and just concerns. She lived in Liberty City, a largely black, poor community in Miami that has been plagued for decades by drugs and violence. Her home had been burglarized several times over the years, and she had taken measures to protect herself, including installing alarms and video surveillance. Jenrette also became a licensed gun owner, precisely because she feared the situation that unfolded. What if she had been unarmed and encountered Mr. Johnson invading her home? Wouldn't her life have been placed in grave danger?

Florida law says yes. Under Florida law, anyone who "unlawfully and by force enters or attempts to enter a person's dwelling, residence, or occupied vehicle is presumed to be doing so with the intent to commit an unlawful act involving force or violence," and that presumption can justify the use of deadly force to protect oneself. While the law was used as intended in this case—that is in order to protect a vulnerable black woman against home invasion and possibly grave physical violence—the reigning psychology expressed by other members of the community and the national media seemed to place the blame on the homeowner who defended herself, rather than the criminal that targeted her.

One of the most important things the black community can do to advance is to reverse this psychology entirely. That is, we should align ourselves with the law, not the lawbreakers, and hopefully begin to see communities solve their crime problems and start to thrive once again.

This perverse psychological and cultural orientation toward crime also puts the hundreds of thousands of blacks serving in the military and in law enforcement in a precarious situation. On the one hand, blacks have pushed for better policing and for adequate representation among law enforcement. But on the other hand, black officers are confronted with an anti-police culture in the very communities they are attempting to serve and protect. Contrast the anti-police attitude among many African Americans with the reality that blacks make up almost 13 percent of all law enforcement in the U.S., and in particular that black men constitute around 11 percent of all police officers, far outpacing their percentage of the overall population— which is about 6.2 percent.[101]

Which situation would be better—the black community overwhelmingly cast as anti-police or a situation in which blacks (especially black men) are welcomed into the police department and ultimately recruited into leadership positions where they can make a significant positive impact on their communities? It seems almost impossible for both to exist simultaneously.[102]

Similarly, symbolic acts of defiance such as Colin Kaepernick's "protest" against police brutality (which has been cynically exploited by the liberal media and corporate brands) are counter-productive to the interests of most African Americans. As stated before, African Americans really do need better and more policing in their communities, perhaps more than any other group. Kaepernick's celebrity gimmick—wearing socks depicting pigs dressed in police uniforms— also hurts black law enforcement officers and undermines that goal. On the one hand, they too feel the sting and the insult affecting how they are perceived by the community as military and law enforcement officials. Four-time NBA champion and future hall-of-famer Shaquille O'Neal voiced it best when he said, in an appearance on *Fox and Friends*, "My father was a military man, and he protected this country. My uncles are in law enforcement; they go out and work hard every day. There are just, you know—other ways to get your point across." O'Neal also took issue with the 49ers quarterback's seemingly "recent" political conversion.

---

101    DataUSA, https://datausa.io/profile/soc/333050/#demographics.
102    Mike Maciag, "Where Police Don't Mirror Communities and Why It Matters," Governing, August 28, 2015, https://www.governing.com/topics/public-justice-safety/gov-police-department-diversity.html.

When President Trump announced in 2017 that he would offer to send federal resources to Chicago to help stem the rate of violent crime, the Democratic leadership in the city rebuked him. They argued that Chicago was not in fact the "murder capitol," as it had been portrayed in the media. Their objection is at best half-true. While Chicago does rank in the middle of the pack among all cities in terms of its homicide rate, it ranks first among the nation's top five cities for gun-related homicides.[103] To put this in context, Chicago has roughly twice the murder rate of Houston, which is second on the list, and nine times the murder rate of New York, which sits at the bottom of the list with roughly 1.8 gun homicides per 100,000 residents.

Nothing exemplifies the Chicago political leadership's ambivalence more than police superintendent Eddie Johnson's boycott of President Trump's October 2019 speech before the largest annual gathering of law enforcement leaders in the world, the International Association of Chiefs of Police Conference hosted in Chicago. Citing Trump's "racial insults and hatred" towards illegal immigrants, Johnson refused to attend the speech. In obstinately insisting on maintaining their status as a sanctuary city, Chicago leaders have signaled that they value the political advantage they can get from Latino voters more than the public safety of African Americans in the city.

In response to Johnson's boycott, Chicago's Fraternal Order of Police issued a vote of no-confidence in Johnson. From the rank-and-file officer's perspective, Trump's willingness to assist Chicago's fight against violent crime by sending in federal resources—including five federal violent crime prosecutors, an eight-member FBI unit, and twenty ATF investigative agents—is welcome and desperately needed help. Imagine, the police rank and file of one of the largest

103    Grace Hauck, "Donald Trump is Visiting Chicago, a City He's Called a War Zone. But What's Really True About Guns There," *USA Today*, October 28, 2019, https://www.usatoday.com/story/news/nation/2019/10/28/trump-chicago-presidential-visit-highlights-gun-crime-violence/4072445002/.

American cities—a city plagued by violence and crime—failing to endorse their own leadership. Morale suffers. Crime-fighting suffers. And the city of Chicago continues to occupy the national spotlight in a negative way.

Except for Chicago, which is an unmitigated failure in terms of crime, and where the political leadership is diametrically opposed to doing anything suggested by the Trump administration to stop crime, other cities have been eager to work with the president.

In September 2018, Attorney General Jeff Sessions announced that the DOJ and ATF would award $5 million in grants to encourage local jurisdictions to use intelligence, technology, and community engagement to identify unlawfully used firearms and to prosecute those who commit violent crimes.[104] The grant recipients included Indianapolis, Indiana, $798,866; Memphis, Tennessee, $714,055; Tulsa, Oklahoma, $800,000; Baton Rouge, Louisiana, $634,971; Detroit, Michigan, $800,000; the Albuquerque, New Mexico, Police Department, $452,108; and the City/County of San Francisco, California, $800,000. The jurisdictions will use these awards to hire personnel to utilize the National Integrated Ballistic Information Network (NIBIN) and to purchase technology required to operate a Crime Gun Intelligence Center and ammunition for ballistic tests of recovered weapons.

The former attorney general also announced awards for Bureau of Justice Assistance's Technology Innovation for Public Safety (TIPS). This program supports the department's priorities of reducing violent crime and supporting law enforcement officers, including prosecutors. While many jurisdictions are making significant progress implementing justice information sharing solutions

---

104     "Department of Justice Will Award More Than $10 Million to Support Crime Reduction Efforts," ATF (Bureau of Alcohol, Tobacco, Firearms and Explosives), Department of Justice: Office of Public Affairs, September 24, 2018, https://www.atf.gov/news/pr/department-justice-will-award-more-10-million-support-crime-reduction-efforts.

to address critical gaps in crime prevention and response activities across organizations and jurisdictions, there remain challenges for the criminal justice system to respond to threats to public safety. This is especially true for efforts addressing significant increases in crime. Grant recipients include Memphis, Tennessee, $417,224; Toledo, Ohio, $492,553; Flint, Michigan, $499,694; and Houston, Texas, $500,000. Other locations include Arizona Criminal Justice Commission, $317,834; and City of Boynton Beach, Florida, $465,860.

More recently, in December 2019, the U.S. Department of Justice has announced "Operation Relentless Pursuit," an initiative to help reduce violent crime in some of the country's most violence-plagued cities. In seven cities—Albuquerque, Baltimore, Cleveland, Detroit, Kansas City (Missouri), Memphis, and Milwaukee—federal agencies will increase manpower and expand partnerships with local law enforcement. Federal grants totaling $71 million will be available to these localities to hire new officers, in addition to paying more to existing staff in terms of overtime and benefits.

These cities were selected because statistics show them to be above the national average in terms of violent crime. Attorney General William Barr says the initiative "seeks to ensure that no American city is excluded from the peace and security felt by the majority of Americans." Once again, the Trump administration recognizes the importance of safety for families and businesses.

For the eight years of the Obama administration, the appallingly high level of crime in these cities was ignored. The traffickers and brutish thugs are now on notice that their days are numbered. Even though these cities have been run by progressives, the families trapped in these jurisdictions have been left to fend for themselves. Unlike Obama, President Trump recognizes the need to protect all neigh-borhoods—even those in the most liberal regions of our country.

It almost goes without saying that adding resources to get illegal guns off the streets and reduce violent crime provides a major benefit to African Americans, who make up a large percentage of the cities being awarded grants under the DOJ programs. Yet the fact that a "law and order" agenda is not perceived to be pro-black should be a sign that blacks need to get on the right side of the law.

If we delve into the crime statistics even deeper, it becomes readily apparent how race and crime become conflated for political purposes. Just as a few bad used car salesmen ruin the impression that people have of used car salesmen as a whole, a few bad apples in the black community ruin the perception of blacks as a group. Here's the takeaway: a minority of black youth have helped to foster a bad impression about blacks in general.

When a police officer observes the race and age of a suspect, this is not a sign of unfair profiling or the conscious targeting of specific people based on their race. No more so than asking a victim to give the racial identity of their perpetrator is a needless form of racial marginalizing. It is instead useful for crime fighting. The actual characteristics matter when looking for context in a situation. Even though all criminals don't fit in a neat little box in terms of their demographic characteristics, it may come as surprise how much correlation between race, age, and socioeconomic status, and violent crime there actually is.

In the case of Black America, a staggering amount of bad behavior by a few young black youths has maligned the reputation of the entire black community—especially black males. This phenomenon, more than any other, drives law enforcement relationships with the black community.

Heather McDonald at the Manhattan Institute conducted research showing that most homicides occur within the same race, but when homicides occur across races, blacks are four times more likely to kill whites than the reverse. The same applies for other violent crimes like armed robbery, carjacking, and rape. Of the known assailants among the more than 7,800 homicides committed against blacks in 2016, only 234 were white. Black males, despite making up only 6 percent of the U.S. population, are responsible for nearly 42 percent of all homicides committed against police officers.

[105] Despite making up only 6 percent of the population, black males constitute over 34 percent of the entire U.S. federal prison population. This number would only be anomalous in and of itself if the victims of rape, home invasions, carjacking, and robbery identified whites, blacks, and browns as perpetrators in numbers proportionate to their population. They do not. And unless these victims (overwhelmingly black) are falsely identifying other blacks, we can only conclude that elevated levels of criminality exist with one particular cohort—black men between the ages of fourteen to thirty-four.

Consider this: prosecutors, judges, policemen, defense attorneys, jurors, prison guards, and crime reporters see a phenomenon practically every day that reveals that a disproportionate number of bad actors are black men between the ages of fourteen and thirty-four. Because such a disproportionate amount of crime is committed by this group of black males, they are disproportionately identified as potential suspects. Blacks as a group need to work to change this perception. We need more mothers and fathers involved in the lives of black youth. We need more institutions like the church and neighborhood organizations like the Boy Scouts to provide activities and modeling in communities of color.

## Return to the Rosa Parks Model of Excellence

Rosa Parks was not the first black person in segregated Montgomery, Alabama, to refuse to give up her seat on a city bus. But she *was* the first black person whose rights had been violated that the nascent civil rights movement was willing to publicly support. Some nine months before Rosa Parks refused to give up her seat, Claudette Colvin, who was discussed earlier in this book, had also been arrested in Montgomery for refusing to give up her seat to a white passenger.

---

105    Heather Mac Donald, "All That Kneeling Ignores the Real Cause of Soaring Black Homicides," Manhattan Institute (MI), September 27, 2017, https://www.manhattan-institute.org/html/all-kneeling-ignores-real-cause-soaring-black-homicides-10655.html.

Miss Colvin was arrested and charged with misconduct, resisting arrest, and violating city and state segregation laws. While the civil rights community initially thought she might be just the person to represent its complaint against racial segregation, reports began to emerge that she was pregnant by a married man, and that during her arrest she had allegedly uttered a stream of obscenities. Learning this, leaders in the civil rights community decided that hers was not the case to rally around.

Subsequently, when Mrs. Parks was arrested, the response was immediate and unequivocal. Fifty leaders of the civil rights community in Montgomery led by a then relatively unknown minister, Dr. Martin Luther King, declared that unlike Claudette Colvin, unwed and pregnant, "Mrs. Parks was regarded as one of the finest citizens of Montgomery—not one of the finest Negro citizens—but one of the finest citizens of Montgomery." They initiated a boycott which lasted for 382 days, forcing the city (because of economic reasons) to suspend the local ordinance segregating African Americans and whites on public buses. The almost miraculous success in Montgomery transformed Dr. King into a nationally known figure and triggered other bus boycotts, ultimately igniting a nationwide assault on the injustice of segregation.

Sadly, this commonsense notion has completely vanished from any discussions of the civil rights movement and Black America. Worse than perhaps the troubling trend towards an ever-expanding definition of civil rights grievance and a glaring failure to acknowledge significant progress and achievements has been *the civil rights community's almost wholesale rejection of the notion of using the finest individuals or causes as occasions to promote their goals.*

Instead, the American people have in recent times been presented with far more morally ambiguous causes and people to support (i.e., Rodney King, crack cocaine prosecutions, Louis Farrakhan, OJ Simpson, odious conspiracies involving an effort to intentionally flood New Orleans, and the like), causes and individuals which not only fail to unify America around the principle of equality, but so taint the concept they almost give even the most fair-minded just cause to reconsider the merits of the principle itself.

Redefining civil rights to include a license for criminality, unjustified racial animus, and even misogynistic "gangsta" lyrics has taken the noble cause of civil rights equality down an unfortunate path that must be reversed.

It is with only a hint of irony that history notes that Rosa Parks, who eventually fled Alabama for her safety and relocated to Michigan, was attacked in her home at age eighty-one by a black youth. This thug would later admit to recognizing her at the time, asking, "Aren't you Rosa Parks?" She handed him three dollars when he demanded money, and an additional fifty dollars when he demanded more. Before fleeing, he would strike her in the face.

We would be well-served to remember Rosa Parks' legacy. Decent and morally upright, she played a key role in a long, primarily nonviolent struggle to bring full civil rights and equality under the law to blacks in America. That battle has largely been won. There is still more work to do. But as we wage the peace, it's vital that it be done in a morally clear and unambiguous manner.

# CONCLUSION

President Trump's defense of the Second Amendment has already provided benefits to the African-American community. Under his presidency, black gun ownership has skyrocketed relative to the rest of the country. Moreover, the president has implemented several measures to curb violent crime and remove illegal guns from the hands of criminals. Trump's rhetorical stance against the NFL protests is good for blacks in that it protects the interests of black law enforcement professionals and military service members. Respecting them, in turn, reverses the trend of subconsciously siding with criminal culture, as evidenced by rap lyrics and the anti-law enforcement group Black Lives Matter. Black Americans also should deny oxygen to the criminal element in its midst. As President Trump makes clear, law enforcement should be welcome in America—especially in communities of color. Similarly, the ownership and use of firearms by African Americans to protect themselves against racial violence is well-documented, and a core feature in the liberation struggle of African Americans. That strategy should be relied upon today. By failing to put additional obstacles in the way of legal gun ownership, President Trump is helping to advance the cause of civil rights for African Americans. Getting inner city communities to be safe places to raise and grow families is a huge step towards bringing greater prosperity to the black community and for America overall.

# Chapter 5

❦

# AT ATTENTION—TRUMP'S STRONG MILITARY HELPS BLACK AMERICA

President Trump's respect and support for the military advances Black America's agenda in important ways. President Trump has helped United States service men and women by successfully pushing to raise stagnated military pay that had been neglected for years under President Obama.

Under President Trump's leadership, pay for members of the military has increased by more than 2 percent during each year he has been in office, including a 3.1 percent increase for 2020, making it the largest overall pay increase the military has received in over twenty years.[106] This more than 10 percent overall pay increase means thousands of men and women will have more of the financial support they need to provide for themselves and their families. Before these increases went into effect, over twenty-three thousand enlistees were receiving food stamps and other forms of public assistance, and

---

106    Slobodan Lekic, "Military, federal civilians to see largest pay raise in years," *Stars and Stripes*, December 31, 2019, https://www.stripes.com/news/us/military-federal-civilians-to-see-largest-pay-raise-in-years-1.613015.

one-in-four children at Department of Defense schools qualified for free meals.[107]

Improving the military helps African Americans in several respects. The first and most obvious is that a strong military defense protects American democracy at home and protects Americans' allies and interests abroad. America's global military strength has undoubtedly been a singularly distinguishing factor in creating and preserving the economic prosperity America continues to enjoy. The U.S. Navy, for example, provides critical protection for oil shipments coming out of the Middle East and is a key asset in America's energy industry. Americans have not been invaded by a foreign power in over two hundred years; it has enjoyed the longest period of peace among any of the world's leading nations. The major factor responsible for the peace we enjoy at home is the incredible deterrent effect of a strong U.S. military.

There are additionally several policy changes that the Trump administration has already made which help to strengthen the military. President Trump announced, after consulting with his generals, that the U.S. government will not accept or allow transgender individuals to serve in any capacity in the U.S. military. While dismissed by progressives as simply an attack on the LGBTQ community, the decision is particularly important. The transgender policy adopted during the Obama administration was expensive, disruptive, and eroded military readiness and unit cohesion.[108]

The expense of medical services related to gender reassignment deserves some attention here because the U.S. government is having to make hard choices regarding where it will allocate resources in an age of trillion-dollar budget deficits. Funding a strong military is

---

107   Dorian Merina, "When Active-Duty Service Members Struggle To Feed Their Families," The Salt, April 19, 2017, https://www.npr.org/sections/thesalt/2017/04/19/524563155/when-active-duty-service-members-struggle-to-feed-their-families.

108   Brooke Singman, "White House defends reversal of 'Obama policy' on transgender military service," Fox News, July 26, 2017, https://www.foxnews.com/politics/white-house-defends-reversal-of-obama-policy-on-transgender-military-service.

one of those choices, but it is increasingly important that resources allocated to the military go directly to the soldiers and veterans that must fight to preserve our cherished freedoms. Making the military the testing-ground for novel social experiments such as transgender psychological counseling and related medical services detracts from the focus the military needs, which is to be the best fighting force it can be. The social cohesion of troops under the myriad "gender" classifications potentially required by transgender troop assignments are disruptive, to say the least. Rather than focus on social engineering, the Trump administration is ensuring that skill development is put in place that enhances military readiness as well as gives veterans a competitive edge when they re-enter civilian life.

# ENDING ENDLESS WARS HELPS RESTORE THE MILITARY AND REFOCUSES DEFENSE PRIORITIES TO THE BORDER

A significant theme endorsed by candidate Trump was ending America's endless wars. When he observed that over the past two decades since the terrorist attacks of 9/11, America had spent almost $10 trillion on war—nearly half the current U.S. national debt—he became alarmed. What exactly had we gotten in return for sacrificing so many American troop's lives and committing so much treasure to wars in far-flung parts of the world?

If America's role as a global policeman was so important to the world order, why weren't we being compensated for our commitments in service of world peace and security? He came to the very same conclusion that many war-weary American families had already reached. We should be "getting out of these ridiculous endless wars, where our great Military functions as a policing operation to the benefit of people who don't even like the USA," he tweeted on October 7, 2019, shortly after he announced American troops would be withdrawing from Syria.

Trump's critics, both on the left and the right, could finally agree on something. They hated Trump's hesitance to commit American military resources to seemingly endless conflicts with no real strategic aim. A child of the Vietnam War, Trump was weary of wars we could not win and yet could not seem to fully extricate ourselves from.

Trump was all for supporting a strong and robust military that would secure our borders and defend our global interests where necessary. But in looking at the far-flung commitments of our military, he recognized that whether by unintentional "mission creep" or policy design, our American fighting force was taking on projects quite unrelated to her core interests. He rejected the notion that it was America's role to take on nation-building tasks that could be far better addressed by local and regional actors who were in a strategic and financial position to do so. This was not a function the U.S. military was designed to perform.

For decades, the U.S. military has operated as both the world's police force and a de facto international Health and Human Services agency. Beyond the nearly twenty years in central Asia fighting in Afghanistan, Syria, and Iraq, we've expended blood and treasure in Somalia, Haiti, Bosnia, Kosovo, and even East Timor. The American taxpayer has literally shoveled hundreds of billions of dollars into these areas and other places, including its financial support of NATO and the United Nations. Wherever our leadership has directed our men and women, they have dutifully saluted and engaged.

These deployments aren't just expensive, they also put hardships on the families of those in the military. Our fighting forces have been strained by multiple deployments, and military morale has noticeably suffered. Suicides among returning veterans jumped 50 percent between 2007 and 2017. Nearly 60,000 veterans lost their lives to suicide in the intervening decade—an alarming epidemic, and a signal that our forces were strained to the breaking point.[109] The VA medical system was in a woeful state of mismanagement and under-performance. It was tragically failing our returning troops and contributing to the already dire stress produced by over-deployment. Something had to give before the whole system collapsed.

While Trump was successful in achieving growth to the military budget in the 2018 and 2019 appropriations, he was faced with the hard reality that America's military commitments were already over-stretching her ability to sustain them. And to compound matters, our focus on military adventures abroad had drawn needed attention away from the budding crisis at our borders. Drug interdiction and immigration enforcement slowed over the preceding decades, while harmful drugs—and the violence that attends their trade—poured over the border and flowed in tandem to major distribution points across the country. The most essential responsibility of any military is to defend its nation's borders, and ours appeared to be particularly vulnerable to a well-organized, festering narco-state just across the Rio Grande.

A shift away from making our nation's military the world's peace-maker would also free us up to commit a greater share of limited military resources to rebuilding and retooling our military hardware and systems capabilities. As it stands, all four critical branches of the military—the Air Force, Marines, Army, and Navy—each need to replenish and update equipment to remain on the cutting techno-logical edge of war-fighting capability. This is especially true amid the rise of geo-political rivalries such as China, which has begun to rapidly militarize, and existential nuclear threats from North Korea, and sooner than later, Iran.

As a leader and lifelong CEO of a major construction busi-ness, Trump new well that the short-term choice to delay plant and

---

109    Leo Shane III, "New Veteran Suicide Numbers Raise Concerns Among Experts Hoping For Positive News," *Military Times*, October 9, 2019, https://www. militarytimes.com/news/pentagon-congress/2019/10/09/new-veteran-suicide-numbers-raise-concerns-among-experts-hoping-for-positive-news/.

machinery maintenance can in many instances balloon into a cost several times what it would take to fix problems in the short term. As widely popular personal management guru Stephen Covey once put it, you have to pay attention to the balance between maintaining production and replenishing productive capacity. Corporate leaders were famous at the time of the publication of Covey's seminal work, *The Seven Habits of Highly Successful People,* for arriving at a company and ramping up production, thereby achieving amazing short-term results—and paying themselves handsome bonuses in the process. Then they would exit the company, "coincidentally," just before the entire plant collapsed due to lack of maintenance, leaving workers and shareholders on the hook for repairs that cost several times what the short-term profits yielded. This was never Trump's style. And in any case, he viewed America as not just another corporate investment, but a unique asset on the global stage. His view was that we cannot afford to run ourselves into the ground.

What was true of military equipment was even more true of the human component—our soldiers. When were we going to pay attention to their needs and support their recovery from the seemingly endless cycles of foreign deployments? How were military families expected to survive in the midst of constant commitments abroad with little time to reconnect to their loved ones and communities? We were creating a permanent warrior class who had an immensely difficult time readjusting to civilian life.

We need a Marshall Plan for America, and that would entail limiting our foreign engagements, requiring more commitments from our strategic allies, and focusing America's defense forces on a few core priorities. America's enlistees also need to focus on rest, replenishment, and reconnecting with their families and communities. They should be supported by a military infrastructure that enables skills development in order to prepare them for successful re-entry into civilian life and a red-hot domestic economy that could use the extra workers.

# HOW TRUMP'S MILITARY POLICIES HELP AFRICAN AMERICANS

Improving the quality of the military and military life improves the lives of black Americans. Blacks, for example, enlist in the military at higher rates than other groups, and they make up a disproportionate part of the enlisted rolls.

In December 2017, President Donald Trump signed into law The Fiscal 2018 National Defense Authorization Act, or NDAA, which authorizes nearly $700 billion for the Defense Department. The authorization bill approved by Congress includes numerous policy-related provisions, including funding for higher pay raises for troops, more weapons, and provides for a higher number of troops.

The increase of 2.4 percent for troop pay in 2018 is significant because it is the first pay raise to soldiers that is not tied to an overall increase in federal worker pay. At the time it was enacted, it was the largest pay raise troops had received since 2010, almost nine years prior. President Trump further cemented his commitment to our military members by including another significant pay raise of 3.1 percent for all troops in the 2020 budget, which was approved by Congress and went into effect on January 1, 2020. This raise produces a significant bump to military paychecks. Junior enlisted troops can expect a yearly pay increase of roughly $815; for senior enlisted and junior officers, it equals about $1,500 more. And some senior officers with more than ten years of service will see more than $2,800 in extra pay.[110]

In addition to the extra pay, one of the most important new benefits that apply to African-American enlisted men and women is the authorization in the 2018 NDAA for a military skills database. The database records all training completed by military members and makes that skills training data available to employers and states

---

110    Leo Shane III, "Biggest Military Pay Raise in Years Takes Effect Jan. 1; Check Out the Complete Chart," *Military Times*, December 26, 2019, https://www.militarytimes.com/news/2019/12/26/biggest-military-pay-raise-in-years-takes-effect-jan-1-check-out-the-complete-chart/.

in order to help veterans obtain civilian certifications or licenses, or claim their military experience when applying for a civilian job. This is a critically important provision in terms of enabling veterans returning from war to enter the workforce and continue to keep pace with the rest of America economically and socially.

Many of the jobs in the military are task-specific, such as maintenance and repair of specific aircraft or programming specific military technology applications. There are service members, for example, who are employed in accounting and finance tasks, graphic design, and welding and electrical work that are part of the war waging functions. It has not always been easy to figure out how that translates into the private sector workforce. When service members leave the military, they often have difficulty in obtaining jobs in the private sector without having more formal college degrees or commercial skills certifications. The new training database helps narrow the gap between military training and private sector skills certification, thus enabling military members to obtain private sector opportunities that may have been foreclosed to them in the past.

One of the most impactful military decisions of President Trump term was the formation of the U.S. Space Force. After announcing his goal early in his presidency, by late December 2019, he had signed into the law the creation of the first new military service since 1947.[111]

Recognizing that outer space is a key source of strategic advantage for the U.S., and that potential foreign adversaries are determined to exploit this area for their own advantage, President Trump successfully pushed its creation. Focused on space based travel, the U.S. Space Force will give its servicemembers a responsibility to augment our space collaborations and capacities and will likely create a large cadre of former servicemembers trained and equipped to compete in

---

111    Ryan Browne, "With a signature, Trump brings Space Force into being," CNN, December 20, 2019, https://www.cnn.com/2019/12/20/politics/trump-creates-space-force/index.html.

the cutting edge field of the future—space travel. Americans of all stripes should race to sign up for this opportunity.

## Blacks Serve Disproportionately in the Military

African Americans have traditionally elected to serve in the U.S. military in high numbers. They have fought and died in all of America's wars, going all the way back to the Revolutionary War. African-American women make up 34 percent of all women serving in the military, and black men represent 17 percent of all active duty military men, far outpacing their respective portions of the American population.

To put this in perspective, one needs to look at the percentage of black participation in almost every other industry. In, for example, the math, sciences, and technology employment sectors, blacks are woefully underrepresented, claiming just under 8 percent of jobs total in that sector. Among all occupations, blacks are underrepresented, constituting around 11.9 percent of the U.S. workforce. The military, therefore, is one of the few employment sectors which Blacks have traditionally been able to access in larger numbers. Seen in this light, continued emphasis on military readiness and elevated compensation as demonstrated by the Trump administration is a critical benefit for African Americans.

You wouldn't know it though, based on the political alignment of black politicians within the Democratic Party. The Congressional Black Caucus routinely submits a proposed military budget allocation that is substantially lower than that proposed by Republicans or Democrats, despite the fact that a purported core constituency is over-represented in terms of military service. In the CBC's "alternative budget" proposal for fiscal year 2018, it proposed roughly $1 trillion in national defense budget cuts over the next ten years—the equivalent of a $100 billion cut annually.[112] By contrast, Trump's military budget for 2018 increased military expenditure by $54 billion in one year alone.

## History of Blacks in the U.S. Military

Blacks were first formally inducted into the U.S. military in large numbers during the Civil War. They were drafted through the Conscription Act of 1863. It is estimated that approximately 186,000 black combat troopers, and another 200,000 blacks in service units, participated in the Union Army. Blacks made up approximately 25 percent of the Union Navy.[113] This marks not only an important contribution by black soldiers in helping to secure freedom of African Americans from de jure slavery, but also an important milestone for measuring the benefit black Americans received from a strong military.

By many accounts, black Civil War veterans found themselves more assimilated to American life than non-veterans, and enjoyed more benefits, including greater job security and geographical mobility, than their non-veteran counterparts. The additional skills they gained from having worked within a large, mission-driven organization like the U.S. Army enabled blacks to enter the federal civil service in white-collar positions. It also inculcated a spirit of "Americanness" in these servicemen, as they had fought and died to secure a free nation.

Military service during the Civil War was generally beneficial for the civilian careers of ex-slaves because they gained new skills in the regimental schools, and a wider perspective of the world in Army service. The experience of serving during war time with a more

---

112    "Congressional Black Caucus Alternative Budget For FY 2018," Congressional Black Caucus, https://cbc.house.gov/uploadedfiles/cbc_fy18_long_doc_10.4.17_final.pdf.

113    Light, Patricia, Danette, "Marching Upward: The Role of the Military in Social Stratification and Mobility in American Society." Ph.D. diss., Virginia Polytechnic Institute and State University, 1998.

diverse group of peers also greatly increased the economic mobility of black Union Army soldiers after the war. Furthermore, social connections with former comrades led Union veterans to live in close proximity to one another and to provide mutual aid in starting businesses and in defending their rights and property.[114] The geographic mobility of Union Army veterans, measured by the probabilities of interstate and inter-regional migrations between 1860 and 1880, was significantly higher than that of non-veterans. Even more strikingly, African-American veterans who were unskilled before the war proved far more likely than non-veterans to attain white collar employment.

Since the very beginning of African Americans' experience with the military, positive assimilative and economic benefits have accrued to them as a result of their military service. Until 1948, though, the military remained largely a segregated force, and blacks, with a few notable exceptions, served in support roles, performing menial tasks such as porters, cooks, janitors, and other low-skilled jobs.

Although the military was segregated for a time, it also has a racial history that is somewhat unique among major American institutions. Racial segregation in the military was abolished in 1948 by President Truman, largely at the urging of African-American Labor leader A. Philip Randolph. To put this in perspective, military integration was carried out in military fashion—with all deliberate speed—several years before segregated schooling was outlawed, and decades before school integration was actually achieved. The military became, at the time, the nation's first large-scale social experiment in integration. To this day, the first experience many Americans have in terms of close interactions with members of other races occurs in the context of their military service. The military is also the only large U.S. industrial sector where one routinely sees blacks having superior roles and direct command over whites. The fact that military service provides opportunities based

---

114    Chulhee Lee, "Military Service and Economic Mobility: Evidence from the American Civil War," PMC (PubMed Central), July 1, 2013, https://www.ncbi.nlm.nih.gov/pmc/articles/PMC3530890/.

on merit and skill rather than social or racial stratification may describe why African Americans tend to gravitate towards military careers.

Black soldiers are, in fact, about one and a half times more likely than whites to complete their enlistments successfully.[115] And black re-enlistment rates are around one and a half times as high as re-enlistment rates for whites. The high rate of re-enlistment of blacks not only affects the representation of blacks in the military overall, but also results in a higher percentage of black enlisted soldiers promoted to the non-commissioned officer ranks, including sergeant, corporal, warrant officers, and Navy petty officers. In contrast to the proportion of African Americans in leadership and managerial roles in private sector organizations, the military offers far more opportunities for African Americans to develop leaderships skills and experience, and to attain actual leadership roles. For example, African Americans make up around 15 percent of the Army leadership ranks, while they constitute only 2 percent of senior leadership in the corporate sector.

## Military Service Works as an Economic Strategy for African Americans

The military can be a viable economic strategy for African Americans, especially for African-American youth without advanced job skills or notable educational attainment. Average basic military pay for an enlisted service member is currently around $35,000 per year. Average annual income for black high school graduates in the private sector is around $30,000. While that may not seem like a substantial difference, when one controls for military service subsidies for housing costs and other benefits, including combat duty pay and special bonuses for training and skills certifications, the difference becomes more significant. With combat pay, training, and

---

115    Light, Patricia, Danette, "Marching Upward: The Role of the Military in Social Stratification and Mobility in American Society." Ph.D. diss., Virginia Polytechnic Institute and State University, 1998.

transportation bonuses, enlisted members can receive more pay and more opportunities for personal and professional development than similarly situated individuals in the private sector. The relatively good pay for non-college graduates combined with the relative lack of income opportunities in the civilian workforce for black males may help to account for the higher re-enlistment rates observed among blacks.

In addition to offering competitive pay, the military offers attractive benefits to be used for furthering education. Benefits include a student loan repayment of up to $23,000 per year for full-time college tuition, as well as cash allowances for books and housing along the way. There are also provisions under the post-9/11 GI Bill program in which the individual pays into an "educational savings program," and the government matches this payment.

The military service offers young black men an honorable and rewarding escape from poverty, unemployment, and crime-ridden streets. After serving, those same black men are better prepared for employment, fatherhood, and higher-paying career opportunities than before they enlisted.

The military is perhaps America's most robust bastion of social and economic equality. Salaries of top military executives are much closer to those of the lowest earner than one sees in the private sector. Senior officers live on the same bases—in the same communities—as junior enlisted personnel, and their children go to school together. The military was the first major American institution to racially integrate, and provides better job opportunities than most other sectors of society.

In the limited number of studies that have been conducted on post-service economic attainment among African Americans, military service resulted in higher levels of income, earnings, and education for all veterans serving since 1950. Compared to their civilian counterparts, veterans had significantly higher incomes, earnings, and educational levels.

# TRUMP'S POLICIES ALREADY IN PLACE MAKE THE MILITARY A MORE ATTRACTIVE OPTION FOR AFRICAN AMERICANS

By putting in place policies that make military careers more attractive, honorable, and rewarding, the Trump administration has made military service more appealing for blacks to serve and improve their skills, careers, and families. President Trump recognizes the value of military service and has already made efforts to reward it by signing the American Law Enforcement Heroes Act, which permits the use of Department of Justice grant funds for hiring and training military veterans for law enforcement positions.

The act gives priority for federal grants to state and local law enforcement agencies that use the funds to hire veterans. The Fraternal Order of Police, the Major County Sheriffs Association, and the Veterans of Foreign Wars all backed the idea of using the grants as incentive. Black males are in a unique position to benefit from this legislation. As disproportionate members of the military fighting force, black men with military backgrounds are equipped with the skills needed to qualify for roles in civilian law enforcement. While African Americans currently make up about 13 percent of the nation's law enforcement work force, black males alone constitute more than 11 percent of the nation's police officers.[116] That is roughly twice the representation of black males in the general population. Black males therefore stand to benefit disproportionately from efforts to recruit law enforcement from the military ranks.

The administration's emphasis on creating opportunities for law enforcement and military careers helps to address the perception that law enforcement is specifically targeting black males for unfair treatment. The reality of black males disproportionately serving in law enforcement roles belies the idea that the police are trying to create barriers to blacks in general. And it also means that America should revisit the idea that blacks—men in particular—are hostile

---

116    DataUSA, https://datausa.io/profile/soc/333050/#demographics.

to law enforcement or the military. This narrative is often implied in the anti-law enforcement rhetoric spouted by many so-called black leaders, including Al Sharpton, lawyer and activist Benjamin Crump, and of course Colin Kaepernick.

## Trump, the Military, and the NFL

President Trump's consistent vocal support of the military helped push the NFL's new national anthem policy, which will honor the sacrifice that so many American veterans—black, white, and brown—have made in service to the country. This issue came to light after then-San Francisco 49ers quarterback Colin Kaepernick was seen kneeling on the sidelines during a preseason game, wearing his signature socks depicting officers as pigs. Fans reacted angrily to his actions, and Kaepernick was ultimately cut from the team; he has not been employed by the NFL since then. But unfortunately, he has become somewhat of a cause célèbre among the leftist elite, who view him as a useful pawn of sorts.

Kaepernick himself seems to be truly lost. Having grown up the adopted bi-racial son of German immigrant parents, he seems to have taken on the mantle of blackness with the naïve fervor of a sheltered white liberal. He loves the symbolism of rebellion, but he has not developed a practical philosophical framework that addresses the real needs of African Americans as a group. It was recently reported that he made a sizeable donation to a non-profit organization called *Assata's Daughters*, named in honor of Assata Shakur, a black "revolutionary" who was convicted of murdering a New Jersey state trooper in 1973. Shakur, who is also deceased rapper Tupac Shakur's aunt, has been hiding out from justice in Cuba, under the protection Fidel Castro and his brother since escaping prison in 1979.[117] If there were any confusion that Kaepernick, in fact, intended to disrespect

---

117   Arturo Garcia, "Did Colin Kaepernick Donate $25,000 to a Group Honoring Assata Shakur?" Snopes.com, September 12, 2018, https://www.snopes.com/fact-check/colin-kaepernick-assata-shakur/.

law enforcement, this brazen act of insensitivity certainly clears things up.

The common misconception about the NFL protests that gets bantered about in the media is that the opposition to the NFL player protests is chiefly a First Amendment issue. It is not. The Constitution's guarantee of freedom of expression gives every American the right to "squawk" about things they don't like about their government. President Regan once told a joke about an American and a Russian arguing about their two countries. "The American said, 'I can walk into the oval office, I can pound the president's desk and say, 'Mr. President, I don't like the way you're running our country!' And the Russian said, 'I can do that, too.' The American said, 'You can?' He says, 'Yes, I can go into the Kremlin to the General Secretary's Office, pound his desk and say, 'Mr. General Secretary, I don't like the way President Reagan is running his country!'"

All jesting aside, the point is that our First Amendment freedoms absolutely guarantee us the right to express our grievances with the government, including the police, without fear of government interference or retribution. But it does not give anyone the right to say whatever he or she wants to say without consequence in a private setting. The NFL owners rightly realized that players protesting the American flag and failing to honor the country during the national anthem did not sit well with the majority of the NFL's customers— the fans in attendance at games or watching on television. It was also bad for business in that the NFL is sponsored by some of the biggest corporate brands in America—and the last thing they wanted to do was invite controversy that would damage their reputations. As for the idea that it is okay to offend the American people, the fans also have the right to choose whether they are going to watch something that they do not like. In the wake of the anthem antics, NFL viewership declined by roughly 10 percent between the 2016 and 2017 seasons. In overwhelming numbers, the American people said with their eyeballs and their dollars, "We don't like what you are doing, and we won't participate."

There has been no government effort to quash the players' protest or interfere with the players' rights to speak. President Trump does not like the protests and believes, along with millions of other Americans, that they are disrespectful to the military and first responders who put their lives on the line to defend Americans' freedoms and safety, and has voiced his opinion about it. Like any American—including the anthem protesters—the president enjoys his own First Amendment right to express his opinion, and to use his bully pulpit to endorse ideas he believes in. But what the president cannot do, and in fact has not done, is issue an edict or order preventing or penalizing NFL players for exercising their First Amendment rights. He does not have hiring and firing authority over the NFL. When the left confuses acts of government with activities of individuals, it is mischaracterizing the First Amendment.

Private organizations like the NFL are generally free to regulate their employees' conduct while on the job. In the NFL this has taken the form of rules banning excessive celebrations and other points of decorum that NFL players must abide by as a condition of their employment. Liberals went virtually apoplectic when rookie quarterback Tim Tebow would bow and pray after every touchdown. It was in their eyes making the rest of the fans endure the spectacle. He's no longer a football player. While he was active, there were whole treatises written about why Tebow shouldn't land another job in the NFL, and some of them quite explicitly stated things like, "If God truly raised up Tim Tebow to be an NFL quarterback (which is debatable), then it was not so that Tim could announce his Christian faith by praying in the End Zone and praising Jesus at press conferences."[118]

Notably Tebow, while honoring his creator, never interrupted any flag ceremony or disrespected anyone at all, and yet in the eyes of many Americans he was blackballed from the NFL—solely because

---

118    Jeremy Myers, "Why The Eagles Cut Tim Tebow," Redeeming God, https://redeeminggod.com/tim-tebow-stop-praying/.

of his moral and religious stance. When this occurred, there was no concern expressed by liberals that somehow Tebow's rights were extinguished, or that it was unfair that he no longer plays football. The double standard applied to these two NFL cases by the left is truly remarkable.

As to the substance of Kaepernick's so-called protest, it is weak at best. Kaepernick seems to conflate the flag and the anthem with police injustice towards black Americans. For most of the NFL's fans, the flag and the national anthem serve as tributes to the brave sacrifices military service members have made in defending, advancing, and preserving America's prosperity and liberty. These two interpretations of the same symbols could not stand in further contrast.

The actual complaint Kaepernick seems to really be venting about is systemic racism in America, the prevalence of which makes it somehow inappropriate to stand for the flag in his opinion. While some players conflate the flag with racism, many black veterans do not. Most of them closely identify with the flag as a symbol of the ideals they fight and are willing to die for. They not only refuse to endorse the symbolic protest of NFL players, but they are offended by what they see as open hostility to American law enforcement and defense forces.

**Black Veterans to NFL Anthem Protestors: Get Off Your Knees!**
Burgess Owens, former star NFL safety and Super Bowl Champion, believes the anthem protests are a symptom of a dangerous ideology that has taken root in the Black community—namely, the ideology of liberalism. He says in response, "My concern with this whole process is what the flag stands for. I remember standing on the sidelines during the national anthem getting teary-eyed at times. I grew up at a time when 70% of Black men were role models and mentors for the youth. They were doing the things they needed to do for their families and their communities. Now, because of liberalism 70% of Black men do not stay around. Therefore, the youth don't have the parents and fathers to tell them what they should do and

what's appropriate. We are dealing with an ideology that first of all bans God, has destroyed the Black family in the 1970s—we once led the country in family cohesion; destroyed our history; and now they want to take away pride in our country."

"At the end of the day," says Owens, "we love our country and we are going to stand against those who take away the hope of our kids. Liberals and corporate elitists—like the NFL—are using my race and using this misery to keep their power. We need to make sure that we are standing against corporate elitists and as Black conservatives go into the Black community and show them how the Democratic Party has harmed them."

Kathy Barnette, a ten-year Army veteran and mother to two young children, has a similar message for NFL players: "Get off your knees already." She says that, "One of the lessons I've learned about America is more of a personal lesson. I am not a victim. My two beautiful Black babies are not victims. Black Americans are not victims." She goes on to say, "we are victors—not so much because of anything we have done, but because of those who came before us and paid the price for us to be here. They were slaves in chains, treated like farm animals to be 'owned' by others. And after Emancipation, those who endured the humiliation of drinking out of the 'dirty' water fountain or taking their child into the 'colored' restroom. We as Black people have a wonderful inheritance—and we have an obligation to live a life that's worthy."

Barnette said the players' protests, which were originally intended to highlight police brutality and social injustice, are not an effective way of getting their message across, and in many respects may have backfired. "There are some real issues in the Black community, some very real, systemic, devastating issues," Barnette said. "But the one that we are seeing almost every day, about police brutality, that probably isn't even in the top five." She said more pressing issues include family instability, lack of education, high unemployment rate and low home ownership. "For these particular NFL players, they have a significant platform. They can go into any community and immediately shine a spotlight on what the real issues are." She pointed out that FBI data reveals that out of approximately 7,800 African-American homicides in 2016, only 233 were killed by police. That's less than 3 percent of all black homicides that year.

Barnett further emphasizes putting the issue of police brutality in perspective. "Seventy-three percent of Black children grow up without a father; we have a poor education system, high unemployment rate and low home ownership among African Americans. All of these issues are much larger than police brutality in terms of how they impact the Black community.

"The narrative behind "Hands Up, Don't Shoot" perpetuates the storyline that around every street corner there's a police officer waiting to shoot a Black man. It is these narratives that have given life to NFL players kneeling during our national anthem. If there was truth behind these narratives, then I would readily support Black millionaire athletes using their national platform to shine a bright light on the systemic racism against the Black community. Racism is certainly not dead, but it's not the powerful monster backed by all the resources of government either. And [Black professional athletes] are not exactly downtrodden, going hungry, being shoved to the back of the bus, or used for target practice by Ku Klux Klansmen dressed up like cops.

"Instead of taking a knee," Barnett urges the players, "take a stand to stomp out poverty by investing in businesses, by creating an environment that promotes family stability, and by fanning the flames of hope, dignity, and direction into the lives of some of our most depressed citizens."

## CONCLUSION

Frederick Douglass was a fierce and unyielding critic of the "peculiar institution" of slavery in America. However, he believed that the principles of the Declaration of Independence and its unequivocal statement that all men are "created equal" would ultimately defeat slavery. Douglass condemned slavery as an impermissible betrayal of American ideals, but he found solace in embracing those very ideals. He encouraged black Americans to sign up and fight for the Union under the American flag during the Civil War, played a crucial role in recruitment efforts, and convinced many former slaves to join the fight for freedom.

Douglass was known to frequently play "The Star-Spangled Banner" on his violin for his grandchildren in the years after the war. He said, in an 1871 speech at Arlington National Cemetery, "If the star-spangled banner floats only over free American citizens in every quarter of the land, and our country has before it a long and glorious career of justice, liberty, and civilization, we are indebted to the unselfish devotion of the noble army."

President Trump also recognizes the noble sacrifices African-American soldiers made to secure their freedom. In his first dedication of a national monument as president, Trump established a 380-acre site in Kentucky to honor African Americans' role as soldiers during the Civil War. Republicans had pushed, for more than a year, to establish a national monument at Camp Nelson in Nicholasville, Ky., which served as one of the largest recruitment and training depots for United States Colored Troops during the Civil War.

Trump's role in bolstering the military—particularly pay for enlisted members, and vocational assistance for those leaving the armed forces—has been a great boon for African Americans. Serving in the military has traditionally been a patriotic duty that African Americans have gladly embraced, and a means of obtaining critical career skills and financial upliftment. Trump's policies honor their service (both present and past) and give them additional tools that they can use for further advancement.

Today, military service is a means for many blacks—especially men—to gather the skills and training needed to compete professionally as they mature and form families. Building on that experience in these truly egalitarian communities is likely to lead to significant opportunities—particularly with the U.S. Space Force.

# Chapter 6

# UNBORN BLACK LIVES MATTER

"Politicians argue for abortion largely because they do not want to spend the necessary money to feed, clothe, and educate more people. Here arguments for inconvenience and economic savings take precedence over arguments for human value and human life… Psychiatrists, social workers and doctors often argue for abortion on the basis that the child will grow up mentally and emotionally scarred. But who of us is complete? If incompleteness were the criteri(on) for taking life, we would all be dead. If you can justify abortion on the basis of emotional incompleteness, then your logic could also lead you to killing for other forms of incompleteness—blindness, crippleness, old age." (Then pro-life) Jesse Jackson, January 1977

The argument of convenience to which Reverend Jackson refers is that because black children are not being born in traditional, supportive family structures (over 72 percent of black children are born to single mothers in America) because they are being born disproportionately into conditions of poverty; it is far more convenient to abort them now than deal with social problems they will experience down the road. The cynicism betrayed by this argument belies the agency that African Americans have in this situation.

They have a choice to raise their children within traditional structures, to forego sexual intimacy until they have the wherewithal to really support a family, and to maintain long-lasting and enduring marriages that model the behavior that young people can emulate going forward. This is the true meaning of family planning—not as the left would have it—have "free" sex, then go and get an abortion.

# PRESIDENT TRUMP IS THE MOST PRO-LIFE PRESIDENT IN U.S. HISTORY

President Trump has already been called by some "the most pro-life president in U.S. history." The Trump administration's pro-life posture is great news for black Americans. With less than two years in office, President Trump had already defended the Little Sisters of the Poor, re-enacted the so-called Mexico City policy (which bans the United States from funding any foreign non-governmental organization providing abortion services), and had begun defunding Planned Parenthood—the largest abortion-on-demand provider in America, an organization that has strategically placed 79 percent of its surgical abortion facilities within walking distance of minority communities. He made history becoming the first sitting American president to attend the annual Right to Life March in Washington, DC.[119]

Also, and probably most significantly, President Trump has confirmed two conservative Supreme Court judges in Neil Gorsuch and Brett Kavanaugh, both of whom are likely to support restrictions on abortion in the United States. The Trump administration could easily be the catalyst for the most significant pro-life legal and policy shift since *Roe v. Wade*, the court case that made abortion the law of the land in 1973.

---

119     Lauren Egan, "Trump becomes first sitting president to attend March for Life rally," NBC News, January 24, 2020, https://www.nbcnews.com/politics/donald-trump/trump-becomes-first-sitting-president-attend-march-life-rally-n1122246.

Trump's appointments to the Supreme Court have prompted a flurry of pro-life laws passed in twelve states in 2019 alone. As of November 2019, states enacted more than fifty abortion restrictions, about half of which banned most abortions. This constitutes a remarkable surge in legal restriction of abortion that stands in stark contrast to the more gradual approach states had pursued under previous Supreme Courts and presidents. Previously, states had acted to restrict access to abortion on ancillary grounds such as medical safety, late-term, and state-funding mandates. The new restrictions on the state level confront abortion head-on. Georgia, Kentucky, Louisiana, Missouri, Mississippi, and Ohio passed "heartbeat bills" that effectively prohibit abortions after six to eight weeks of pregnancy, when a fetal heartbeat can usually be detected.

In contrast to the gradualist approach, the new, more aggressive abortion restrictions seem tailored to provoke litigation that will ultimately wind up before the Supreme Court, which is solidly poised, thanks to President Trump, to deliver a death-knell to the *Roe v. Wade* framework which invented, out of thin air, a constitutional right to kill unborn children.

Advocates on both sides have acknowledged that 2020 is different. Pro-lifers saw the appointment of Justice Brett M. Kavanaugh in 2018 as tipping the balance of the court in their favor, and state legislators were energized to pass more aggressive pro-life legislation. Elizabeth Nash, state policy director at the pro-abortion Guttmacher Institute, admitted as much, stating, in an interview for *The New York Times*, that, "The appointment of Kavanaugh focused legislators across the country…to pass abortion restrictions that they hope will be challenged and end up before the court, so the court can undermine or overturn abortion rights."[120]

---

120    K.K. Rebecca Lai, "Abortion Bans: 9 States Have Passed Bills to Limit the Procedure This Year," *The New York Times*, updated May 29, 2019, https://www.nytimes.com/interactive/2019/us/abortion-laws-states.html.

As a result of this renewed pro-life fervor ushered in by President Trump's election, the U.S. abortion rate dropped to 13.5 abortions per 1,000 women in 2019, the lowest rate recorded since abortion was legalized in 1973.

For the millions of Americans who view the legalization of abortion as a civil-and-human rights abomination, this is a truly exciting time. The Trump administration's broad mandate to curb abortion represents the culmination of decades of organizing and mobilizing against abortion by many, including the Republican Party and especially non-partisan, faith-based organizations and individuals. But for African Americans, the Trump administration's power to limit abortion may represent the single-most impactful civil rights development since the Voting Rights Act.

## Trump's Executive Order Restricting Federal Funds From Going to Planned Parenthood Is a Generational Win for the Pro-Life Movement

Early in the Trump administration, the White House signaled that it would make changes to Title X (the federally-funded contraceptive program and women's health service program) to bar these organizations from making abortion referrals unless there is a medical emergency. According to the Department of Health and Human Services, this proposed rule reflected the underlying law, which bars Title X funds from going to programs "where abortion is a method of family planning."

The rule ultimately was implemented, and in August of 2019, Planned Parenthood announced that it would formally exit the Title X program. The Trump administration may have made the greatest contribution to the pro-life movement in a generation simply by causing this outcome. Rather than comply with the regulation, Planned Parenthood willingly walked away from $60 million in annual funds to their bottom line. Choosing their abortion business over cancer and pregnancy services demonstrated the real motivation of Planned Parenthood and simultaneously reduced taxpayer support for a morally reprobate organization.

## Trump's Executive Order Protecting Religious Freedom Is a Significant Win for the Pro-Life Movement

While the main thrust of the pro-life movement is to legally forbid the barbaric practice of killing unborn children, de-linking "health care" law from "abortion" services has been a major strategic aim. As things stand, most insurance policies, including those provided by the federal government, include coverage for abortion-related services like so-called "family planning" counseling, surgical abortions, abortifacient contraception, and attendant pre-and-post abortion medical care. Pro-life activists have long sought to restrict their tax dollars from supporting what they view as a morally reprehensible practice. At the very least, faith-based organizations have sought specific accommodations that permitted them to opt-out of government mandates that required even private health insurance providers to include abortion-related services.

Although certain accommodations were made under the labyrinthine legal and bureaucratic rules that govern health care, to exempt strictly religious institutions—that is, churches and closely affiliated faith-based non-profit organizations—the law did not generally exempt non-religious services such as hospice care, day care, social services, and book publishing provided by faith-based organizations. This still left hundreds of organizations subject to government coercion in the form of fines and other sanctions to cover abortion-related services that are strictly forbidden by their religious convictions.

### Little Sisters of the Poor

Perhaps no example is more illustrative of the insanity of abortion laws invading religious freedom than the case of the Little Sisters of the Poor. Founded in France in 1839, the Little Sisters is a Catholic religious order of nuns. Like most Catholic religious orders, the Little

Sisters take vows of chastity, poverty, and obedience to God. But the Little Sisters also ascribe to a fourth vow—the vow of hospitality to the elderly and poor. They believe hospitality brings their religious consecration to the lives of everyday people, giving a spiritual dimension to the humble tasks of serving the poor. This small group of Catholic nuns was probably one of the most unlikely of all the religious orders to become symbols of government encroachment on religious freedom. They did not go out looking for a fight.

But when the Obama administration signed into the law the Affordable Care Act, it brought into effect a set of sweeping mandates that not only required employers to provide health insurance for employees under a drastically expanded set of circumstances, but also prescribed the features that had to be included in such coverage. Surprisingly—to them, at least—the Little Sisters of the Poor found that their religious work of providing hospice care for the elderly and sick brought them squarely into conflict with the requirements of the new health care law.

The Little Sisters employed health care professionals and support and administrative employees in their hospice care centers across several cities in the U.S. As an employer, they were mandated to provide health care coverage under the new laws. However, because they were not classified as a "church," their organization did not fall within the religious carve-outs for providing contraceptive and other sexual reproduction services included in the broad Obamacare mandate. On the other hand, their religious beliefs explicitly prohibited them from any involvement in the provision of both contraceptive and abortion-related services which are mandated by the law. They found themselves stuck between offending God on the one hand and offending the United States on the other. The penalties for either were grave. Offend God, and they violated their sacred vows. Offend the United States, and they faced stiff penalties for non-compliance with Obamacare, penalties and fines that would quickly bankrupt the organization and prevent them from practicing their faith. Keep in mind that an essential part of their religious practice involves providing hospice care and other services for the elderly poor. They were truly caught in an unwinnable situation.

When President Donald Trump signed the executive order on religious freedom on May 4, 2017, the Little Sisters could finally breathe a sigh of relief. The order directed the federal agencies responsible for implementing the Affordable Care Act issue to new regulations. The president is ordering the agencies to do what the Supreme Court and the Constitution actually require.

Sister Constance Veit, Director of Communications for the Little Sisters, said, "We are trusting in the Lord that he will see this through to the end. He's never let us down as a community. We never thought we'd end up with any kind of a legal case. We thought that through the mechanism of the U.S. Bishop's Conference, this would all be resolved fairly quickly, because Cardinal Dolan has received some assurance of that through President Obama. On the one hand, this has been a cause of anxiety for us, because the fines, humanly speaking, are insupportable. They are so huge, over $70 million per year. But on the other hand, it has been a wonderfully eye-opening experience to bond with different faith groups."

This religious victory should be of particular interest to blacks, who are by and large significantly more likely to identify as people of faith than other ethnic groups. Blacks pray more, are more devout in their belief in God's existence, and are more likely to believe that the admonitions of the Bible should be believed and adhered to. Among African Americans who identify as Christians, nearly three-quarters consider themselves born-again or evangelical Christians, and 84 percent of black evangelicals say they pray every day.[121]

While culturally, black and white evangelicals appear to be similar in terms of their beliefs about prayer, abortion, and family values,

---

121    "How Does Pew Research Center Measure the Religious Composition of the U.S.? Answers to Frequently Asked Questions," Pew Research Center, July 5 , 2018, https://www.pewforum.org/2018/07/05/how-does-pew-research-center-measure-the-religious-composition-of-the-u-s-answers-to-frequently-asked-questions/.

they differ sharply when it comes to political affiliations. White evangelicals tend to overwhelmingly support Republicans (66 percent), according to the latest Pew study, while black evangelicals tend to overwhelmingly support Democrats (80 percent). Fully, 92 percent of black evangelicals voted for Hillary Clinton in the 2016 election. So why the political disconnect, when in purely religious and cultural matters, the two groups seem to behave quite similarly?

Just as the white evangelical community was at an earlier point more politically diverse, there is likely a political reckoning coming for black evangelicals. As late as 1976, white evangelicals were split between the Republicans and the Democrats, at least at the presidential level. Since then, white evangelicals have voted as a bloc in higher and higher percentages for the GOP, including their most recent effort in 2016 for Donald Trump. Their support for faith-based institutions and family, traditional values and related biblical principles often puts them at odds with national Democrats.

There are nascent signs that a similar phenomenon is starting with black evangelicals. Consider, black evangelicals are closer in their view with white evangelicals on same-sex marriage than they are with Democrats.[122] Also, issues like school prayer and abortion place black evangelicals apart from Democrats as a whole. Perhaps the biggest challenge has been the rise and strength of the "secular Democrat," a rapidly growing force on the left, defined by adherents who are not just apathetic regarding matters of faith, but express antipathy to the notion that religion is in any way relevant in the public square.

In 2004, black evangelicals provided George W. Bush a significant boost in Ohio and to a lesser degree in Florida, which many

---

122    Kate Shellnutt, "For Black Evengelicals, How Does Masterpiece Cakeshop Compare to Jim Crow: Four Views On Why African American Christians Have Mixed Feelings About the Supreme Court's First Ruling on Refusing Services for Same-Sex Weddings," *Christianity Today* (CT), June 10, 2018, https://www.christianitytoday.com/ct/2018/june-web-only/masterpiece-cakeshop-jim-crow-service-refusals-gay-weddings.html.

analysts credited with giving him his margin of victory in winning re-election. In the 2018 statewide races in Georgia and Florida, with blacks at the top of the ticket, Democrats were unable to prevent black evangelicals from defecting—a major factor in the margin of Democrats' defeat in statewide offices that year.

If a sizeable bloc of black evangelicals shifted their support away from Democrats nationally, say between 20 percent and 35 percent, the reverberations would be explosive and deadly for Democrats. And yet if the secularists who are ascendant in the progressive movement continue their efforts to marginalize faith in the public square, this outcome could likely occur.

## TRUMP'S POLICIES PUSH BACK AGAINST AN ABORTION INDUSTRY THAT HAS TARGETED THE BLACK COMMUNITY

The Trump administration's staunchly pro-life policies are pushing back against an abortion industry that historically has targeted the black community for more than a century. Today, black women remain far more likely than women of other races to have an abortion. Black women account for roughly one-third of all abortions in the United States, but constitute only 13.7 percent of the female population; Hispanic women received 25 percent of the abortions, while Hispanic women constitute only 17.4 percent of U.S. females. Combined, these minorities received 55 percent of the abortions, but comprise only 30 percent of the U.S. female population.[123] Many in the pro-life black community believe that such high and disproportionate percentages are no coincidence, but are a result of intentional efforts.

Alveda King, the niece of Martin Luther King, Jr., and long-time pro-life civil rights activist, is encouraged by President Trump's

---

123 "Abortion and Race: For Decades, Abortion Has Disproportionately Eliminated Minority Babies," Abort73.com, https://abort73.com/abortion/ abortion_and_race/.

pro-life agenda and believes that his presidency may offer the pro-life black community a "historic opportunity." But there are still those in the African-American community who have cynically adopted the liberal agenda of genocide. Contrast, for example, the humanitarian work of Alveda King with the pro-abortion practice of Dr. Willie Parker, who goes around the Southern United States performing abortions on poor blacks, under the auspices of "Christian ministry."

## Alveda King: Drum Major for Unborn Justice

Alveda King is probably one of the most powerful and yet unheralded voices in America when it comes to drawing the line between abortion and denial of blacks' civil rights. Over the past twenty years, she has worked tirelessly to be a "voice for the voiceless," defending the rights of the unborn, particularly African-American children killed by abortion.[124]

Her personal story is riveting. After giving birth to one child as a married teenager in 1969, she learned about a year later that she was pregnant again. When her doctor informed her that she was pregnant, he declared that because she was a young, poor woman who already had a baby at home, it might not be a good idea for her to carry the baby to term. "My doctor made a decision for me," recounts King. "He did an involuntary DNC. It changed my body— my mammary system was messed up. I ended up having surgery to repair my cervix. It changed my personality so much, that first one, that the doctor did without telling me. It was the year after my uncle MLK was assassinated, and I had all of that trauma and tragedy, including all of the post-abortive syndrome, that I ended up getting divorced."

Alveda King's tragic case undermines one of the central tenets of abortion rights advocates, namely that access to legal abortion

---

124     "Alveda King: A Voice for the Voiceless," CBN (The Christian Broadcasting Network), https://www1.cbn.com/700club/alveda-king-voice-voiceless.

reduces the risk to the mother of having unsafe abortions. Abortions are, by definition, an unsafe and unnecessary procedure in most cases, and actually pose a far greater health risk to the mother than carrying a child to term. About twenty-three thousand women die each year from unsafe abortions. And the number of women who report catastrophic physical and psychological injury from having an abortion is immensely higher.

Sadly, Alveda's tragedy did not end there. In 1973, shortly after *Roe v. Wade* made abortion the law of the land, Alveda King was once again faced with an uncomfortable choice. As she recounts, "It was in 1973 when I made that decision [to have another abortion], and for a minute I became a pro-choice voice. I was out saying a woman has a right to choose what happens to her body, and that's true. But those children are not my body. I knew those babies were not my body because I actually bore six living children, and they were not my body. My testimony is that I was fooled into believing my baby was a lump of tissue."

Alveda credits two men with helping her to change her position. "I got pregnant again in 1977, and the baby's dad said 'no, we are not killing that baby.' Then I went to my grandfather Dr. Martin Luther King, Sr., and I told him the same junk, 'it's just a blob of tissue.' And he told me, 'No, that's the real civil rights issue. Injustice anywhere is a threat to justice everywhere. Ripping babies apart is a very unjust act. It is very violent. Dr. King [Jr.] was nonviolent. And he said the Negro cannot win if he's willing to sacrifice the future of his children for personal comfort and safety. And that's what we do when we have abortions.'"

No clearer, more poignant or personal story could better illustrate the point that abortion, especially as it relates to the black community, is one of the most egregious forms of injustice ever practiced. Not only did Dr. King's niece become an unwitting target of the pro-abortion movement, but in doing so, she acknowledges she was betraying the very goals of justice and freedom for which her uncle, Dr. Martin Luther King, Jr., had fought and died.

Since making the decision to keep her babies, not only has Alveda King become a courageous voice for unborn children, she has birthed and raised six healthy children. "All abortion is genocide," says King. "All abortion is eugenics. It's designed for population control for various reasons.[125] When we consider the history of abortion in the African-American community, and abortion in the community of America. Slaves were counted as chattel. Women did not have the right to vote. The Caucasian women and the slave women had an uneasy alliance, pretty much like Hagar and Sarah. And so the slave master's wife, when the slave master preferred the slave and she became pregnant, said, 'We've got to come up with a solution.' The slave woman said, 'I'd rather my baby die than be born into this life.' And so there were chemicals and procedures to induce abortions all the way back to slavery in America."

Like Alveda King, Norma McCorvey, the "Jane Doe" from the original *Roe v. Wade* case, had a religious conversion and later formed her own group, the "Roe No More" ministry. She traveled the country speaking out against abortion, stating, "I am dedicated to spending the rest of my life undoing the law that bears my name." McCorvey died in 2017, still speaking out about the horrors of abortion.[126] It is telling that both Martin Luther King, who is widely regarded as one of the fiercest champions for human rights in modern history, and Norma McCorvey, whose story became the basis for the landmark case legalizing abortion, both staunchly opposed abortion on human rights grounds.

---

125 Barbara Hollingsworth, "Alveda King on Disproportionate Abortion of Black Babies: 'That's Certainly Black Genocide,'" CNSNews.com, December 5, 2016, https://www.cnsnews.com/news/article/barbara-hollingsworth/genocide-what-black-pro-life-leaders-call-disproportionate-number.

126 Joe Carroll, "After 31m abortions, legal victor regrets role," *Irish Times*, January 24, 1998, https://www.irishtimes.com/news/after-31m-abortions-legal-victor-regrets-role-1.127818.

## Dr. Willie Parker: Genocidal Monster

Dr. Willie Parker is another African American who professes to be doing justice for black women. Like Alveda King, Dr. Parker is an African American who grew up in a deeply Christian Baptist household in the Jim Crow South, during the 1950s and '60s. He was the first person in his family to go to college, and ultimately graduated from medical school with a specialty in obstetrics. According to Dr. Parker, after becoming an obstetrician he was initially hesitant to perform abortions because of his Christian beliefs.

Parker has worked in abortion clinics in eight states, and he was formerly a medical director at Planned Parenthood in the greater Washington, D.C., area. In his book, he describes patients exercising a legal right to make "private health care decisions for themselves, facing a variety of problems—certain medical, social, financial or other personal conditions." In Dr. Parker's practice, they are often women in poverty and women of color.

But the notion that somehow Dr. Parker is helping women seems oddly incongruent with Jesus's message.

Willie Parker's macabre medical practice is a primary example of how even people who profess Christian beliefs can be misled into making horrible choices. Abortion is not only a moral abomination akin to murder, it is also, in most cases, bad public health care practice. A 1993 Howard University study that examined black women and breast cancer showed that African-American women over age fifty were 4.7 times more likely to get breast cancer if they had any abortions, compared to women who had not had any abortions. And pointedly, the actual deaths of the pre-born is also a horrific health practice. According to Arnold Culbreath, Founder/CEO of Breath of Life, LLC, and Breath of Life Foundation, LLC, abortion is the leading cause of death for African Americans, more than all other causes combined, including AIDS, violent crimes, accidents, cancer, and heart disease. Tragically, more than sixteen million black babies have died by abortion since 1973.

This is no accident. The history and context of abortion politics and practice in the United States is rife with racism and eugenics, pointing to a policy choice designed to support the elimination of black children and families. By some estimates, abortion has reduced the black population in the United States by as much as 35 percent, and caused a significant reduction in black political power and cultural representation as a consequence.[127]

It bears mentioning that in accepting responsibility for children—if black lives really do matter—it is essential that the black family structure be restored. It is undoubtedly a crisis that three out of four black children in the U.S. are born to unwed mothers. And that is often used as an excuse by politicians to assert the need for abortions. The logic being that if black children are going to face severe disadvantages from their station in life, it would be better if they were killed before they had a chance to live. This is backwards thinking. It is akin to the logic that Jesus would have saved the life of a pregnant adulterer from stoning even though she was a social outcast, but then encouraged her to kill her unborn child. Jesus was both pro-marginalized people and pro-life.

While it is, of course, a Christian's duty to have deep compassion and action on behalf of other human beings, and even to defend women against the shame and stigma of single motherhood, it is manifestly not an act of compassion to ask her to kill her unborn child.

# THE INCREDULOUS RACIST HISTORY OF THE PRO-CHOICE MOVEMENT IN THE UNITED STATES

The history of abortion in the United State is replete with the once outspoken but by now forgotten racist propaganda of leading

---

127   Anunkor, Ifeoma, Daniels, Christina, Davis, Catherine, Parker, Star, "The Effects of Abortion on the Black Community," Policy Report, Center for Urban Renewal and Education, June 2015, https://docs.house.gov/meetings/JU/ JU10/20171101/106562/HHRG-115-JU10-Wstate-ParkerS-20171101-SD001.pdf.

pro-choice advocates at the turn of the 20th century. Furthermore, there are clear parallels between the Supreme Court's language describing black slaves in the infamous *Dred Scott v. Sandford* slavery case, and the court's language describing unborn babies in *Roe v. Wade* (1973) and *Planned Parenthood v. Casey* (1992).

## Margaret Sanger: The Eugenicist in Sheep's Clothing

Margaret Sanger, the nurse turned activist, who founded the American Birth Control League (which became, in 1942, the Planned Parenthood Federation of America), opened the first birth control clinic in the United States in a slum in Brooklyn, New York, in 1916. She styled herself an advocate of women's rights, focusing most of her efforts on the poor and mostly black communities in New York and elsewhere in the U.S. What is not so well-known is that Sanger was also a staunch eugenicist. In her own words, "The most urgent problem today is how to limit and discourage the over-fertility of the mentally and physically defective."

Sanger was no mere dabbler in eugenics, the belief that the human race can be improved by selectively breeding only the most dominant and successful traits among certain populations. She was obsessed with the topic. Most of her closest friends were well-known eugenicists of the day.[128] She was, in fact, the main organizer behind the First World Population Conference in Geneva, Switzerland, in 1927. Most of Sanger's friends believed that population improvement should be accomplished by encouraging the wealthy and "competent" to have more children, thus outpacing the less competent in the population race.

Sanger's solution, however, was much different. She believed that the goal of eugenics could be most effectively accomplished by

---

128    Alana Varley, "Margaret Sanger: More Eugenic Than Fellow Eugenicists," Care.net, January 16, 2018, https://www.care-net.org/abundant-life-blog/margaret-sanger-unintelligent-people-are-a-drain-on-society-0-0-0-0.

limiting the births of those she considered to be mentally and physically defective—i.e., the poor. Her "final solution" was to promote
population-reducing practices, such as birth control and abortion,
among the poor by dressing them up in the language of "family planning" and "women's reproductive rights." However, women's rights
were always merely the window dressing for a far more sinister aim,
the reduction of the black population in the United States. She wrote,
"As long as civilized communities encourage unrestrained fecundity
in the 'normal' members of the population…and penalize every
attempt to introduce the principle of discrimination and responsibility in parenthood, they will be faced with the ever-increasing
problem of feeble-mindedness."

This cold calculation and the methods she proposed to achieve
it horrified her fellow eugenicist friends. Many of them were Jewish
and were witnessing in real-time the eugenics policies of Hitler, who
was using gas ovens instead of abortion clinics, as a form of population control. They vigorously opposed her methods and never got
behind her movement.

Sanger then went out in the poor and minority communities
across the United States, trying to spread her message. She primarily
targeted Christian ministers in the black community, and was even
on record in one of her letters to supporters in 1939, stating, "We
do not want word to go out that we want to exterminate the Negro
population, and the minister is the man who can straighten out that
idea if it ever occurs to any of their more rebellious members." Note
here that Sanger did not say in the letter that she did not aim to
exterminate the Negro population, only that she "did not want word
to get out" of her true intentions.

From its earliest inception through today, Planned Parenthood's
chief mission is to achieve population control among minority—
primarily black and Latino—communities. It is no coincidence
that, according to statistics gathered by ProtectingBlackLife.org,
"Planned Parenthood, the largest abortion provider in the country,
targets African Americans by locating 62% (approx. 2 out of every

3) of their surgical abortion mills in black and minority communities." Planned Parenthood does not operate in Beverly Hills or Boca Raton, or any of the wealthiest communities in America. It targets the poor. As a result, because blacks are disproportionately poor, they are subjected to a disproportionate share of abortions conducted in the U.S. According to The Alan Guttmacher Institute, black women are more than five times as likely to have an abortion as white women. In the powerful words of Alveda King, "Whatever her [Sanger's] pain was and whatever her misguided dream was, abortion has killed 60 million children in the twenty-first century. A third of those were African American. Abortion is by far the number one killer of African Americans."

## The Competing Moral (and Legal) Fallacies of Slavery and Abortion

Both the institutions of slavery, as it was defined in the lead-up to the Civil War, and that of abortion as it exists today, rest on almost identical lies. Namely, that the subject at issue is the property of another and not a human being with inalienable rights endowed by God. They also rest on similar legal fallacies—that a judge should depart from "saying what the law is" (that is, interpreting the Constitution in light of what the text and words actually mean) to making laws by edict based on political necessity or evolving standards. The former is what judges should do. The latter is what they actually did in *Dred Scott v. Sandford*, the infamous slavery case, and in *Roe v. Wade* (1973) and *Planned Parenthood v. Casey* (1992), the seminal abortion cases.

In *Dred Scott*, the Supreme Court erred in describing the litigants that came before the court to sue for their freedom as "property." Human beings in the U.S. have inalienable rights, among them life, liberty, and the pursuit of happiness. It follows simply, therefore, that human beings cannot be property and also enjoy these natural rights. Writing for the majority of the Supreme Court in a 7–2 decision, Justice Taney said that under the U.S. Constitution, blacks "had no rights which the white man was bound to respect; and that the negro might justly and lawfully be reduced to slavery for his benefit. He was bought and sold and treated as an ordinary article of merchandise and traffic, whenever profit could be made by it." This statement was, in many respects, overkill. The Constitution never specified that blacks were property.

Even when making distinctions between enslaved individuals and citizens for apportionment purposes, the Constitution made a compromise—slaves would be counted as three-fifths of a person for allocating representation in the Congress. In other words, states with large slave populations could not obtain the same number of congressmen in the House of Representatives as non-slave states with similar populations. Notably, the U.S. Constitution explicitly gave Congress the power to ban the importation of slavery, which Congress did within weeks of being authorized to do so. The Constitution, then and now, refused to expressly authorize slavery or declare that the race of any person was a basis to limit rights.

To square the issues, Taney also had to invalidate the Missouri Compromise, which was the law that all the new states being formed west of the Mississippi would be non-slave states. He declared that act unconstitutional.

What Taney and the other justices on the Supreme Court did in the *Dred Scott* case was rule by edict. That is, he did not interpret the law, but created a whole new legal regime that never existed— that blacks were "property" under the U.S. Constitution, and that acts of Congress inconsistent with this new "property" rule would be struck down by the courts. Taney was a staunch supporter of slavery and seemingly wanted to do everything in his power to protect it. However, his decision was so repugnant to the will of the people in the non-slavery states (essentially saddling them with the obligation to drag human beings back into bondage), that it forced people who had been mildly uncomfortable living in a country that practiced slavery in certain parts where they didn't live, into an extreme position. Even if you were white and wanted to escape slavery as an institution, you could no longer do so by going to a non-slave state. For these Americans, slavery anywhere was now a direct threat to their views about the rights of every person everywhere.

Many Americans of moral conscience found slavery to be an abhorrent institution, one that flouted the ideals upon which America was founded. Abigail Adams, wife of America's second president, John Adams, was adamantly opposed to slavery. Even before she became First Lady of the United States in 1800, she decried the failure of the drafters of the Constitution to ban slavery outright, saying, "How could they [Southern States] reconcile human bondage with the ideology of freedom that Americans had fought for?" Abolitionists like Frederick Douglass argued passionately against the evils of slavery, arguing that it corrupted both slave owner and slave alike. John Brown actually staged an armed rebellion at Harper's Ferry, Virginia, in 1859, in hopes of stoking a slave revolt in Virginia. People of conscience were disgusted that the institution of slavery was operating in their name and under the auspices of the U.S. Constitution. And they felt that the efforts by Democrats in Congress to extend slavery to the newly incorporated Western states was a bridge too far. They would not stand for it.

And in fact, that is exactly what happened. The anti-slavery Whigs broke off from the rest of the party and formed the Republican Party in 1854, specifically to fight the problem of slavery spreading to the Western territories. Democrats in Congress threatened to secede from the nation if Republicans won the 1860 election, which they did, electing Abraham Lincoln as the first Republican President of the United States. Six weeks after Lincoln took office, South Carolina declared its secession, followed shortly by five other Southern states. By 1861, the Civil War had begun, and by 1865, there were no slaves in the United States after a conflict that saw more loss of American lives than any war before or since. So much for the effectiveness of judicial edicts.

When it comes to abortion, a similarly fictional legal and moral regime has governed since *Roe v. Wade* in 1973, when abortion was declared to be a constitutional right. Before that time, states enforced various abortion laws, and women who wanted abortions in states that restricted them could travel to the states with fewer restrictions.

But the court's decision to take on the case of Norma McCorvey, a Texas woman who had been denied an abortion (and bore a healthy daughter before the case would be decided) marked a stark departure from the social evolution that was taking place around the U.S. In *Roe*, the court ruled seven to two that a right to privacy under the Due Process Clause of the Fourteenth Amendment extended to a woman's decision to have an abortion—a right that had never been referenced by the founders or even earlier members of the Supreme Court. They further created one of their famous balancing tests, setting up different standards of scrutiny for abortion regulation, predicated on whether the regulation affected abortion in either the first, second, or third trimester of gestation.

All of this legal fiction writing was crafted, purportedly, to protect a woman's health and to protect the potentiality of human life. Arguing that these state interests in restrictions became stronger over the course of a pregnancy, the court resolved this balancing test by allowing greater state regulation of abortion in the third or final trimester of pregnancy. *Planned Parenthood v. Casey* almost twenty years later essentially amended *Roe* by removing the "third trimester" limitation and substituting the concept of "undue burden" on a woman's ability to have an abortion instead, meaning that restrictions adopted by a state may occur at any point during a pregnancy.

But *Roe*, like *Dred Scott*, rests on a legal fiction. That is, it implies that an unborn child is either the property or an appendage of its mother, and therefore, the state shouldn't interfere with any reproductive decision made by the mother in consultation with her doctor.

In deciding *Roe*, the court had to get into the business of deciding when a developing fetus becomes a "life," and therefore, a citizen with its own set of constitutional rights. And to do so, it had to invent the fiction of "viability" to give the state a "compelling" interest in interfering with the privacy rights of the mother at late stages of gestation since most Americans at the time would have been horrified at the idea of a right to abortion through nine months of pregnancy.

*Roe* developed a faux-scientific framework out of thin air and then used that framework to apply to the decision about the relative rank between the constitutional rights of two citizens: the right to privacy on the part of the mother, and the right to life on the part of the unborn child. However, the author of *Roe* chose a weak reed to rest his argument on—viability. Perhaps since Justice Harry Blackmun, who wrote the majority opinion in Roe, was not a biologist, he didn't realize just how unsound viability as a basis of constitutional rights would be. Every decade since 1973, viability of an unborn child has come closer and closer to the point of conception.[129] Pre-natal surgery is expanding, and births of so called "preemies" continue to occur with babies of younger and younger ages.

Notably, there is no other constitutional right that is predicated on whether science advances. The legal argument also goes against what the practice often looks like. In the recent controversy over Planned Parenthood, a sting operation revealed the organization is engaged in the regular practice of selling fetuses based on the maturity of certain types of tissue—brain and organs in particular—to scientific research labs. This is the type of macabre market for human—notice, not merely "fetal"—tissue that the organization regularly engages in for profit. And of course, they are harvesting a large amount of this tissue from the unborn children of poor, African-American women.

As bad as it sounds, Planned Parenthood's despicable practices are a best-case scenario. The abortion industry is so under-regulated that "abortuaries" often get by with dirty facilities and medically unsafe procedures.

That was the case with the horrible serial killer Dr. Kermit Gosnell, who's Philadelphia abortion clinic regularly killed babies—that is,

---

129    Maria Pyanov, CPD, CCE, "What's The Earliest a Baby Can Be Born And Survive," BellyBelly.com.au, September 6, 2017, https://www.bellybelly.com.au/baby/whats-the-earliest-a-baby-can-be-born-and-survive/.

delivered live, viable babies and then murdered them by severing their spinal cords with scissors. He also killed at least two of his female patients, who died from botched abortions. In 2013, Gosnell was finally caught after decades of operating in the shadows, convicted of multiple counts of murder, and is now serving a life sentence in prison.

While this case was an outrage, it received very little coverage from the mainstream media. It just did not jibe with the story they wanted to tell about the clean, clinical, and ultimately liberating practice of abortion. A movie released in 2018 detailing the Gosnell case received critical acclaim, but very little coverage in the mainstream media.

After the Civil War three separate constitutional amendments were adopted to end the debate once and for all as to whether the rights of all Americans are protected in America. But perhaps the way in which *Roe v. Wade* is most like *Dred Scott* is the way in which it has galvanized American society. The issue of abortion is now one of the most divisive issues of our time. Like *Dred Scott*, both major political parties have been forced to line up on opposite sides. The Supreme Court itself has become a source of conflict, because as American society organizes itself around the abortion dispute, other important issues are pushed from the center of civic life. And like *Dred Scott*, individual households are divided; as was the case with *Dred Scott*, today, Americans under *Roe* are forced to live with an edict that has no moral truth associated with it—to wit: unborn babies are merely property. That falsity can be seen as such with our own eyes merely by viewing a sonogram. Is it any wonder that so many states have passed laws challenging this judicially-created edict?

In theory, slavery was about property rights, at least as far as the Supreme Court in the *Dred Scott* case conceived of it. In practice, it was a horror of incredible atrocity, as most thinking human beings can readily acknowledge. In theory, abortion is all about a woman's privacy, as far as current law is concerned. In practice, it is a dirty business replete with charlatans, macabre body-parts merchants, racist eugenicists, and serial murderers. Hopefully the Supreme Court will overturn this ruling and prevent the kind of societal fracture that *Dred Scott* created.

## CONCLUSION

The Trump administration has made it clear that it supports the right to life and wants to end the practice of widespread abortions in the United States. He has appointed two conservative Supreme Court justices who are likely to vote to weaken, or eliminate, the "undue burden" limitation on abortion restrictions. President Trump has openly sided with the faith community and implemented a sweeping review of governmental insurance coverage regulations that will permit a far broader number of faith-based organizations to opt-out of providing insurance coverage that includes abortion and contraception services; and he has forced Planned Parenthood to exit Title X, one of its most significant sources of taxpayer support.

The abortion industry has its genesis in the racially odious desire for a genocidal destruction of blacks as well as the "weak" and the poor. Even today, abortion clinics target communities of color in a manner quite consistent with Margaret Sanger's racist ambitions. Profiting from the harvesting of baby organs is something expected in mainland China, not the U.S.A.

Black people are better off when the laws protect the lives of their children, whether born or unborn. Abortion has wrought untold sociological and psychological trauma on the black community as well as the rest of America, even as it has been marketed as a means of avoiding the consequences for unwanted pregnancies. Untold millions of black Americans have had their lives snatched away at their most vulnerable point—in their mothers' wombs—since 1973. By disproportionately impacting blacks, has *Roe* snuffed out the lives of the 21st century Frederick Douglass or Harriet Tubman? Or a modern-day brilliant scientist in the mold of George Washington Carver? Blacks are far better off having children within traditional family structures than following the eugenicists' plan of aborting themselves into non-existence. President Trump's support for pro-life policies helps promote and protect unborn black lives as well as the lives of Americans of all races.

# Chapter 7

❦

# PRESIDENT TRUMP RESTORES MLK'S VISION OF A COLORBLIND AMERICA

On July 30, 2019, President Trump stopped on the White House lawn on his way to board Marine One, and delivered, as is his custom, an impromptu press conference. What emerged was a stream of consciousness reply to reporters who questioned whether his rhetorical attacks on four liberal congresswomen known collectively as "The Squad" were racist. In response, Trump replied, "I'm the least racist person you'll find anywhere in the world."

While the statement embodies Trump's penchant for hyperbole, it does not miss the mark entirely. The Trump administration has purposefully avoided targeting Americans using race-based appeals. Instead, Trump's approach to Making America Great Again has focused largely on issues of common concern to all Americans—the economy, immigration, and restoring American prosperity.

At his rallies, the president frequently announces the latest economic achievements for the country, including those for blacks, women, and Hispanics, to loud approval from the audience. Encouraging campaign crowds to join in lauding economic gains for minorities is quite a strange approach for a racist.

For a quick refresher: racists order the National Guard to block entry to universities. They segregate federal facilities, and they order the police to fire water cannons at peaceful protesters seeking basic human rights. Please note, when you actively work to enrich and empower blacks, like Donald Trump has done for the last three and a half years, you are at odds with racists.

## "THE WAY TO STOP DISCRIMINATION ON THE BASIS OF RACE, IS TO STOP DISCRIMINATION ON THE BASIS OF RACE..." - CHIEF JUSTICE JOHN ROBERTS

President Trump has signaled an eagerness to deal with the vestiges of de jure discrimination that still exist as a matter of law in America, by challenging race-based quotas in employment and racially targeted efforts, such as affirmative action, in government and higher education. By erasing these harmful attempts at social engineering, the Trump administration is helping to advance Martin Luther King's noble dream of a colorblind America.

One of the things that modern-day progressives need to understand is that racial separation is wrong, regardless of motivation. While most Americans consider the Jim Crow era a time of great evil, its advocates did not see themselves that way. Just as some today argue that it would be helpful to have all-black graduation ceremonies or all-black student housing, in the early 20th century there were those who thought the same about water fountains and restaurants.

We are a nation of over 320 million of every race and creed. It isn't possible to operate as if we won't interact at the grocery store, the workplace, or in our neighborhood, in scholastic and athletic endeavors, and increasingly—even within our own family settings—with people of other races. Encouraging our brightest (those in college) to assume that they should find solace in being with just their own, in racially separate housing and graduation ceremonies is coddling of the worst kind. It hinders their knowledge of how diversity actually works, and more importantly it undermines their ability on a practical basis, to observe that regardless of skin color, height, or age, we are all Americans equal in the eyes of God.

Getting us all to see that we're all the same is not helped by staying racially separate. This was true in 1954, and it is true today. We may not be able to force people to interact, but government policy shouldn't force us to stay separate.

This brings up another important point. Racial separatism isn't natural. It has always needed the assistance of government coercion to occur. There's a reason that it was illegal in the state of Virginia for whites to marry blacks—because without the law, whites would marry blacks and vice versa. Same with laws that separate shoppers or passengers on public transports. Those laws are only needed precisely because in their absence people will integrate rather than separate.

But just because it isn't natural to separate doesn't mean that race separation can't be political. Political interests have regularly used racial solidarity to gain or keep political power in the U.S. and abroad. Today, there are those who push raced-based policies to maintain political power—affirmative action, so-called racial justice, and the like. But this was also true in the early 20th century. In other words, some modern-day politicians espouse the separatist ideas of "identity politics" not out of any actual affinity for the group them-selves—Joe Biden's presidential campaign which led him to repudiate his sponsorship of one of the most significant anti-crime bills in a generation comes to mind—but out of political necessity.

Political necessity didn't get invented in the 21st century. It existed in the 19th and 20th centuries, too, and likely explained why so many politicians embraced Jim Crow and segregation. This fact doesn't excuse those individuals for failing to stand for principle, but it also doesn't license today's separatists. Either separate treatment is wrong or it isn't. Pretending that there is "good" segregation versus the old "bad" segregation is pure nonsense. Yielding to separation is a temptation in the political arena that should always be avoided. The history of separation by race is that blacks have been harmed. Why any blacks would advocate racial separation today is nonsensical.

Advancing the ideal of colorblindness helps blacks, who have been subjugated for the majority of their history in this country by laws and private attitudes that have operated against them merely because of their race and not their abilities or character. By removing such explicit references to race from our laws and policies, the Trump administration advances the cause of African Americans to be evaluated on their merits and character, rather than their skin color. This was the original hope of the folks who made significant sacrifices in the struggle for civil rights in America. They are honored when we honor the principle of colorblindness in how we conduct our society.

## REDUCING VOTER FRAUD PROTECTS BLACK VOTERS

The Trump administration's efforts to reduce voter fraud helps protect the right to vote—a right that blacks have fought long and hard to secure. Votes cast by "ghost" voters, illegal immigrants and felons, which effectively dilute the legal votes of citizens, are just as much an infringement of the right to vote as if the racist clerk rejected a black voter's ballot, set up a "whites only" primary, or used physical intimidation to discourage black voters—just like Democrats did during the period of de jure segregation in the South.

Our republic is predicated on the notion of self-government. The residents of a given community, town, state, or nation are responsible for selecting who their representatives will be and what policies will be adopted. When outside forces—those who are not lawful voters or residents of a community, town, state, or nation—make these choices for those jurisdictions, they prevent the lawful residents from having control, and they defeat the very notion of self-government upon which our republic is predicated.

Most cynically, progressives, both black and white, are not concerned about the ability to vote. They are troubled by what happens when voting occurs. If actual living, breathing residents of a community are asked to make decisions about their political leadership, they are more likely to be interested in "parochial" concerns such as the cost and scope of the proposals in a candidate's platform. Real residents care about tradition and the pace of the change being advocated for. A consequence is that in most political jurisdictions in America, there is a preference for the "small government" candidate. But the "big government" groups don't like this consequence, so they prefer to "rig" the vote to make it more likely their candidates can win.

If everyone shows up with identification and are lawful residents eligible to vote, it's harder to get them to agree to higher taxes, greater expansion of government, and so on. But if you can allow a few ghosts in the mix, maybe some felons, or especially people who aren't bona fide residents, you can increase the likelihood that the "big government" candidate can prevail.

Many on the left might argue that, in the end, the "big government" policy agenda is good for blacks, so the end justifies the means. But this isn't true, and even if it were true, stuffing the ballot is antithetical to self-government. Imagine what the progressives might say about municipalities in the 1950s justifying barring black voters because in the end, the policy agenda selected by white voters was good for the community?

The Trump administration has both initiated efforts at the federal level (The Presidential Advisory Commission on Election Integrity[130]) and supported activities on the state and local level to assure integrity in the voting process. The efforts come up against intransigent insistence, often on the part of black leaders and public officials who declare that efforts to secure voting integrity are intended to disenfranchise African Americans. This is not true. In fact, the opposite is the case.

Voter fraud is far more likely to occur in places with higher concentrations of African-American voters. It is likely to occur and be most impactful in local elections, especially in small towns and

---

130    "Presidential Advisory Commission on Election Integrity," The White House, July 13, 2017, https://www.whitehouse.gov/articles/ presidential-advisory-commission-election-integrity/.

rural areas with higher concentrations of elderly African-American people. Liberals have argued that in-person voting fraud has had an almost negligible impact, and that instances of fraud occur so rarely that efforts to curtail voter fraud must somehow be a pretext for voter suppression. But their arguments fail in certain respects.

Unlike most crimes, the ability to ferret out vote-related fraud is very difficult. If ballots go missing, election machines appear to malfunction, or more votes occur than there are registrants in a juris-diction, showing intentional violations is quite difficult. Not unlike sexual harassment, many incidents of misbehavior, often referred to as "he said, she said," are difficult to prove. Normally, that difficulty isn't used as an excuse to argue that the misbehavior doesn't exist.

Vote fraud can take many forms. Fake registration, ballot manip-ulation or destruction, or false identity vote casting. While looked at as a whole—in terms of numbers of votes shown to be fraudulently cast across all elections in the United States—fraudulent votes may not number in the millions, but the overall effect is still notable.

Take, for example, the 2015 case of the voting fraud in the Dothan, Alabama, race for City Commissioner. Campaigners for the ultimate winner of the City Commissioner District 2 seat, an Afri-can-American local politician, Amos Newsome, were subsequently convicted of dozens of counts of absentee ballot fraud for mailing in more than fifty absentee ballots. Newsome's margin of victory in the election was fourteen votes. Election officials' suspicions were raised when 119 of the 124 absentee ballots cast in the election were for Newsome. It was subsequently determined that one of Newsome's campaign supporters, Olivia Reynolds, had fraudulently cast over twenty-four absentee ballots—more than the ultimate margin of victory in the campaign. [131]

---

131    Lance Griffin, "Commissioners Call for Amos Newsome to Resign After Voter Fraud Convictions," *Dothan Eagle*, September 4, 2015, https://www.dothaneagle.com/news/government/commissioners-call-for-amos-newsome-to-resign-after-voter-fraud/article_008fc1d0-531c-11e5-bc02-1f2f99a77d33.html.

The point is that people who commit voting fraud do so with the intention of defrauding the voters of their real choices in elections. When measures are put in place to curb these abuses of the system, they protect African-American voters by allowing the real voters to make the choice rather than having someone make the choice for them.

An existential question was put to voters in another small town in Texas, namely, *Is it possible for dead people to cast a vote?* Apparently the answer was yes. Deceased local judge Blas Chapa, who died in 2010, was not only still registered to vote, but apparently had voted in Starr County, Texas, three times since his death. According to local records, the deceased Judge Chapa has apparently been voting in South Texas, in the name of a deceased voter, for years—and it took a federal lawsuit over dirty voter rolls for local election officials to discover the problem. A civil lawsuit filed in federal court against Starr County's elections administrator, in 2016, prompted the voter roll investigation. The lawsuit, filed by the Public Interest Legal Foundation on behalf of the American Civil Rights Union, alleged that Starr County's voter rolls "contain more voters registered to vote than there are citizens eligible to vote residing in the county." That includes deceased voters, ineligible felons, and non-citizens— all of which have been found on the county's registration rolls and casting ballots.[132]

## Voter Fraud Is Real and Significant

Here's a sample:

*Virginia*: *The Richmond Times Dispatch* reported in early July of 2012, that convicted felon Sheila Peterson was one of forty people who had been charged with engaging in voter fraud. Ms. Peterson,

---

132    Erin Anderson, "Voter Fraud Case Reveals Deceased Texans Still Voting: A Civil lawsuit Over Starr County's Voter Rolls Reveals Ballots Being Cast in the Name of a Voter Who Died in 2010," Texas Scorecard, March 8, 2018, https:// texasscorecard.com/local/voter-fraud-case-reveals-deceased-texans-still-voting/.

along with career criminal Michael Harris and several other felons, was targeted in an investigation that led to prosecutions for the crime of "registering felons to vote" heading into the 2008 presidential election.

Bonnie Nicholson, a felon living in Louisa County, was charged in mid-July 2018, with having used pre-printed forms from the leftist Voter Participation Center to register to vote, and then casting a ballot in the 2008 presidential election.

*Texas*: Testimony in the voting rights lawsuit Texas filed against U.S. Department of Justice efforts to block its voter ID program revealed that more than fifty thousand dead people are registered to vote in Texas. The state can prove that at least 239 dead people voted in the May election, 213 of them in person. A state senator testified that his long-deceased grandfather is among those recorded as having voted.

The Texas State Attorney General's office reported fifty election fraud convictions since 2002, and promises that prosecutions are ongoing.

*Arkansas*: In the spring of 2018, a special prosecutor was appointed to handle a case involving allegations of voter fraud in Mississippi County, in an election held in June of 2017.

*Kentucky*: In 2018, the U.S. Attorney for the Eastern District of Kentucky brought a blockbuster voter fraud case involving drug dealers selling and exchanging marijuana and cocaine in order to manipulate the outcome of local elections.[8] U.S. Attorney Kerry B. Harvey has taken the lead on a number of recent federal prosecutions involving vote-buying schemes in the Eastern District. In a recent case, drug dealers are accused of having spent nearly $400,000 buying votes, at $50 apiece. In the previous two years alone, more than twenty public officials and others have either been convicted or pleaded guilty in various vote-buying schemes.

*New York*: Much of the state's media reported on the trials and plea deals of officials involved in a scheme to shut out the Working Families Party's participation in the state's primary by casting forged absentee ballots. Four defendants have already pleaded guilty, including a city clerk and a city councilman.

*Pennsylvania*: In July of 2017, Philadelphia City Commissioner Al Schmidt released a report focused on sixteen of the nearly 1,700 polling sites in Philadelphia, and found several instances of voter fraud, including "double voting," voter impersonation, and voting by non-citizens. The report also documented twenty-three cases of people being allowed to vote despite not even being registered. One polling site recorded six more votes than the actual number of registered voters in the district, and there were multiple instances of people voting in legislative districts where they didn't reside.

## Black Communities Are More Likely to Be Victims of Voter Fraud

Today's voter suppression doesn't come from men wearing hoods. It comes through voter dilution due to phony voters on the rolls—convicts, illegals, and ghosts. The effect is the same—bona fide black citizens have their votes canceled or drowned out.

Blacks are more likely to be victims of voter fraud than other Americans. Former New York political operative Anthony DeFiglio, who pled guilty to falsifying business records, explained to the police why this is: "[We] targeted [for voter fraud] those who live in low-income housing…there is a sense that they are a lot less likely to ask questions." When identity thieves cast votes of registered voters or on behalf of people long deceased, the votes of legitimate black voters are diminished. This is akin to the discriminatory polling tactics practiced in the 19th and 20th centuries.

According to an analysis by Aristotle International, more than three million dead people were found on America's election rolls in 2009. The same analysis found that 12.9 million people on voter rolls were listed at addresses where they no longer lived. In total, the study found about 8.9 percent of all registered voters fell under the category of "deadwood" voters who should not be allowed to vote. Additionally, a 2017 state-by-state analysis by Judicial Watch's

Election Integrity Project yielded 462 counties where the registration rate exceeded 100 percent, and found that 3.5 million more people were registered to vote nationwide than the amount of living adult American citizens.

Black voters are not under-represented or, in fact, prohibited from participating in their most fundamental civic activities, as some self-proclaimed civil rights leaders suggest. The bigger problem is that their interests are woefully misrepresented by their leadership. The lack of voter integrity weakens the true voice of voters and may cause many to become disillusioned, thus reducing their enthusiasm about turning out to vote. In fact, the leading reason Americans—black, white, or brown—give for not voting? A belief that their vote won't matter.

A little-known fact is that in the United States, there are more voter fraud indictments than there are income tax fraud indictments. Surely the measure of how many convictions occur isn't evidence of the severity of the problem. If so, when will progressives ask to repeal tax payment penalties and fines?

I suspect that the overwhelming tendency of blacks to vote for Democratic candidates is rooted in another fraud: that is, that the color of one's skin is the primary determinant of one's political interests. This is not a ballot box fraud that the government can regulate. Rather, it is a symptom of misrepresentation that is prevalent among blacks. It rests on the false notion that Republican candidates and market-based solutions to social ills do not benefit blacks, and in fact, will harm them. Increasingly, black voters are waking up to the inherent contradiction between what they see in their wallets and what they hear from their so-called black leaders.

The 2018 midterm elections for governor in Florida and Georgia are a case in point. Both races were framed as a leading black Democratic candidate—Gillum in Florida versus a white Republican DeSantis, and Stacey Abrams in Georgia versus Brian Kemp, the Republican candidate. Both states had outgoing governors who were Republican, and the electorate of both states had voted majority

Republican for most statewide races in the recent past. There was controversy over racial dog whistling and voter suppression, particularly in Georgia. But when it was all said and done, there was record turnout in each state. Moreover, each candidate received a record number of votes. What made the difference in the outcomes in each state, however, was not voter suppression, but voter turnout. Whites and Republicans in Florida turned out more than 70 percent of their registered voters, while Democrats barely achieved more than 50 percent voter turnout. Moreover, nearly five hundred thousand registered black voters in Florida failed to show up at the polls. Of those that did vote, over 250,000 voted for the Republican candidate. In the end, fewer than thirty-four thousand votes separated the governor-elect, DeSantis, from the losing candidate, Andrew Gillum.

The failure of African Americans to show up and elect a black governor in Florida—something that, given their numbers, they could have easily done—is not the story we hear about in the media. Instead of a story about agency, all the media focused on was voter suppression. Viewed through a lens not shrouded by race, however, the Florida election for governor tells a far different story. There was record turnout, but ultimately, Republicans (with slightly fewer registered voters) turned out in greater numbers than Democrats, who hold the numerical advantage in the state. Blacks did not vote monolithically for a black candidate, and in fact voted in far greater number for the Republican candidates (roughly 14 percent of black voters chose the Republican candidate) than they had in the most recent presidential election.

Anyone doubt what the outcome would have been if the election wasn't restricted to living, breathing, bona-fide residents in these two elections?

In the Florida midterms, while DeSantis won by a slim majority of the vote, a ballot measure restoring voting rights to ex-felons passed by an overwhelming two-to-one margin. Black folks, who are disproportionately arrested and incarcerated, stand to benefit the most from the new law. In 2016, more than 418,000 black people out of a black voting-age population of more than 2.3 million, or 17.9 percent of potential black voters in Florida, were denied the vote due to a felony record. If the Florida election were truly a referendum on race, as liberal prognosticators would have us believe, why did both white and black voters clearly choose to restore the voting rights of nearly half-a-million African Americans?

And what of the racial minorities who voted for DeSantis and Kemp? Do their aspirations not matter? Are their views on small government or gun control meaningless? If the racism and voting narrative in these two elections is so clear, why didn't they join the effort to support the black candidates?

The tendency to view political outcomes purely through the lens of race may have, in fact, hurt Tallahassee Mayor Andrew Gillum in his quest to win the governorship. And this again comes down to the failure to distinguish between race-neutral government policies and well-intentioned but racially-biased efforts to address past injustices. The former fights racism, but the latter reifies race as a distinguishing factor.

When my grandparents lived in the Jim Crow South during the 1920s–1950s, and someone said to them, "I am here to defend your civil rights and stop the racism and segregation you are experiencing," they had a fairly clear understanding of what that meant. It meant that the law that prevented you from being able to shop in a large department store, to use public facilities, to vote, or to attend quality public schools needed to be abolished. We no longer have this universal understanding of what it means to pursue civil rights and end racism, and that division is leading to a lot of people speaking past one another.

Today, when people say racism is a serious problem, it probably means that the guy who is on the homeowner's association security team does not like you because of your race. My grandparents were not ever concerned about individual people's "beliefs" or prejudices. They knew and accepted that everyone may have some degree of prejudice. They were concerned with government mandated prejudice.

Today's race conversation is largely a debate by folks who complain about government sanctioned prejudice, versus those who believe that the personal views of whites in their private roles—"white privilege" or "institutional" racism—are the most prominent and destructive expressions of racism.

Traditional measures of racism, including violence and separatist measures in the public square, have receded to a historic low. Instead of celebrating this achievement, the move to redefine racism to include measures that are almost impossible to identify or regulate has led many in the country today to argue that our racial problems are greater than ever.

Not only is this a migration away from public sector sanctioned racism (a challenge we can collectively fight), but now the move primarily centers around the private sector and private actors. It is dangerous for a society to embark on an effort to insist that every American's private thought and action demonstrate that they are not acting out of bias. What if, as a society, we embarked on a policy of insisting that every teenager go on a date with a person of a different race? Would the resulting restriction on the right of free association result in a more, or less just society? Or consider a goal that every household have a least one member of a minority group? Or perhaps that every dinner party include a minority?

Some see no issue with these scenarios, but it is because they fail to appreciate how such crude attempts at social engineering would trample on the legitimate right of Americans to associate with others that they choose in the circumstances and times of their own choosing. People become friends or date or socialize with others based solely on their own initiative, and for the reasons they choose, and that is fundamental to freedom. Being forced to interact with others won't create more harmony, it will instead lead to greater acrimony.

Going on a date with someone who genuinely likes you is far more pleasurable than going on a date with someone you are forced to associate with. This commonsense concept is often ignored in the quest to ban racism, especially in its newly redefined form.

Finally, every group contains bigots. While axiomatic for many, this concept often eludes the progressive elites. This reality can be observed most every day. The one-sided or "one-racial" portrayal, if you will, of bigotry is, however, yet another hurdle in creating racial harmony and prosperity for all.

## TRUMPS "COLORBLIND" POLICIES VS. THE OBAMA ADMINISTRATION'S RACE PROPAGANDA

The colorblind policies of the Trump administration actually help to advance the cause of freedom and justice for African Americans. On the other hand, identity politics espoused by the Obama administration was designed to appeal to blacks, but in the end did very little to advance blacks socially or economically. One of the clearest signs that blacks did not feel empowered by Obama policies was the turnout in Obama's second election. While Blacks voted overwhelmingly for Obama (as they had done consistently for Democrats in elections past), his level of support dropped from 96 percent in 2008, to 93 percent in 2012.

This reduction actually represented the first time in over a hundred years in a presidential election that a candidate was re-elected with fewer black votes than in their first win. In 2016, a-third fewer blacks showed up to vote on election day than had for Barack Obama in 2008, and of that diminished turnout, an even smaller percentage voted for Democrat Hillary Clinton. Her support dropped to only 88 percent of the black vote. A review of the neighborhood demographic data, conducted by Ryne Rohla, revealed two distinct trends that gave rise to the Trump presidency. The first is that white turnout for Trump narrowly surpassed that for candidates Romney and McCain in the 2012 and 2008 elections, respectively; and black turnout for Hillary Clinton fell far below that for Barack Obama in both 2008 and 2012.[133]

The trend here suggests that more and more blacks are rejecting the view of progressive politics that rely on racial policies for the advancement of blacks. Increasingly, the black electorate looks to policies that will benefit them and their families as Americans, not specifically as African Americans. This is a good thing.

President Obama's administration—for all its racial posturing—failed to protect the people of Flint, Michigan, while the Trump administration has already awarded $100 million for Flint's clean-up efforts. Similarly, President Trump has posthumously pardoned black boxer and world heavyweight champion Jack Johnson, acknowledging his unfair prosecution and conviction—a step that President Obama refused to take. President Trump has taken these steps and others, not because of the color of anyone's skin, but because those steps were the right steps to take.

President Obama, for example, made a great show of issuing presidential pardons for dozens of African Americans who were given heavy federal prison sentences for drug-related offenses. While it made for great public relations, it did little to address the systemic problem of black incarceration, or aid in the devastating effects of drug abuse in inner-city communities. Nor did he take a leadership role in promoting the cultural change in these communities necessary to truly end this cycle of deprivation.

In fact, many of those pardoned under Obama emerged from lengthy prison sentences, only to be re-incarcerated because they were not given social support such as job training and economic opportunities that would allow them to thrive as free citizens. By contrast, President Trump passed the First Step Act with bipartisan support,

---

133    Phillip Bump, "Mostly Black Neighborhoods Voted More Republican in 2016 Than in 2012," *The Washington Post*, September 25, 2017, https://www.washingtonpost.com/news/politics/wp/2017/09/25/mostly-Black-neighborhoods-voted-more-republican-in-2016-than-in-2012/.

setting up a system that not only has freed almost three thousand non-violent criminals, but also provides post-release support to help them assimilate to a law-abiding, productive life.

## THERE SHE GOES AGAIN: THE AGE OF RACIAL HOAXES

Black prosperity and achievement frustrate the liberal race-based civil rights groups that need racial strife and unrest in order to fundraise and remain relevant. Much to their dismay, the Trump administration's colorblind policies which focus on merit rather than melanin are helping to make blacks more prosperous as they create new opportunities for even greater achievement.

In order to justify the continued alarm about racism in the absence of de jure discrimination, it seems that a series of racial hoaxes have been fabricated and persistently foisted upon the general public. In some cases, such as the person trying to get out of a speeding ticket by claiming he was pulled over because of his race (not a winning defense against the radar speed readout in any courtroom I've ever visited), the racial hoaxes are fairly benign. In others, they take on an insidious and wholly counterproductive tenor.

The discovery of racist graffiti galvanized the Air Force Academy in 2017, and the superintendent of the Colorado campus turned that into a teaching moment with a speech about diversity and tolerance that found more than a million viewers on the internet. Now officials say the scrawled slur in a dormitory was a hoax by one of its so-called targets, a black cadet candidate. The episode renews concerns that falsely reported hate crimes could make it more difficult for people with legitimate grievances to be taken seriously, particularly in a time when the reports of hate crimes are highly politicized.[134]

---

134    Christine Hauser, "Target of Racist Graffiti Wrote It, Air Force Academy Says," *The New York Times*, November 8, 2017, https://www.nytimes.com/2017/11/08/us/air-force-academy-racist.html.

In 2016, Yasmin Seweid, an eighteen-year-old Baruch college student was charged with obstructing government administration after her claims that three white men screaming, "Donald Trump!" attacked her on a subway train were proven false. She told the police that the men had called her a terrorist, and that when she tried to move to the other end of the subway car, one of them followed and tried to pull off her traditional head scarf.[135] And there are myriad other racial hoaxes emerging, including Jewish people who defaced a synagogue and blamed white supremacists, and the list goes on and on.

*Smollet Hoax: Getting foreigners to fake the hate that Americans just won't do.*

Many Americans are all too well aware of the Jussie Smollet case in Chicago. On a cold morning in January of 2019, Smollet, who is black and gay, called police and reported that he had been attacked by two men yelling, "this is MAGA country." Police painstakingly investigated the case, and then subsequently announced that they were charging him with sixteen felony counts for making a false police report. It turns out that instead of experiencing a racial/anti-gay attack, the police discovered that Smollet had paid the two men—who were Nigerian, not white—to stage the attack on him. The investigating officers surmised that the stunt was intended to enhance his salary negotiations with the producers of the TV show *Empire*.[136]

Laird Wilcox, author of the book *Crying Wolf: Hate Crime Hoaxes in America*, told Fox News, "It's widely recognized now that college campuses have become the perfect incubators for fake hate crimes. I would say now 80 percent of the events that happen on campus

---

135    Christopher Mele, "Muslin Woman Made Up Hate Crime on Subway, Police Say," *The New York Times*, December 14, 2016, https://www.nytimes.com/2016/12/14/nyregion/manhattan-yasmin-seweid-false-hate-crime.html?module=inline.

136    Thanks to a sweetheart deal, the charges were subsequently dropped leading to a lawsuit filed by the Chicago Police Department against Smollet for the costs associated with the investigation. A special prosecutor has been named to determine the circumstances of the decision to drop the charges and that investigation continues.

are hoaxes or pranks. It's a place where consciousness of discrimination, sexism, and homophobia is at a peak, and when there's nothing happening, and they need something to happen, they can make it happen."[137]

We are migrating away from the core definition of racism (government action that explicitly favors one race over another) and towards hoaxes which attempt to substitute phony instances of bigotry to demonstrate that racial hostility is alive and well in modern-day America. By some accounts, they number nearly five hundred instances over the last five years alone.[138] While they take undue investigative resources. their most pernicious effect is two-fold—they hide the truth that Americans are increasingly less bigoted in attitude and behavior, and even more damningly, they cause us to question the remaining few actual instances of mistreatment, thus depriving victims of the moral support they deserve.

## TRUMP'S POLICIES CONFRONT A HISTORY OF RACIAL DISCRIMINATION IN HIGHER EDUCATION

Racial discrimination in education has long been a contentious civil rights battleground. For much of America's history, blacks fought for the right to receive educational opportunities legally denied them by state and federal laws, on the basis of race. The Supreme Court case of *Brown v. Board of Education* explicitly forbid discrimination on the basis of race in the provision of public education, including in the awarding of federal and state educational scholarships and also with

---

137    Doug McKelway, "What is Fueling Fake Hate Crimes Across the U.S.," Fox News, April 20, 2017, https://www.foxnews.com/us/what-is-fueling-fake-hate-crimes-across-the-u-s.

138    Wilfred Reilly, "Hate Crime Hoaxes, like Jussie Smollett's Alleged Attack, Are More Common Than You Think," *USA Today*, February 22, 2019, updated February 22, 2019, https://www.usatoday.com/story/opinion/2019/02/22/jussie-smollett-empire-attack-fired-cut-video-chicago-fox-column/2950146002/.

grants to private institutions that maintained racially discriminatory policies. But ever since *Brown* was decided in May 1954, the country wrestled with how to deal with the effects of past discrimination.

### Affirmative Action: New Bigotry to Undue Old Bigotry

One of those responses was affirmative action. Originally proposed as a means of proactively recruiting qualified black (and later female) candidates to attend the nation's colleges and universities, the effort was later modified to mean quotas—that is, allocating specific numbers of seats at universities—and expanded to include corporate boards and general hiring, as well as in government contracting. In fact, the federal and state governments went as far as to create explicit minority set-asides to go along with the general contracting for services. While well-meaning in many cases, affirmative action itself became a form of discrimination based on race and produced a set of incentives that both corrupted the ideal of "colorblind" America and disadvantaged the very populations it purported to help.

### Forced Integration: Better Than the Old Separation?

Rather than merely removing the enforced strictures of de jure segregation, law and policy shifted during the late 1960s and 1970s to forcing integration. Probably the most controversial social experiment in education came in the form of busing, in which minority students from the inner city were sent to predominantly white suburban schools, and white students from the suburbs were sent to the inner city. Busing not only failed as a remedy to the educational problems of inner-city schools, it created all sorts of racial resentment among families on both sides of the transaction.

Take affirmative action at the university level: racial quotas at universities not only discriminate against qualified white and Asian applicants, but it puts black applicants with less competitive academic backgrounds in a precarious position. The applicants displaced were unhappy, and their replacements frequently struggled in their place to keep up with the academic load.

By the mid-1990s, the cynical calculus seemed apparent. Though some schools and universities achieved almost precisely racially proportional entrance classes, often by lowering the admissions standards for some black students, their graduating classes four years later looked quite different.

By graduation day, many of the minority applicants had noticeably disappeared; many of whom dropped out and were discouraged, never to return to college again. Many of those, however, were faced with student loan burdens from their time in college that they found almost impossible to pay, given their earning status as college dropouts. Some colleges and universities attempted to correct this by creating almost entire departments (e.g., African American Studies and Women's studies) designed to shelter minority students from competing with the wider student body (in fields that actually held the potential for job readiness and further educational attainment such as physics, science, mathematics, and economics). This, of course, merely kicked the ball down the road and then exposed the minority graduates to workplace challenges they were ill-equipped to overcome due to the substandard education or degree they received.

A policy that results in B students competing with A+ students is harmful to both groups. Just as a football game where players from the University of Maryland play against the Baltimore Ravens doesn't reveal much about the relative talents of either, even if the outcome is pre-ordained. It can, however, wrongly leave spectators with a misimpression about the capabilities of the two teams.

Similarly, when MIT admits a 75th percentile ranked student to compete with fellow 95th percentile students in an engineering program, the results can be disastrous without giving any real insight into the two different students. The 75th percentile student can erroneously conclude that he is not college material due to the pace of the coursework, and might ultimately fail or drop out. Similarly, the 95th percentile students—some of the brightest in the country— might erroneously conclude that 75th percentile students are not academically equipped for the demands of any college. Clearly, a policy that results in these two outcomes isn't working. One that lets the students reach either conclusion on the basis of race is an abject failure.

The Trump administration has opposed all forms of discrimination in public education, and also signaled its intention to join private lawsuits alleging racial discrimination by even private educational institutions. In 2018, the administration announced in a joint letter published by the Education and Justice Departments that it would abandon Obama administration policies that advocated that universities consider race as a factor in diversifying their campuses, and instead called on schools to champion race-blind admissions standards. The Obama guidance to universities was being abandoned, the letter said, because it "advocate[d] policy preferences and positions beyond the requirements of the Constitution."

In a public statement supporting the administration's policy, Roger Clegg, the president and general counsel of the conservative Center for Equal Opportunity, said, "The whole issue of using race in education is being looked at with a new eye in light of the fact that it's not just white students being discriminated against, but Asians and others as well. As the demographics of the country change, it becomes more and more problematic."

In April 2019, Texas Tech University's medical school entered into an anti-discrimination agreement with the Trump administration for admissions. This agreement represented a first for the Trump administration in successfully resolving a probe into racial discrimination in university admissions. Pursuant to the agreement, Texas Tech's medical school will "discontinue all consideration of an applicant's race and/or national origin" in admissions.

By attempting to stamp out racial discrimination in university admissions, the Trump administration is signaling that, unlike the Obama administration, it is serious about the spirit of civil rights, including enforcing laws that forbid discrimination on the basis of race.

Importantly, since there are actually enough schools to go around in America, without schools putting their thumbs on the admission scale, every student will be able to find a school somewhere in the country that they can attend. Ultimately, that school will be one where they meet or exceed the requirements to attend. Overall matriculation rates will rise, and a higher number of students can enter the workforce with skills to cover the costs of their student loans, as well as make it possible for them to earn middle-class or higher incomes.

## Racial Quotas at Harvard: A Relic of a Bygone Era

Where the absurdity of the "racial hoax" writ largely occurs is when it starts to seep into public policy and private administration. The issue of affirmative action in public colleges was initially justified on the basis not of remedying past injustices against black Americans as a group, but of using racial diversity as a proxy for diversity of thought and experience. In many respects though, the diversity rationale was a pretext for the desire of many institutions to show as quickly as possible that they had indeed created their own colorblind, multi-ethnic society that perfectly matched the demographics of America. This was and is a fantasy built on a house of cards. In a free society, the number of participants in any group will never be proportionate to the population at large.

Except in the mind of a Soviet commissar, careers and professions will never break down into neat and proportionate boxes. The greater the level of freedom a society offers, the more the differentiation is likely to be. Take health care. How many nurses should there be? How many should be male? How many should be Asian? In a free society, these answers are unknowable. Unfortunately many on the left believe they know the answers to these questions and are willing to impose their belief on the rest of us.

The Trump administration recently tested the frailty of that edifice when the Department of Justice, led by former Attorney General Jeff Sessions, joined in a racial discrimination lawsuit brought by several Asian Harvard University applicants, against the school. The DOJ supported the claims of the plaintiffs, who had been rejected by Harvard, that the university systematically discriminated against them by artificially capping the number of qualified Asian-Americans from attending the school to advance less qualified students of other races. The filing said that Harvard "uses a vague 'personal rating' that harms Asian-American applicants' chances for admission, and may be infected with racial bias; engages in unlawful racial balancing; and has never seriously considered race-neutral alternatives in its more than 45 years of using race to make admissions decisions." The DOJ later joined a similar lawsuit brought by Asian students suing Yale University.

The reaction from the liberal left has been to cry foul. They claim that the DOJ is essentially using the Asian students' lawsuit in an effort to destroy affirmative action, and thereby limit the opportunities for blacks to attend universities. Their implicit argument is, of course, if Asian students are admitted in numbers adjusted to their qualifications, that will limit the number of black students admitted. Therefore, according to liberals, Asian students—a minority group that had nothing to do with America's history of de jure discrimination—should be discriminated against purely in order to preserve black seats at the institution. Even if the argument is more nuanced on both sides, the basic principle being argued by the left is that discrimination against Asians is fine as long as it benefits blacks and Latinos.

This tactic by liberals flies directly in the face of the principal advanced by the civil rights lawyers in *Brown v. Board of Education*, that "no State has any authority under the equal-protection clause of the Fourteenth Amendment to use race as a factor in affording educational opportunities among its citizens."

Imagine what liberals would say if Google or Amazon said that as a private company they were "prioritizing" hiring Asians and white males in order to advance their companies' status globally, as well as to reflect the racial and gender makeup of their international competition?

By tortuously attempting to violate the principle of equal treatment and racial neutrality, the race-based admissions scheme reaches perhaps its most absurd expression. If anything, blacks should be pushing for everyone, especially another minority group, to be treated equally. Setting aside for the moment the fact that Harvard as a private institution should be permitted to develop its own rules of admittance in accordance with the First Amendment to the U.S. Constitution, under what circumstances would we praise an institution using that right to block applicants solely or primarily on the basis of race?

Black prosperity and achievement on terms that are not explicitly race-infused tend to frustrate the liberal race-based civil rights groups—groups that need racial strife and unrest in order to fundraise and to remain relevant. Much to their dismay, the Trump administration's colorblind policies focusing on merit are helping to make blacks more prosperous in practice as they create new opportunities for even greater achievement.

A curious fault line in race politics lies in the often-overlooked distinction between eliminating government-sponsored racism and attempting to shape private attitudes and behaviors via law and regulation. It is important because the original intent of the civil rights movement was to achieve what Martin Luther King saw as an American ideal—namely that we as a nation could "one day live in a nation where [we] will not be judged by the color of their skin but by the content of [our] character." The civil rights era laws were enacted for the very purpose of getting government out of the business of enforcing racial oppression and aligning government policies with the spirit and letter of the U.S. Constitution that all men are created equal and should be treated equally under the law. The Supreme Court found that de jure segregation had violated the post-reconstruction constitutional amendments guaranteeing equal citizenship rights to former slaves and their descendants. That was the extent of what the law should do, which is to eliminate barriers explicitly premised upon race.

However, as politicians began to see blacks as a potentially lucrative voting bloc concerned about the effects of racism, there began a push to expand laws to regulate private behavior and assign political rewards based on group membership. And why stop with blacks? Women, gays, immigrants, and so on, are lucrative voting blocs that merit expanded laws to regulate private behavior of others. Look at mis-gendering laws in New York and California that punish individuals solely based on their (mis)use of pronouns. The ability to expand regulation to cover private behavior in the quest for political gain is boundless. It does, however, serve to reinforce many of the us-versus-them attitudes that progressives claim they seek to reduce.

Affirmative action programs do not ensure equal opportunity, but merely substitute race for competence in the allocation of scarce goods and resources. Like many other government interventions, racial quotas create market distortions that harm both the recipients (blacks in this case) and those excluded from consideration for admission based on lower standards (Asians and whites in many cases). For blacks, the crush of race-based public policy helps to reinforce the notion expressed by the writer and Stanford psychology professor Shelby Steele, "[that] since the social victim has been oppressed by society, he comes to feel that his individual life will be improved more by changes in society than by his own initiative."

Once again, personal agency is discounted in favor of circumstance. Here's the truth: blacks, like all Americans, are capable of attaining remarkable accomplishments in science, mathematics, and medicine. Rules that interfere and regulate careers, education, and training make that progress harder to see. Policies that mismatch individuals competitively create the very sense of inadequacy they seek to avoid.

Clarence Jones, who was a speechwriter and attorney for Dr. King, says King's position on affirmative action would have been colorblind and based on need. He says he believes that King would support affirmative action policies that help poor people, not one particular race. He was already headed that way with the "Poor People's Campaign," says Jones, author of, *Behind the Dream*, which offers a behind-the-scenes look at the making of King's dream speech. King had already decided during the last year of his life to push for the congressional passage of an economic bill of rights for the poor, Jones says. King's Southern Christian Leadership Conference debated whether to include non-blacks in the bill of rights, but King insisted that they do so. "We came to the conclusion that the economic circumstances of poor people transcended the issue of color and race," Jones says.

## CONCLUSION

"Is color the test of competence?" Richard Nixon thundered at the Republican National Convention, in 1972. "You do not correct an ancient injustice by committing a new one." During the 1980 campaign, then-candidate Ronald Reagan argued against affirmative action in the following way: "I'm old enough to remember when quotas existed in the U.S. for the purpose of discrimination. And I don't want to see that happen again." Reagan did not wish to see King's dream die on the altar of racial vengeance.

Simply put, the Fourteenth Amendment provides that no state shall "deny to any person...the equal protection of the laws." The Equal Protection Clause guarantees every person the right to be treated equally by the state, without regard to race. At the heart of this lies the principle that the government must treat citizens as individuals and not as members of racial, ethnic, or religious groups. Furthermore, the Constitution does not control private prejudices, but neither can it encourage them.

By enacting policies that are colorblind with regards to race, and that seek to remove the explicit use of race in the allocation of public goods and services, the Trump administration continues in the tradition led by former Presidents Nixon and Reagan in helping to restore Martin Luther King's dream of a colorblind America. A colorblind society is a place where all Americans, black, white, or brown, can thrive and prosper. By pursuing MLK's dream, President Trump promotes the real interest of black Americans, which is to live in a society where the evil of racism has no hold on individual opportunity or achievement and the government neither favors or disfavors any particular racial group.

# WHEN HISTORY IS EPILOGUE —THE STATE OF BLACK AMERICA IN 2020 AND BEYOND

As 2019 came to a close, Black America found itself at a crossroads. The largest percentage of black voters remained at least nominally committed to Democrats in Washington according to polling data. All the while, a dawning recognition of the reality that blacks have fared, on the whole, better under Donald Trump's leadership than under the previous Obama administration has occurred. Signature legislation and executive initiatives spearheaded by the Trump administration resulted in significant gains for blacks in the preceding year. These included enhanced resources to law enforcement in black communities to reduce violent crime, aggressive interdiction of illegal immigration, and the correlated reduced labor market competition from illegals, dedicating unprecedented resources to compensating and supporting America's military service members many of whom are black; groundbreaking criminal justice reform that has impacted thousands of African American prisoners and—not to mention the 800-pound gorilla in the room—the lowest black unemployment rate ever recorded. A rate that has dropped faster for blacks than for the nation as a whole.

Rather than offer a more compelling case for black voters, Democrats joined in a hyper-partisan effort to impeach the president in the fall of 2019. This process, if successful, threatened to impede further progress for blacks and for Americans generally who have benefited from the policies of Donald Trump.

Conversely, fundraising numbers for the final month of 2019 show a marked increase in donations to the Trump 2020 re-election campaign—with Trump far outpacing his Democratic primary challengers to raise more than $47 million in the month of December alone.

Demonstrating the frailness of the left's reliance on "identity politics", all of the non-white candidates either dropped out of the Democratic Primary or failed to meet polling/fundraising requirements to participate in official DNC debates, leaving only white candidates vying to represent the hopes and dreams of the vast majority of African Americans who vote Democrat.

Although black Americans made gains in employment and wages relative to White America, Black America continues to experience a significant wealth gap relative to all other groups. As things stand, African Americans are experiencing a drastic reorganization of the traditional Democratic coalition—along the lines of a radically left Democratic Party largely patronizing highly educated whites and economically downtrodden Hispanics at the expense of the economic interests of blacks. Thus far, blacks have not demonstrated the desire to enhance and benefit from non-government institutions (family, business, religious, educational, and community civic organizations) in the way they did early in the 20th century. Today, too many black leaders continue to pine for the largely receding tide of federal government largesse that heretofore had kept African Americans on the Democrat plantation since the Johnson administration and Big Society programs of the 1960s and 1970s.

Democrats' cynical use of identity politics reached its pinnacle with the election of Barack Obama in 2008. While many blacks at the time viewed Obama's election as the dawn of a new era of black progress in America, it proved to be just the opposite. Under the

Obama administration, blacks fell further behind in almost every measure that counts—employment, income, home ownership, wealth attainment, and family formation. Rather than representing the culmination of Black America's achievement, Obama's presidency signaled a new era of depredation—what Velma Hart called the return of the "Franks and beans" era.[139]

But this reality was masked by the shiny, new toy Democrats found to distract Black America from the obvious signs that it had been losing ground, socially, economically, and politically since the 1960s coalition with Democrats was started: you live in a country that has a black president.

As Obama began a global apology tour which focused on repairing America's image on the world stage, his administration's domestic policies compounded the pressing needs of everyday Americans who were suffering amidst historic unemployment and wealth destruction. Black Americans led the pace in America's reversal of fortune. According to a Pew Research report released in 2014, black home ownership rates retreated nearly 8 percent to early 1990s levels. For blacks, whose largest source of wealth is in home ownership, declining rates of home ownership had a devastating effect on their economic prospects and greatly hampered their recovery during the remainder of the Obama administration.

Furthermore, the Obama administration took a decidedly antiquated approach to the economy. Rather than implement pro-growth, pro-business policies that could get America back to work, Obama focused instead on artificial government stimulus

---

139    Tim Perone, *"It's franks & beans time,"* *New York Post*, November 23, 2010, https://nypost.com/2010/11/23/its-franks-beans-time/.

In September of 2010, Velma Hart told President Obama that she was exhausted from defending him and waiting for his policies to start working. ""I've been told that I voted for a man who said he's going to change things in a meaningful way for the middle class," Hart said. "I'm one of those people, and I'm waiting, sir. I'm waiting. I don't feel it yet." She also told the president she feared her family would have to go back to the "hot dogs-and-beans era."

and social-welfare-based wealth transfers—such as the Affordable Care Act, expanded food stamp access, and tax increases. Obama raised barriers to business growth by implementing a staggering 667 new regulations in his first two years in office alone. To compound matters, the economic stimulus designed to bail out Wall Street ended up crowding out Main Street. Moreover, the steady abandonment of family, faith, and community blacks had experienced over the preceding four decades left the black community without adequate organizational and institutional resources to compensate for the reduced attention provided by the government.

This was not the first time that Washington had abandoned blacks. In the aftermath of the Civil War, Washington abandoned the newly freed slaves and left them at the mercy of the vengeful southerners, who were themselves a war-torn nation seeking to rebuild. When Federal troops eventually pulled up stakes and left the South, a series of repressive codes were put into place in the vacuum that operated. These actions impeded blacks' civil rights and ultimately were transformed into a pernicious system of de jure discrimination. Blacks were also terrorized by white vigilante groups that unleashed a horrid campaign of lynching and mob violence across the post-bellum South.

What was Black America's response to the end of the first reconstruction? In essence, it began to build coalitions with industry and commerce—signaled in large part by Booker T. Washington's "Atlanta Compromise" speech in 1895 at the Cotton States and International Exposition. Blacks agreed to participate in our nation's mutual economic success, while also agreeing to a strategic retreat on matters of civil rights. Some black Americans at the time, notably the black elite, objected to the compromise and broke off from the majority of the black community to form its own "Talented Tenth" led by liberal black elites like W.E.B. Dubois.

But the majority of black folks in the post-Civil War South adopted, out of necessity, a more pragmatic approach. They often returned to the plantations upon which they had formerly been enslaved, this time as free laborers. Black men sought out family members—spouses and children that had been dispersed throughout the South during the ugly scourge of commercial slavery—and rebuilt strong family units. Blacks formed religious institutions, and in most communities, religion became the cornerstone of black society. With the assistance of Republican Party-aligned philanthropists and the Federal government, blacks built land-grant colleges, which taught the trades necessary at the time to participate in industry—masonry, agricultural trades, electrical, and mechanical trades—and some became schoolteachers, doctors, and lawyers. Also, blacks began to arm themselves, and in several instances, defended themselves effectively against racist mob violence.

These core strategies—faith, family, and industry—helped blacks survive from the end of the first reconstruction up until the end of the first world war, when the war economy began to falter amidst the "forgotten" recession of 1920–21. In a response reminiscent of what President Obama would do almost a century later, Democratic President Woodrow Wilson implemented a host of job-killing regulations and raised taxes, in addition to drastically increasing the national debt. President Wilson remains the second-largest contributor to the national debt, in percentage terms. He added $21 billion, which was a 727 percent increase over the $2.9-billion debt of his predecessor. In addition, in response to the deflationary conditions of the Great Recession, he raised interest rates on top of increasing the debt—which further dampened economic growth. After Wilson lost the nation's confidence, Republican President Harding rose to leadership in 1920, on a campaign that promised "less government in business and more business in government."

According to historian George Soule in his book, *Prosperity Decade*, The Harding administration's "avowed purpose was to withdraw as far as possible from exerting any influence on the economic life of the country except the encouragement that might be derived from a balanced budget and nonintervention with private enterprise." Harding raised tariffs on imports, reduced regulation, and reduced government's crowding-out effects on private industry by drastically curtailing government spending. Not surprisingly, this strategy worked. Within eighteen months, the economy had fully recovered. Black workers overwhelmingly benefited from this economic strategy and record numbers of black men were employed—indeed at employment rates not seen for much of the 20th century.

Does all this sound familiar? It should. President Trump has drastically reduced regulations, cut government bureaucracy across almost every agency, and even attempted to dissolve entire agencies. President Trump's strong immigration and "fair trade" policies have led to a resurgence in job opportunities for those at the lower end of the labor market—a principal reason why black unemployment has reached its lowest level ever recorded.

If we observe them critically and apply the lessons they provide, historical antecedents can point the way forward towards progress for Black America in 2020 and beyond. The education, familial, and social institutions blacks established in the aftermath of the first reconstruction and through the 1920s, ultimately created a robust black middle class. They were educated, affluent, and socially prepared to once again press for political rights when the opportunity arose in the mid-1950s. The dividends of economic prosperity—earned by generations of hard work, family and community cohesion, and moral striving in the aftermath of slavery—ultimately set the stage for individuals like Martin Luther King, A. Phillip Randolph, Ralph Bunche, and other black civic leaders to successfully push for civil rights.

Black America today would do well to return to the values that helped it achieve greatness in the past. Those include, as Booker T. Washington would say, "cast[ing] down your buckets where you are"; aligning with industry and commerce in beneficial ways; placing family and faith first. This is really a simple prescription. It does not rely necessarily upon having a "black face" in the office of the president, or moving "black issues" to the forefront of the national legislative agenda. Rather, it sees Black America as an integral part of all America. What is good for Americans is also good for black folks.

President Trump then, is, for blacks, a blessing in disguise—or rather—in plain sight. But the worsening partisanship in Washington threatens to impede the progress our nation has made over the past three years since the Trump administration took office. Rather than contribute to the partisan rancor, blacks should seek to align themselves with the positive aspects of Trumpism and build coalitions of friendship and mutual interest with like-minded people of all races and political orientations.

If left to his devices, Trump will likely accrue a legacy of a Reagan-style conservative. He has already signaled dovish intentions regarding foreign policy, exhibiting a restraint in the exercise of U.S. military power that even Barack Obama might envy. Despite his bellicose threats to foreign leaders, Trump has signaled an intention to extricate America from costly foreign wars and draining international military commitments such as NATO, and he is committed to rebuilding and retooling our overstrained military forces. We need a peace economy, not a war economy. Blacks should mirror Trump's strategy in terms of retreating from costly political fights over identity politics—which largely benefit only elites and politicians—and focus instead on rebuilding the core foundations of the black community. The masses of black Americans are in no position socially, structurally, or economically to wage a major race-based struggle at this time. In the words of Booker T. Washington, in 1895, we should not "permit our grievances to overcome our opportunities."

Perhaps even more counterintuitively, blacks would fare far better in the long run if, instead of opposing Trump's presidency, they joined with Trump to help establish more effective leadership on a national level. Leadership, especially leadership attempting to turn around a massive organization the size of the United States, rarely looks like a straight line. In order to change course and move towards a more beneficial destination, sometimes the ship has to sail east in order to arrive in the west. But the ship will go nowhere if the helmsman and the person operating the rudder are working at odds with each other. By unifying and attending to matters of mutual advancement, our nation can certainly restore itself to prosperity and retain its former glory. In the process, Black America can also be made great again.